Praise for *Perforn.*

"*Performance Feedback Strategies* is one of those rare business books that are rooted in rock-solid science and deliver principles that can be put into use by everyone in your organization. The suggested models for performance feedback are incredibly useful and have withstood the test of time."

—Joel A. DiGirolamo, International Coaching Federation, Vice President of Research and Data Science

"Ken and Sandra combine their considerable experience in serious research, hands-on consulting, training, and coaching as well as innumerable dialogues with other performance leaders to deliver a performance feedback framework that works. You cannot close this book without finding at least three great takeaways on how to improve performance feedback."

—Beverly Kaye, Co-Author, *Love 'Em or Lose 'Em*, *Help Them Grow or Watch Them Go*, and *Up Is Not the Only Way*

"Sandra Mashihi and Ken Nowack's book is an invaluable resource offering strategies that anybody can implement immediately to improve their feedback skills and drive positive organizational change. The integration of AI in feedback processes makes this the business book of our time."

—Theresa Edy Kiene, CEO, Girl Scouts of Greater Los Angeles

"*Performance Feedback Strategies* masterfully blends the science of feedback with the practice of coaching to bring forth pragmatic approaches to navigating the challenges of feedback conversations with both high and low performers. A must-read for people managers!"

—Woody Woodward, PhD, PCC, Clinical Assistant Professor, Executive Coaching and Director, NYU School of Professional Studies Coaching Innovation Lab

"Ken and Sandra review the science of feedback and use examples to show how sharing candid, concrete, feedforward information effectively facilitates employee professional development and improves operational performance. This entirely practical book gives managers the strategies and checklists they need to make communication easier and more effective."

—Paul J. Zak, PhD, Distinguished University Professor, Claremont Graduate University; Founder, Immersion Neuroscience; Author, *Immersion: The Science of the Extraordinary and the Source of Happiness*

Sandra Mashihi and Kenneth Nowack

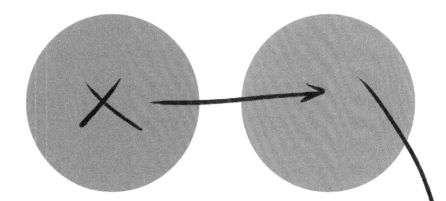

PERFORMANCE FEEDBACK STRATEGIES

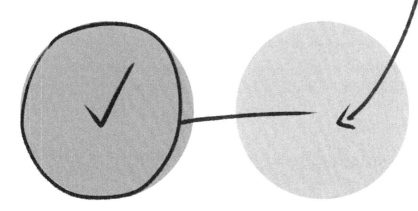

Driving Successful Behavior Change

PRESS

ALEXANDRIA, VA

ATD Press is an internationally renowned source of insightful and practical information on talent development, training, and professional development.

ATD Press
1640 King Street
Alexandria, VA 22314 USA

Ordering information: Books published by ATD Press can be purchased by visiting
ATD's website at td.org/books or by calling 800.628.2783 or 703.683.8100.

Library of Congress Control Number: 2024944239

ISBN-10: 1-957157-86-0
ISBN-13: 978-1-957157-86-3
e-ISBN: 978-1-957157-88-7

ATD Press Editorial Staff
Director: Sarah Halgas
Manager: Melissa Jones
Content Manager, Senior Leaders: Ann Parker
Developmental Editor: Shelley Sperry
Production Editor: Katy Wiley Stewts
Text Designer: Shirley E.M. Raybuck

Text Layout: PerfecType, Nashville, TN

Cover Designer: Faceout Studio, Elisha Zepeda

Printed by BR Printers, San Jose, CA

Contents

Introduction 1

Part 1. The Science of Feedback

1. The Power and Purpose of Feedback 11
2. Ouch, That Hurt! The Neuroscience of Feedback 23
3. Feedback for a Diverse Workforce 43
4. Feedback: The Prerequisite for Successful Behavior Change 81

Part 2. Performance Feedback Coaching

5. The Performance Feedback Coaching Model 103
6. Performance Management: How to Coach High Performers
   With Low Interpersonal Skills 119
7. Performance Acceleration: How to Coach High Performers
   With High Interpersonal Skills 137
8. Performance Enhancement: How to Coach Poor Performers
   With High Interpersonal Skills 161
9. Performance Improvement: How to Coach Low Performers
   With Low Interpersonal Skills 181
10. Performance Feedback Meets Artificial Intelligence 201

Conclusion 207

Acknowledgments 209

**Appendix. A Selected List of AI Tools for Performance
Feedback and Coaching** 211

References 213

Index 235

About the Authors 247

About ATD 249

Introduction
Bridging the Feedback Gap

> "If you just communicate, you can get by. But if
> you communicate skillfully, you can work miracles."
> —Jim Rohn, entrepreneur and author

"We want to create a feedback culture in our company that fosters open, candid, and constructively helpful feedback," explained Kostas in a Zoom meeting with Ken and Sandra. "And we want all our leaders and employees involved."

Kostas had reached out to our team for help improving his organization's feedback culture after completing a company-wide survey that confirmed his gut feeling: The company's approach to feedback—up and down the chain of command—needed an overhaul.

What was clear right away was that we had to address the poor quality of communication between the company's leaders and employees at all levels if we were going to solve his problem. Kostas's company was not unique. A 2022 survey of more than 700 employees across a wide range of industries reported that less than half believed their leaders could "manage difficult conversations effectively" (Garr and Mehrotra 2023).

All the leaders in Kostas's global enterprise had years of experience and deep knowledge of how their industry worked, but few knew how to handle people and give candid feedback—whether positive or negative—to their direct reports. Making matters more difficult, the company's international team represented many different cultures and spoke many languages. In some cases, divisions between leaders and team members along gender, cultural, and generational lines created serious misunderstandings and rifts.

Kostas ended our discussion with a challenge: "Sandra and Ken, the bottom line is that the leaders in our company need to learn how to deliver better, timelier, and more constructive feedback, and they have to understand that the feedback style that works with one employee might not be effective for another."

In less than an hour, our candid conversation with Kostas summed up many of the daunting communication and feedback challenges that contribute to dissatisfaction among employees and the difficulty in getting them to make and maintain changes to improve their performance.

As we strategized over the next few weeks about how to address the needs of this one company, we realized that most organizations could benefit from the model we were recommending as a solution for Kostas—a model based on our years of research and conversations with hundreds of global leaders. So, we decided to share that model in this book.

A strong and effective performance feedback culture starts with leadership practices and behaviors that are sensitive to today's diverse workforce. Leaders must be introspective and check in on the biases and stereotypes that shape their thoughts and actions, and then modify their behavior and communication styles to provide the most effective feedback possible to each employee. Using the four-part Performance Feedback Coaching Model we've developed, leaders can create simple, individualized feedback plans that inspire growth and successful behavior change in each employee, meeting them where they are and taking advantage of their unique technical knowledge, skills, and interpersonal strengths.

Employee Disengagement and Lack of Supportive Feedback

We know that good leaders adapt and change over time to help their organizations overcome challenges and grow stronger. We watched this happen in the wake of the COVID-19 pandemic and during periods of economic and technological change. Timely communication and collaboration are crucial when organizations are at a crossroads, and leaders must rise to the challenge and find innovative ways to maintain effective relationships with their team members. And of course, when leaders face sudden, unfamiliar management challenges, employees face equally unfamiliar expectations that require new kinds of support from their organizations. Unfortunately, many organizations aren't prepared to provide that support, which contributes to employee disengagement. Our post-pandemic "new normal" includes not only hybrid schedules and more virtual meetings but also varying degrees of disengagement, discontent, and open feedback cultures across almost every industry.

If we condense the many definitions and measures of engagement into a few core truths, we see that performance and retention are strongly associated with the way people feel about their jobs, managers, and organizations. When we understand the roots of employee disengagement and resistance, we can move forward to solve the frustrations plaguing so many organizations today.

In 2023, Gallup reported that only 33 percent of employees were engaged at work. And 18 percent were actively disengaged (Harter 2024). Much of the current dissatisfaction among employees can be traced to inadequate or poor feedback from leaders and a lack of support on the job.

At this point, we believe the research is clear: Much of the current dissatisfaction among employees can be traced to inadequate or poor feedback from leaders and a lack of support on the job. In our coaching and consulting work with diverse organizations, employees tell us that performance standards and expectations are *ambiguous and limiting*. Other perceptions we see consistently include that employees:

- Have a lack of connection to the mission or purpose of their company
- Find fewer opportunities to learn and grow professionally than in the past
- Find fewer opportunities to leverage their signature strengths
- Do not see demonstrations of caring and support from senior leaders

Bridging the Feedback Gap

Through decades of working with people across global organizations, we have watched leaders struggle to package and deliver feedback in a way that helps employees understand and accept it, and then feel motivated to make the necessary behavior changes. More important, the problem is not usually that employees don't want to listen to feedback and improve their performance. In fact, one 2018 study found that 87 percent of employees wanted to "be developed" in their careers but only a third reported receiving the feedback they needed to engage and improve (Rock, Jones, and Weller 2018). Recent studies support our own observations of a wide *feedback gap* between employee expectations around performance feedback and what leaders are providing. Employee engagement and satisfaction surveys consistently show that while employees want specific, helpful, and constructive feedback, most say they don't get it.

The disconnect between employees' eagerness for constructive feedback and leaders' reluctance to provide it was observed in five experiments by a team of researchers at the University of California, Berkeley Haas School of Business (Abi-Esber et al. 2022). These researchers concluded that leaders truly underestimate how much employees crave feedback. The Eagle Hill Performance Management and Feedback Survey asked 1,000 US employees about their feedback preferences. Only 48 percent of those surveyed reported that they received feedback once every six months or annually, and another 8 percent reported never getting feedback at all (Eagle Hill 2022).

In our consulting, training, and coaching projects, we hear a range of complaints about performance feedback. Leaders' complaints tend to focus on employees being too needy, entitled, or unwilling to listen to corrective feedback. They'll often say things like:

- "I've given feedback numerous times, and my employees don't change."
- "Every time I have a performance-feedback conversation with my employee, I get backlash."
- "I've spent hours training and coaching my employees and they are still not satisfied."

- "We need to focus on the bottom line. . . . I don't have time to spend hours checking on my employees."
- "I'm not sure how to increase the motivation levels of my team."
- "I am spending more time trying to fix the mistakes of my direct reports than developing other employees."
- "I don't have time to work on strategic initiatives because I am so focused on trying to engage and develop my staff."
- "I just can't communicate with millennials (or Gen Zers). They are too entitled."

In contrast, employees often share frustration about leaders who refuse to listen, don't support career development, or are disrespectful. More often than you might expect, we hear employees say, "I'm considering leaving my organization because of my supervisor." Here are a few other things we've heard:

- "My supervisor's feedback style is one-sided. I'm not included and there's no attention to my career growth."
- "My boss does not listen."
- "My boss doesn't understand me or my needs."
- "My boss is not challenging me."
- "I get minimal feedback from my supervisor."
- "My career is not growing under my supervisor's leadership."
- "My leader is not empowering me."
- "My supervisor only focuses on what I do wrong. I never receive positive reinforcement."
- "My leader is not clear or transparent."
- "My leader is not respecting me working from home."

Given that this feedback gap contributes to frustration for both leaders and employees, we believe it is more important than ever for organizations to create *a participative culture that facilitates psychological safety and interpersonal trust in the workplace.*

Our Performance Feedback Coaching Model bridges the feedback gap by providing a road map leaders can use to drive engaging conversations tailored to each employee. Thousands of leaders around the world have already used our model to enhance engagement, improve on-the-job performance—and most importantly—retain high-potential talent. Now you can use it and evaluate too.

Based on two universal dimensions of the way we perceive others—*warmth* and *competence* (Cuddy, Fiske, and Glick 2008)—our model is designed to help leaders categorize direct reports into one of four coaching groups to enhance individual performance:

- **Performance management:** Employees with high overall performance and low interpersonal competence
- **Performance acceleration:** Employees with high overall performance and high interpersonal competence
- **Performance enhancement:** Employees with low overall performance and high interpersonal competence
- **Performance improvement:** Employees with low overall performance and low interpersonal competence

These four groups then become the model's foundation and guide leaders to engage in tailored feedback conversations that improve motivation for employees who want to perform, grow, and learn. In this book, you'll find practical strategies, tips, and tools to facilitate collaborative, supportive, and empathetic conversations between leaders and employees in each group of our model.

Understanding and using the common characteristics in each of the four categories provides a level of analysis and insight not available through other methods. Of course, there is no one-size-fits-all approach to sharing feedback and leading others. Every employee is unique, bringing their skills, interests, values, motivations, personalities, and styles to the workplace. In addition, as employees grow and develop, their performance levels may vary over time depending on many work and nonwork-related factors. The same is true for each leader. Our model is not designed to relegate employees to a restrictive category, but to help leaders provide *individualized development plans* for each of their direct reports.

We want to make all feedback conversations effective and worthwhile, so they result in both enhanced performance and successful behavior change.

What's Ahead in This Book

As organizational psychologists with decades of experience researching, coaching, and training leaders all around the world, we have written this book to help leaders at every level effectively manage performance and behavior change in employees across cultures, genders, and generations. Our performance feedback model is based on the latest research in neuroscience, social psychology, and organizational psychology, in addition to our own executive coaching experiences with diverse clients. It will help you become a better communicator and influencer so you'll be able to help your direct reports leverage their signature strengths, enhance their engagement, and foster their ongoing professional growth and development.

> Organizations that create a culture of continuous feedback are 3.5 times more likely to sustain high performance and employee well-being (Guggenberger et al. 2023).

In the chapters that follow, we share stories from our own experiences and from clients in a range of industries, drawing on lessons from large corporations, small businesses, international organizations, government entities, nonprofits, and startups. In sharing our stories, we have changed names and situations to ensure clients' anonymity and confidentiality.

This book is divided into two parts, both built on the science and practice of performance feedback coaching. In part 1, we discuss the challenges of providing feedback and the impact of feedback on employees from a neuroscientific perspective (Williams and Nowack 2022). We build upon our 3E Model of Successful Individual Behavior Change and explain the science of initiating new behaviors and making them automatic.

The key to successful sustained behavior change turns out to be *self-insight*, which is largely brought about by direct feedback from others (Nowack 2009). So, we also include information about how to establish working relationships that are collaborative, psychologically safe, and trusting to encourage self-awareness and avoid potentially damaging social interactions. We share the factors that contribute to perceived trustworthiness and their importance in giving and receiving feedback. And we summarize what makes for effective feedback, considering important individual factors such as gender, race, culture, and age.

In part 2, we introduce our complete Performance Feedback Coaching Model. Each chapter in this section includes specific techniques, strategies, tools, and tips for conducting effective feedback conversations with the four categories of employees. We end with a look at how artificial intelligence (AI) is helping and challenging the performance feedback process and a brief conclusion.

We've designed this book to help leaders like you—at all levels up and down your organization's hierarchy—appreciate the latest science around feedback and habit change and deploy that science to enhance your ability to communicate with, re-engage, and retain your diverse and valuable group of employees.

Let's start now.

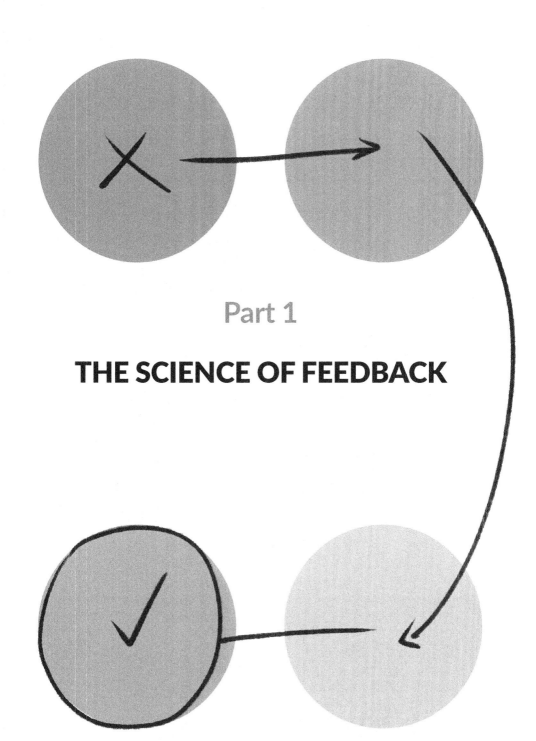

Part 1

THE SCIENCE OF FEEDBACK

Chapter 1

The Power and Purpose of Feedback

Sandra is now the mother of two beloved children, but like many women, her path to motherhood wasn't easy. When she finally became pregnant at age 38, Sandra chose a world-renowned obstetric gynecologist known for handling high-risk, complex cases with incredible skill. Patients traveled from all over the US to seek Dr. T's counsel, literally placing their lives and their children's lives in his hands.

Unfortunately, with each visit to Dr. T's office, Sandra felt increasingly unsettled. Despite his talent and reputation, she found that Dr. T also had profound deficits—including a lack of empathy and an inability to communicate effectively with his patients. For example, when medical staff dropped subtle hints about a potential complication with Sandra's pregnancy, Dr. T never clearly addressed or explained the situation.

Sandra's uneasiness only worsened during her first trimester screening. Dr. T didn't utter a word while performing the ultrasound.

"What's happening? Is everything OK?" Sandra asked eagerly.

"I see something here," was all he said—his face blank and body stiff.

"What is it?" she prodded.

In a calm, matter-of-fact tone, Dr. T replied, "There are some spots on your placenta."

While his demeanor indicated the spots could be a minor issue—Sandra somehow knew they weren't. So, she asked again, "What does that mean? Is the baby going to be OK? What do I do now?"

Her questions were clear and direct, but Dr. T refused to reply or make eye contact. Instead, all he said was, "Let's continue to monitor it." And he then immediately left the room.

Over the next few weeks, Sandra tried to speak to Dr. T by phone, but only got messages delivered by his nurses in return. She was anxious and frustrated by the doctor's curt, cold responses, but she told herself his exceptional skills and stellar reputation were what mattered.

During the final ultrasound, Dr. T simply said, "There is no heartbeat. . . . I'm sorry." Then he left the room and asked his nurse to tell Sandra what would happen next. For Sandra, the anguish of losing her child was made even more painful because in that moment she felt completely isolated and uncared for by the physician she had trusted. He expressed no empathy, offered no explanations, and made her feel like she was just another patient on a long list.

We share this personal story to shine a light on how essential it is for people in powerful positions to communicate with sensitivity rather than making others feel ignored, unimportant, or anxious. If you're a leader with people who look to you for guidance, your skills and reputation simply aren't enough. Unfortunately, many people we coach aren't aware of how they come across or how their words, tone, and body language are perceived. We often say that leaders who lack self-awareness and don't understand their influence on others were born with a "no-clue gene."

On the other hand, we all know people with a strong, innate sense of self-awareness and empathy for others. They have a gift that enables them to forge productive interpersonal relationships and communicate effectively with anyone. They can sense when they're coming across as jerks, need to listen more carefully to other people's views, or even when their jokes aren't funny.

In the workplace, most of us fall somewhere between being fully empathetic and having that no-clue gene. We're sometimes able to connect with and support colleagues and employees when they need it most. And sometimes, like Dr. T, we're oblivious to the impact our words and behavior have on others. We have to learn good communication skills through trial and error, and if we don't come by self-awareness naturally, we must cultivate it—especially if we want to lead others effectively.

In our work as leadership coaches, the same questions arise again and again: Why do so many leaders fail the self-awareness test? Why can't they see how they're perceived by others? In other words, why is the "no-clue gene" so dominant, and how can we counteract it to improve our leaders' ability to communicate with their teams and provide feedback that gets results? We've found some of the answers to these questions in recent social science research, and in this chapter, we'll begin to explore what that research can teach us about providing performance feedback in a way that leads recipients toward the goals of *understanding*, *acceptance*, and *action*.

The Science of Self-Awareness

We all face daily challenges at work that can erode our self-esteem, confidence, and well-being. We adapt in numerous ways, including inflating our own skills and abilities, imagining that we have more control over events than we really do, and looking at the future through an overly optimistic lens. To maintain enough self-confidence to thrive, we may need to tell ourselves we are more competent, skilled, and knowledgeable than other people. For example, a classic study at US universities found that 90 percent of college professors believed their teaching was above average compared with that of their colleagues (Cross 1997). This positive illusion or self-enhancement bias is a normal human adaptation, but it can become a big problem in the workplace if leaders and employees over- or underestimate their abilities relative to how others evaluate them in feedback (Taylor et al. 2000).

How Leaders Rate Themselves

In collaboration with the University of Barcelona, we did a study comparing self-ratings of more than 178 leaders at different levels of their organizations (Alzina and Escoda 2007). The study also compared those scores against two validated measures of emotional intelligence (EI) to see how accurate leaders were when assessing their own EI:

- A self-assessment of 22 emotional and social competencies (Nowack 2013).

- The Mayer-Salovey-Caruso Emotional Intelligence Test (MSCEIT), a well known ability-based assessment that measures EI through an individual's abilities to perceive, comprehend, act on, and manage emotional information.

Our analysis found that 23.6 percent of study respondents provided high self-ratings but scored low on the MSCEIT. We also found that 30 percent rated their EI competence low but scored high on the MSCEIT. **In other words, more than half of the leaders in our study either overestimated or underestimated their demonstrated ability to understand, manage, and use emotional intelligence.**

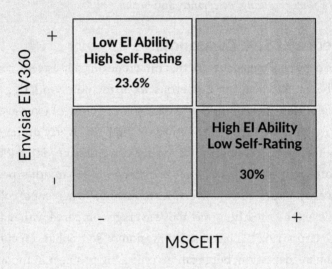

Self-enhancement bias in the larger population can lead to the illusion of one group's superiority over other groups. In organizations, this bias may cause leaders and employees to overestimate their skill levels and abilities, and we see this frequently in our consulting work. For instance, if an executive board asks a leader to assess their skill at building a team and effectively developing others by comparing themselves to other leaders in the company, that leader will likely rate themselves above average. Of course, some leaders and employees chronically underestimate their true skills and abilities, but that's a much less common occurrence.

Weak Skills, Strong Confidence

The tendency of leaders and employees with weaker skills to provide skewed positive assessments of their abilities is known as the Dunning-Kruger effect. Many leaders simply don't recognize what they don't know about their own competence and how they are perceived by others (Kruger and Dunning 1999). They are also prone to expressing unfounded confidence and a lack of judgment about their actual skill levels (Sanchez and Dunning 2018).

Despite some suggestions that the Dunning-Kruger effect is nothing more than the better-than-average effect (Gaze 2023), our experience coaching and teaching executives has convinced us that overestimation of skills and misinterpretation of their influence on others is more common in those who are less competent. So, if most leaders and employees inaccurately judge their skills, communication styles, and personalities, then receiving feedback from others should be quite useful for navigating interpersonal relationships at work. The congruence between how leaders evaluate their skills, abilities, and blind spots (their "identity") with how other colleagues experience them (their "reputation") is an important focus in most executive coaching assignments (Vergauew, Hofmans, and Willie 2022).

Windows Into Ourselves and Others

The Johari Window model provides a wonderful way to help people better understand their relationships with themselves and colleagues at work or elsewhere, and we often include references to this model in our coaching. The Johari model was created in 1955 by two psychologists, Joseph Luft and Harrington Ingham (they chose the name by combining their first names; Luft 1963). Its primary goal is helping leaders and employees understand the differences between how people see them and how they see themselves. The components are a person's *self-knowledge* and *self-disclosure to others* and yield four quadrants within the larger window:

- **Open**—known to yourself and to others; these are your *traits.*
- **Hidden**—known to yourself but not known to others; this is your *identity.*
- **Unknown**—not known at all to yourself or others.

- **Blind spot**—not known to yourself, but known to others; this is your *reputation*.

Imagine each quadrant as a window you can widen or narrow to different sizes. Let's use Ken's characteristics to look at each window in more detail.

Those who know Ken well, including Sandra, would describe the traits in his open window as intellectually curious, supportive, collaborative, humble, and willing to coach and mentor others. In the workplace, the *open window* is visible to all and is a match between how we describe ourselves (our identity) and how others experience us (our reputation).

Ken's *hidden window* includes key parts of his identity that others are not aware of. For example, in 1975 he was involved in a high-profile kidnapping and bank robbery in California, which resulted in the death of an innocent woman by armed radicals billing themselves as the Symbionese Liberation Army (SLA). Curious to know more? Feel free to search on the internet, ask an AI engine or chatbot, or seek out government records using the Freedom of Information Act; but you won't learn more than the sentence shared above (unless you get an AI hallucination!). Ken's involvement in this case is an integral part of his own identity, but it's completely hidden from others. In your organization, employees' hidden windows are those private parts of their identities and experiences that mark the separation of work and external relationships and activities.

What about the *unknown window*? A few years ago, neither Ken nor anyone else knew that he and Sandra would write and publish a book in 2025. So, while that was once part of his unknown window, it isn't anymore. When a new employee joins your organization, their unknown window is large: How will they interact with other members of the team? Will their ideas conflict with the leader's? Which of their strengths will be the most important to their success and which weaknesses will be the most problematic? We can all shrink our unknown windows over time through careful observation of ourselves, counseling or therapy, and expanding our interactions with others.

As you may have guessed by now, the *blind spot window*—those things not known to us but known to others—is what most people want to shrink. Fortunately, through feedback, we can become more aware of how others view our skills, abilities, habits, and actions and respond accordingly.

One of Ken's former blind spots was that he sometimes came across as inadequately recognizing the knowledge, skills, and abilities of others, which eroded their confidence and self-esteem. By listening to understand more frequently and asking more questions rather than providing his own experiences and expertise first, Ken was able to become a better performance coach and shrink this blind spot. In your organization, you'll want to consider each employee's blind spots and how your feedback can help them become more aware of how others experience the impact of their behavior. Specific feedback to employees—such as, "Have you noticed that you interrupted others on more than one occasion?" or "For your next presentation, consider repeating the questions from your audience before responding"—can help illuminate blind spots and provide constructive suggestions for improvement.

Social Feedback Loops to Cultivate Self-Awareness

Our internal, personal experiences and our external experiences with others involve complex feedback loops. For our purposes, a *feedback loop* is an interaction that provides people with information about their actions. The feedback can be positive or negative, and the interaction can be biological or social. For example, when people have a "normal" circadian wake-and-sleep rhythm and experience normal zeitgebers (events like sunrise and sunset that set our biological clocks), their brains create a biological feedback loop that tells them when to go to bed at night and when to rise in the morning—all repeated within a 24-hour cycle. In the workplace, leaders create social feedback loops to educate, inform, and share observations, seeking specific behavioral changes in their employees.

Let's return to the Johari model for a moment. If you have a small blind spot, there's a greater congruence between your self-evaluation and how other people perceive you, which is an ideal situation for most of us. We can use feedback to illuminate our blind spots and gain self-awareness, increase the size of our open window, and make improvements on and off the job.

Good social feedback targeted to our blind spots can lead to three important outcomes, each culminating in a change in thought, feeling, or behavior. Let's now look at these social feedback outcomes and consider how leaders can use them to pave the way for success.

Feedback Outcome 1. Understanding

To ensure that employees understand feedback, leaders need to provide information, data, and observations that are educational. The employee needs to learn how others perceive their behavior and how their behavior affects others. Feedback can be positive such as praise, recognition, reinforcement for desired behaviors, or future-oriented with tips and suggestions for improvement. Feedback can also be critical and negative if it is framed, received, or experienced as a harsh judgment or a put-down of the recipient.

Critical or negative feedback in a workplace is rarely helpful, because leaders and employees quickly ignore or dismiss it. In addition, the employee typically reaches out to others to seek more encouraging or positive feedback, which is called "shopping for confirmation" (Green, Gino, and Staats 2017).

Research suggests that 72 percent of employees prefer corrective feedback (or suggestions of better ways to do things in the future or ways to improve), over both negative and positive feedback (Zenger and Folkman 2014). The timing and use of positive versus corrective feedback may be related to the employee's personality, their level of experience, and their maturity. For example, positive feedback is much more motivating for novices and employees beginning a goal that requires new knowledge or skills (Schroeder and Fishbach 2015).

The lesson for leaders is to pay attention to new employees, those in new positions, or those acquiring new skills, and emphasize what they are doing well in immediate corrective feedback to reinforce their behaviors.

Feedback Outcome 2. Acceptance

Leaders need employees to not only understand but also accept the feedback they're given. Employees' reactions to feedback vary widely and can include surprise, hurt, anger, and even depression. In the workplace, reactions matter because if an employee is upset, angry, or dismissive about the feedback they receive, it will have little or no impact on their thoughts, beliefs, or future behaviors. In other words, their blind spots will remain the same.

When we sit down to coach a leader, we often check not only how well another person understood the leader's feedback, but also whether the individual truly sees value in the feedback shared with them. Accepting the value of feedback is related to the recipient's intrinsic motivation to act and commit to change at an interpersonal or emotional level.

Does Feedback Lead to Positive and Lasting Behavior Change?

Research suggests that only 47 percent of initiatives that consisted of feedback alone—not in combination with things like goal setting or behavioral consequences—had a positive effect on employee performance, while 53 percent had a mixed effect (Alvero, Bucklin, and Austin 2001). This suggests that in some cases, feedback not only has little or no impact on actual behavior change, but could also lead to discouragement, disengagement, and strong negative emotional reactions (Nowack 2014, 2016).

Leaders need to think about the best way to frame employee feedback and what they can do to minimize any possible defensive reaction or rejection of the message. When performance feedback is delivered frequently and perceived as helpful and supportive, good individual and organizational outcomes will result. For example, a recent meta-analysis found a significant association between performance feedback to employees and positive organizational citizenship behavior, including discretionary effort and cooperation with others (Tagliabue, Sigurjonsdottir, and Sandaker 2020). This leads us to ask about the best strategies and techniques for enhancing people's acceptance of the feedback. Let's look at a few now.

The Feedback Sandwich

One popular feedback technique is to initially offer praise—such as a compliment or a meaningful positive observation about the person's performance or behavior—and then provide constructive feedback, criticism, or suggestions to improve, followed by more encouraging feedback. This "feedback sandwich" is intended to avoid defensiveness and dismissal of the more constructive or critical feedback.

However, recent studies suggest that the criticism-sandwiched-between-praise approach is ineffective and can create disengaged employees and erode trust. This outcome is magnified in the context of teaching new skills, and is the opposite of what feedback is intended to accomplish (Bottini and Gillis

2021). The sandwich approach can also cause a greater stress response in employees if they're anxious about your true intent and message.

A better option is to be direct and candid—provide feedback without starting the conversation with a compliment or praise. Leaders need to get over their discomfort about delivering constructive feedback because employees really just want to know how they are doing.

Feedforward

Establishing a future orientation to feedback does seem to significantly increase both understanding and acceptance and enhance performance and effectiveness. In two separate studies, people were significantly more motivated to improve when they perceived feedback as concentrating on future actions rather than their past performance (Gnepp et al. 2020).

The main takeaway for leaders is to frame feedback as a set of tips, suggestions, recommendations, and ideas for the future, with the ultimate goal of helping the employee. This approach is often referred to as *feedforward*, and it is universally met with less resistance (Kluger 2006). After all, who doesn't want trusted advice and encouragement to be a better version of ourselves in the future?

Feedback Outcome 3. Commitment to Action

The gold standard by which you measure your feedback's effectiveness is whether the employee pays attention, increases their motivation to improve, and then takes observable action to do so. This is the purpose of feedback—not idle chatter or thoughts shared with employees without a goal in mind. In our executive coaching practice, we often see the first two feedback outcomes—understanding and acceptance—without firm commitments to action focused on specific behaviors. Sometimes, leaders and employees share their intentions to change with us, but the intentions don't result in any meaningful or sustained change over time. In fact, intentions to change are quite weak predictors of actual behavior change over time (Nowack 2017).

There is no guarantee that effective feedback will lead to successful goal setting and change in an employee's job performance. However, without structuring, framing, tailoring, and delivering feedback to employees in ways they can understand, accept, and follow up with an attempt to act, nothing will change.

Unfortunately, for some people we have coached over the years, natural skills and abilities simply limit their range of success. In other words, executive coaching probably won't transform many competent jerks into lovable stars.

In chapter 5, we will expand upon our approach to individual habit and behavior change, which we call the 3E Model of Successful Individual Behavior Change. This model supports the three outcomes of feedback we've just discussed and provides a variety of useful steps leaders can use to help employees translate insights they understand and accept into deliberate actions. Before we introduce this model and our practical tips, we will provide some background into the neuroscience of feedback and how that translates into the practical challenges leaders face when feedback is deemed judgmental, unfair, incorrect, or biased. Armed with this basic understanding of how feedback works in our brains, leaders can reflect on their current biases around delivering feedback and apply evidence-based strategies and techniques to minimize the pain that may inadvertently occur during conversations with employees.

Key Points

Let's review a few key points from this chapter:

- Most people have inaccurate and biased estimates of their knowledge, skills, and abilities relative to others. Exposing blind spots and increasing self-awareness are essential steps toward effective leadership and improved employee performance.
- When providing feedback, leaders should strive for one or more of these three outcomes:
  - The employee understands the feedback.
  - The employee is willing to accept and try on the perspectives, experiences, and perceptions provided in the feedback.
  - The employee commits to action, which leads to goal setting, deliberate practice, and changes in behavior.
- Leaders can use specific strategies to help ensure that others accept their feedback and then stop, increase, decrease, or change specific behaviors as needed. It's a truism that only wet babies like change, but if we are ready to accept feedback and committed to changing our thoughts, emotions, and behaviors, we can rewire our brains and create new habits.

Tool 1-1. Tips for Facilitating Successful Feedback Outcomes

Understanding

1. Structure the environment to minimize distractions and maximize focus.
2. Introduce and structure the feedback session with clearly defined goals and intended outcomes.
3. Check your biases about the feedback receiver's current performance and potential.
4. Explain what information you will be sharing with the employee (your observations, observations of others, 360-feedback results, or performance behavior).
5. Schedule enough time to adequately cover all the feedback information you want to share.

Acceptance

1. Before jumping into sharing feedback information with the employee, take time to ask about their perceptions of their current performance and their ideal or future self.
2. Listen for responses that suggest employee defensiveness, negative emotional reactions, or dismissal of the credibility or accuracy of the feedback information hared.
3. Periodically check with the employee to summarize their perceptions about what is validating and what is surprising in the feedback information presented.
4. Regularly check with the employee and ask them to summarize what they agree and disagree with in terms of the feedback shared.
5. Focus on the areas the employee agrees with and accepts.

Commitment to Action

1. Ask the employee what, if anything, they might be motivated to further consider or take specific action to leverage concerning the strengths you shared or potential development areas.
2. Ask the employee how their commitment to action can be translated into a goal they want to work on that will be helpful for them in the future.
3. Ask the employee what barriers might prevent them from successfully reaching this goal.
4. Ask the employee what you can do as a coach, mentor, or peer to help support their success in reaching the goal.
5. Ask the employee how they can measure and evaluate their success in translating feedback from the meeting into successful behavior change perceived by others.

Chapter 2

Ouch, That Hurt!
The Neuroscience of Feedback

Can you think of an emotionally charged moment in your past that shocked or saddened you, hurt your pride, or bruised your ego? We bet it wasn't hard for you to recall. One of Ken's most vivid childhood memories is the gasp his second-grade teacher let out when she answered the red telephone that usually hung silently on the classroom wall. The date was November 22, 1963, and after the gasp, his teacher turned to the class and announced, "President Kennedy has just been assassinated."

But an emotionally charged memory doesn't have to involve a world-changing event or violent disaster. Often, simple social interactions at home, school, or work create lasting impressions due to emotional meaning that only we understand. For Ken, one of those memories is from a high school biology class project about acupuncture. He learned that his baseball idol, Hall of Fame first baseman Willie McCovey of the San Francisco Giants, was one of the first players to get an acupuncture treatment. Ken's high school baseball coach, a former New York Mets pitcher, happened to have a side gig throwing batting practice for the Giants, so Ken summoned his courage and asked the coach to ask McCovey if he'd be open being interviewed about his acupuncture treatment.

McCovey agreed to the interview, and Ken was even able to join him on the field during pregame batting practice, capturing all his answers on a tiny tape recorder. After the interview, Ken stayed to watch the rest of practice from the dugout. He can still recall the feel of the breeze and smell the oil on the baseball mitts. He felt like one of the coolest 17-year-olds in San Francisco.

Then he heard a loud ringing and turned toward two black phones at the far end of the dugout.

"Hey kid, will you answer the phone?" yelled McCovey from his first-base position in the infield.

"Sure!" Ken yelled back. "Which one?"

"Well, the one that's ringing!"

Ken's coach and all the players standing near the dugout burst into laughter and continued to tease him mercilessly throughout the rest of batting practice. He felt embarrassed in the way only a teenager can over a little blunder like that. Today, more than 50 years later, when he plays back that tape and listens to the interview with his idol, Ken still can't help but cringe and feel ashamed of his tiny faux pas all over again.

Have you ever experienced teasing or bullying in school? Were you ever verbally abused by a person close to you or belittled by a colleague in front of others? If so, you can probably recall the exact words they used, the precise location where the interaction took place, and the emotions you felt. Our memory chains are always the longest for deeply emotional events and our most embarrassing situations. Researchers have demonstrated that our recall of socially painful situations in the past elicits greater emotional pain than reliving a physically painful event (Chen et al. 2008).

How is this relevant to our efforts to improve performance feedback? Researchers now understand that for many people, workplace feedback, even if well intentioned, can hurt deeply on an emotional level and remain in employees' memories long term. As a leader, you always want to avoid creating an indelible, embarrassing, or painful memory for an employee, and to do that, you need a basic understanding of how the brain processes feedback—for both the giver and the receiver.

In this chapter, we provide an overview of the neuroscience behind giving and receiving feedback. This explanation should help you understand how feedback works in our brains and why it can create very real emotional hurt and pain, even when the feedback is a direct, candid, and helpful conversation between a leader and an employee to point out how they are performing and ways to improve.

Neural Links: The Impact of Feedback on Our Bodies and Brains

Most of us know from experience that *receiving feedback* can be an emotionally charged experience, but did you know that *giving feedback* creates even more anxiety and a stronger stress response (Thorson and West 2018)? You may be surprised to learn that all conversations focused on feedback, whether at work or home, activate a potential social threat response in our bodies, and it is not unusual for heart rates to jump as much as 50 percent during such interactions.

Our neurological systems rapidly respond to potential harm and threats. The brain functions to ensure our survival by avoiding pain and seeking pleasure, and humans have evolved so well that activation of our threat-and-reward circuitry happens a fifth of a second *ahead* of activation in our planning, problem-solving, and decision-making neocortex. This means we react to threats on a physiological level before we can thoroughly analyze the best way to respond (Hambley 2020). In other words, we react physically and emotionally to the threat of feedback *before* we can consciously make rational decisions about it. Our brains perceive feedback as a potential threat, whether we are giving or receiving it, and this can become a tremendous source of tension and stress.

Let's dive into what this powerful link between emotional and physiological systems means for leaders who are providing performance feedback and the employees who receive it.

Warning: Feedback May Be Harmful to Your Health

Based on recent research, we believe all leaders should work harder to provide timely constructive feedback to employees, create a psychologically healthy culture, and promote positive mental health. Unhelpful critical feedback by leaders significantly contributes to feelings of shame, negative effects, and end-of-workday emotional exhaustion for employees (Xing, Sun, and Jepsen 2020,

2021). Indeed, toxic leaders can even become dangerous to the overall health and mental well-being of their employees (Nowack and Zak 2020).

Unfortunately, many leaders are oblivious to how often their interactions with others cause what we call the "cringe factor"—strong emotional reactions that leave lasting negative impacts on employees' attitudes, levels of engagement, and overall well-being. Many of our high-profile executive coaching assignments have focused on the emotional and social-competence deficits of such leaders, with the goal of minimizing potentially negative interactions and the mental and emotional pain that results (Nowack 2016).

The Impact of Critical and Hostile Feedback on Our Bodies

Feedback perceived to be unfair, microaggresive, uncivil, and negative can elicit more than just an emotional reaction. Research suggests it can also create short- and long-term meaningful reactions that affect our health and well-being. For example:

- Female participants who were systematically ignored and ostracized by colleagues during a laboratory social interaction task showed significant increases in cortisol (Stroud et al. 2000).
- The risk of major depressive disorders in adolescents who are bullied is 2.77 times higher than that of those who are not bullied (Tian et al. 2023).
- Children rejected by their peers had higher cortisol levels than those who were popular or accepted within their social group (Gunnar and Donzella 2002).
- Newlyweds who used hostile verbal feedback (such as criticism, put-downs, and disapproval) during discussions of their marital problems showed significant increases in stress hormones. Twenty-four hours later, these couples exhibited bigger negative changes in immune function than less hostile couples (Kiecolt-Glaser 2018).
- People who receive negative feedback and negative social comparisons experience amplified physiological stress reactions (Dickerson and Kemeny 2004).
- The impact of de-energizing interpersonal communication and relationships (those perceived as unfair, bullying, or draining) is four to seven times more negative than the impact of energizing, positive relationships (Parker, Gerbasi, and Porath 2013).
- Criticism from workplace supervisors leads to *greater* relational distancing than criticism from mothers, fathers, or even romantic partners (Neoh et al. 2022).

Why Feedback Hurts: The Neurobiology of Pain

In most languages, people use words related to physical pain to describe negative interpersonal interactions and social distress; for example:

- "That public rejection was really painful."
- "Her mocking tone hurt my feelings."
- "I was crushed when he ignored what I said."
- "My heart is just breaking now."

Words can indeed be powerful, punishing, and even physically harmful, whether they are spoken aloud or written in an email, social media post, or text message. Neuroscience research suggests that the old playground taunt, "Sticks and stones may break my bones, but words will never hurt me," is not at all scientifically accurate. Words can hurt. But how do we know?

About 20 years ago, an elegant study by University of California, Los Angeles, psychologist Naomi Eisenberger and her colleagues (2003) demonstrated for the first time a direct overlap of the neurobiological systems that govern social and physical pain. The emotional pain of social rejection, ostracization, bullying, incivility, unfair treatment, and verbal abuse were all found to activate neural pathways long associated with physical pain and suffering. More recent neuroimaging research has revealed that one specific area of the brain—the dorsal anterior cingulate cortex (dACC)—is most associated with the unpleasantness of physical pain. But breaking an arm or stubbing a toe aren't the only things that activate the dACC—distressing negative interpersonal interactions, especially self-reported social distress also activate this region (Dickerson and Kemeny 2004).

The experimental paradigm Eisenberger and her colleagues (2003) first discussed is called the "Cyberball paradigm." *Cyberball* is a virtual ball-toss game widely used for psychological research on ostracism, social exclusion, and rejection; it has also been used to study discrimination, prejudice, and interpersonal interactions. In the studies, participants believe they are playing Cyberball with two or three other people, but in fact, the other players are all controlled by the researcher, and no other human interaction occurs. The researcher can modify the speed of the game, the frequency of inclusion, and players' information and iconic representations.

Eisenberger and her team conducted functional magnetic resonance (fMRI) brain scans while participants were playing the game to measure how social interactions were working at the neural level. In the first scan, participants were told that there was a technical problem, and they were able to play but not watch the other two participants. In a second scan, the participants were told they were playing with the other two participants. In a final scan, the participants tossed a ball on the screen seven times in a row, but then, they were suddenly excluded from the game while the two other players threw the ball between themselves for the next 45 throws.

At the end of the experiment, participants were asked to complete a questionnaire to capture their emotional reactions to the game, level of social distress, and explanations about what had occurred during their time interacting with the others. As expected, participants universally reported that they were puzzled and felt ignored and excluded during the game's final round. Unexpectedly, the experience of the brain-scan data also demonstrated that the key brain areas associated with physical pain were significantly more active during the exclusion period of the study.

The brain patterns recorded in Eisenberger's study repeated those found in earlier research, demonstrating that negative social interactions do indeed share a common neural network with physical pain.

Take 2 Acetaminophen and Call Me in the Morning: Suppressing Social Pain

Many people take over-the-counter pain killers to address physical discomfort from minor ailments such as a sprain, headache, or backache. We rely on these medications because they are easy to obtain, relatively inexpensive, and usually work well to alleviate our everyday aches and pains.

Given what we've learned about the common neural network of physical and social pain, you might wonder: *If physical and social pain processes overlap, will taking an analgesic reduce both neural responses?* Science suggests that should be the case, and an over-the-counter painkiller could at least temporarily mitigate the pain related to social distress as well as physical discomfort.

C. Nathan DeWall, who collaborated with Naomi Eisenberger in her initial fMRI findings, decided to test this hypothesis. He conducted two experiments using the same Cyberball manipulation game, dividing the participants into two groups—one took a daily dose of 1,000 milligrams of acetaminophen (also known as paracetamol) for three weeks and another took a placebo for the same three-week period (DeWall et al. 2010).

In the first experiment, 62 healthy participants used the Hurt Feelings Scale (a widely accepted self-assessment tool) to report how much social pain they experienced daily. DeWall and his team observed that while the amount of self-reported negative emotions didn't change for the placebo group, the group taking acetaminophen saw a decrease in negative emotions. Neither group reported a change in positive emotions.

In the second experiment, 25 healthy participants took 2,000 milligrams of acetaminophen daily or a placebo for three weeks. The participants then played the Cyberball game using the same protocol as in the original study. Not only did the participants taking the painkiller report less subjective social distress, but they also demonstrated significantly less neural activation of the physical pain networks in their fMRI scans. Subsequent research studies using similar virtual online games and alternate analgesics have validated these initial groundbreaking studies.

Other neuroimaging studies of feedback have shown a strong link between specific neural networks and specific types of feedback. For example, positive feedback activates the reward areas in the brain, including the medial orbitofrontal cortex and ventral striatum. Additionally, negative feedback activates punishment-related areas, such as the anterior cingulate cortex, insular cortex, and prefrontal cortex (Zak 2018; Kim, Hwang, and Lee 2018).

The takeaway for our purposes is simple: Social pain hurts, just like physical pain. Feedback that we interpret as unfair, negative, discriminatory, or mean-spirited can cause great distress. Leaders who are concerned about the well-being of their direct reports should strive to deliver negative feedback in a way that increases positive effects and decreases negative ones (Young et al. 2017). In the next sections, we'll look at how to accomplish that difficult task.

Balancing Act: Positive-to-Negative Feedback Ratios

As we pursued a deeper understanding of feedback culture in researching this book, we began to wonder: Is there a ratio of positive to negative interaction between leaders and employees that can lead to the most valuable outcomes in work and life? As it turns out, researchers studying the expression of thoughts, feelings, and behavior across various disciplines have discovered a few interesting ratios that predict things such as our longevity or how effectively teams will function. Let's look at some examples of those ratios at work, and then we'll apply them to building an effective feedback culture.

Positive Emotions Equals Long Lives

Developmental psychologist Deborah Danner and her colleagues from the University of Kentucky analyzed one-page, handwritten autobiographies from 180 Catholic nuns. In the documents, the nuns (whose mean age was 22 at the time of writing) were asked to include their place of birth, parentage, interesting childhood events, schools attended, influences that led them to join a convent, their religious life, and outstanding events. The autobiographies were scored for emotional content and the researchers then compared that score with the nuns' longevity based on death certificates.

The study revealed that the nuns who wrote more sentences expressing *positive emotions* lived an average of seven years longer than those whose stories contained fewer positive emotions. Lifespans were longer by 9.5 years for nuns whose autobiographies contained the most words referring to positive emotions and by 10.5 years for those who used the greatest variety of words expressing positive emotions (Danner, Snowdon, and Friesen 2001).

This study suggests that leaders who can enhance the positive emotions of their employees by providing supportive and encouraging feedback might promote both psychological well-being and higher engagement. Leaders who can focus on the positive and model such emotions might find that it "rubs off" on others—a concept often referred to as *emotional contagion.*

Negative Interactions Poison Relationships

John Gottman, a professor emeritus of psychology at the University of Washington, conducted a 10 year study in which he followed 700 couples for 10 years to investigate the positive-to-negative ratio of their interactions. He examined thousands of videotaped interactions, each lasting just 15 minutes, and found that a less than five-to-one positive-to-negative ratio predicted divorce with a high accuracy of 81 to 94 percent. In his "love lab," Gottman analyzed and wrote about some of the most telling negative interactions, including:

- **Criticism**—expressions indicating a defect in a partner's personality; for example, "You always talk about yourself."
- **Contempt**—expressions of superiority; for example, "You just can't get things right."
- **Defensiveness**—expressions of righteous indignation; for example, "It's not my fault that we're always late—you're the one holding us up."
- **Stonewalling**—emotional withdrawal from interaction, such as ignoring the other person.

These kinds of negative expressions predicted early divorce, an average of 5.6 years after the wedding. Surprisingly, behaviors we might consider more extreme, such as emotional withdrawal and anger, predicted later divorce, an average of 16.2 years after the wedding.

What's important for our purposes is that Gottman's research appears to be just as relevant for relationships between leaders and team members working closely together every day as it is for intimate partners (Gottman and Gottman 2015). Therefore, leaders who are highly critical, demonstrate a defensive posture while communicating, or refrain from even discussing important issues will likely lead to disengagement and a willingness on the part of employees to explore other job and career opportunities. Gottman's research becomes even more important in the context of workplaces where many of us cope with a variety of "arranged marriages" with our leaders and team members.

Positive Emotions Encourage Psychological Well-Being

Perhaps most interesting in terms of the leader-employee relationship is University of Michigan psychologist Barbara Fredrickson's study of the power of positive emotions to enhance well-being and coping mechanisms, allowing them to flourish.

Frederickson found the positive-negative ratio of emotions in college students' month-long diaries differentiated those who were languishing from those who scored high in psychological well-being. Students in her study who expressed three times as many positive emotions as negative emotions also reported significantly higher levels of life satisfaction and happiness than the other students.

In another study, Frederickson analyzed a single day's emotions as expressed by three groups:

- People who were fully flourishing (defined as functioning optimally in terms of goodness, growth, and resilience)
- People who were not flourishing
- People who were depressed

Again, Fredrickson's findings indicated that *positive emotions promoted a state of flourishing*; they were not just a by-product. Her well-respected *broaden-and-build theory* suggests that a high ratio of positive versus negative emotions helps expand our awareness, relative to negative emotions, and contributes the raw materials needed to build enduring coping resources and responses on all levels—physical, intellectual, social, and psychological (Fredrickson 2004).

In your organization, Fredrickson's findings translate into continuous monitoring and attending to the mental health and well-being of your employees. Leaders might refer struggling employees to internal and confidential employee assistance programs (EAPs) and explore work-related factors contributing to their overall emotional health and ways to support them.

What the Science Means for Leaders

There is no guarantee that your employees will be motivated to change because of your positive or negative feedback, but without any feedback, spontaneous behavior change is unlikely. Few employees wake up in the morning saying, "I want to be a better listener today and make sure I don't interrupt my colleagues as much as I usually do," or make other commitments to behavior change on their own. However, when packaged and delivered well, your feedback can be the necessary—though not always sufficient—condition that increases an employee's self-awareness and motivation to change.

Based on the research we've examined here and elsewhere, we've concluded that one key to delivering good feedback to your team is finding the right positive-to-negative ratio. When perceived too negatively by recipients, feedback contributes to the breakdown of relationships, shame, and physical and mental anguish, as we discussed already in this chapter. All these results can in turn negatively affect individual and team performance. When the ratio of positive-to-negative feedback is higher, employees are more likely to flourish on many levels (Smither and Walker 2004).

If as a leader you want the members of your team to thrive, what can you do to optimize the positive emotions and minimize the negative when giving feedback? Let's now review some science-based suggestions and a few of our own hacks to make the interactions easier.

Taking the *Ouch* Out of Feedback

As we have already emphasized, without constructive criticism—including some carefully delivered negative feedback—employees are not likely to improve. However, most leaders find it stressful and difficult to give negative feedback. Many even avoid the practice entirely because negative and constructive feedback, even when well intentioned, can elicit defensiveness in recipients, reducing the likelihood that the message will be heard and acted upon.

Unfortunately, while leaders tend to focus on the stress and discomfort of delivering constructive feedback, they underestimate how much employees want to know about where they stand and how to grow and improve (Abi-Esber et al. 2022). If you are a leader who is hesitant about offering feedback, try to take the perspective of your employee—the potential feedback receiver. This may help you recognize that employees truly want to hear feedback and appreciate it when they get it.

When to Give Critical Feedback

In a paper published a few years ago, two researchers at the University of Toronto examined the conditions in which people would be most open to receiving negative feedback (Ruttan and Nordgren 2016). They conducted five separate studies focusing on the impact of self-regulation on defensive information processing—in other words, the way people deny, distort, or avoid processing negative feedback. As it turns out, our capacity for self-regulation and self-control is a bit like a phone battery that runs down as the day progresses. People are likely to be more resistant, more defensive, and less open to criticism as they become more fatigued. In each of their five studies, the researchers found that people who were running low on the capacity to self-regulate were significantly more apt to reject the message and the importance of any negative feedback they received. More importantly, they were also *less willing to seek improvement* based on the feedback provided. Anecdotally, we can confirm that defensive rejection of feedback by employees tends to get worse as the day wears on.

However, in 2019, researchers from Hokkaido University tested when social stressors—such as providing negative feedback, giving a speech, or being evaluated in front of a senior team or other colleagues—would elicit key physiological markers of a stress response by analyzing their subjects' cortisol levels and using a popular tool called the Trier Social Stress Test (Yamanaka, Motoshima, and Uchida 2019). The participants were told not to drink caffeine or exercise throughout the day because those activities were known to influence the rise and fall of cortisol levels. The researchers also carefully controlled for other factors, including duration of sleep, age, gender, and health.

At the end of the study, they found significant and consistent elevated physiological stress responses following social-stress situations in the morning but not later in the day. This suggests that *feedback scheduled earlier in the day might lead to an exaggerated stress response*, which would include strong emotional reactions such as frustration, anger, and defensiveness.

Because the science supports two contradictory conclusions, we believe leaders must use their personal preferences and their knowledge of their employees—including circumstances on the job and outside the workplace—to decide when to hold difficult feedback conversations. Practical steps, like being prepared and making sure to get a good night's sleep before the feedback meeting, can make all the difference. Leaders who don't sleep enough or experience poor quality sleep are less able to read the emotional reactions of others, less in control of their own emotions, and show less sensitivity and caring when interacting with others (Nowack 2017).

The Power of Supportive Relationships

Effective feedback and communication are important factors in defining the overall quality and satisfaction of our social-support relationships at work and home. Current research suggests that strong relationships with a partner, family members, co-workers, bosses, and friends are all associated with emotional and physical health. Findings consistently support a predictive and positively correlated association between the quality of our friendships (in terms of support, feedback, and communication) and our physical health and overall psychological well-being (Pezirkianidis et al. 2023).

Recently, we used StressScan, a well-known published psychological stress and health-risk appraisal, to analyze the differences in perceived *availability*, *utility*, and *satisfaction* around social support for a sample of more than 800 working adults of varied ages (Nowack 2013). Highlights of some of our findings, which demonstrate key differences based on gender, are summarized here:

- **Women reported greater availability and use of their social-support networks**—including supervisors and bosses, colleagues and co-workers, partners, family, and friends—than their male counterparts.
- **Women reported significantly more availability and use of friends and greater satisfaction with their friends** compared with men's reports. Women also reported greater availability and use of partners and families, which is consistent with the "tend-and-befriend response" for successfully coping with work and life stress (Taylor et al. 2000).

In addition, a total of 785 men and women responded to questions about their satisfaction with specific sources of social support in meeting their emotional and instrumental needs. For our purposes, the first item is the most important. When asked about their satisfaction with levels of social support:

- 31 percent said "not at all" or only "slightly" about their boss or supervisor.
- 16.8 percent said "not at all" or only "slightly" about their colleagues or co-workers.
- 13 percent said "not at all" or only "slightly" about their families.
- 9.9 percent said "not at all" or only "slightly" about their partners or significant others.
- 8.3 percent said "not at all" or only "slightly" about their friends.

Perhaps unsurprisingly, given all we've learned in this chapter so far, people in our sample who reported *greater overall social support and openness to feedback* also reported:

- Significantly lower perceived levels of work and nonwork stress
- Significantly greater resilience and cognitive hardiness
- Significantly greater overall happiness

The US Surgeon General's *Advisory on the Healing Effects of Social Connection and Community* (2023) report also highlights the impact of social support on well-being and overall health. According to the report, men and women who lack meaningful social connections and support run the same mortality risk as people who smoke 15 cigarettes a day. Additionally, such individuals have a 29 to 32 percent higher risk for heart disease and stroke, respectively, and a 26 to 29 percent higher risk of premature death.

Finally, recent research highlights the importance of our evolutionary need for social connections. A study led by Giorgia Silani from the University of Vienna investigated the effects of social isolation using comparable methodology across two contexts: in the laboratory and at home during the COVID-19 pandemic. Those who experienced social isolation for eight hours reported higher levels of tiredness, suggesting that low energy may be a basic human response to a lack of social contact (Stijovic et al. 2023).

We can't always have "best friends" at work or even connect on a social level with everyone on our team or with our boss. However, research-based evidence does suggest that the quality of peer relationships is indeed linked to short-term health and well-being (Shirom et al. 2011).

Science-Based Feedback Hacks for Less Distress

Figure 2-1 illustrates the importance of emphasizing employee growth and professional development in all your feedback. Over the years, we've developed some strategies (or hacks) that have proven useful for our clients who are trying to minimize the potential emotional distress of providing feedback to their employees. Four of our best science-based feedback hacks are presented here.

Figure 2-1. The Neuroscience of Feedback Versus Feedforward

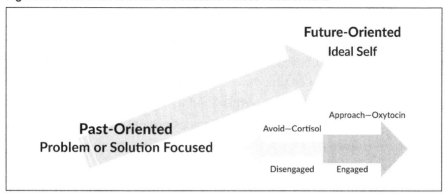

Provide Forward-in-Time Feedback

People who remember the feedback they get from others tend to have an advantage in improving their skills. In six separate experiments, subjects consistently recalled feedback focused on the past better than feedback focused on the future (Nash et al. 2018). However, tips, suggestions, and recommendations for improvement in the future (feedforward) are universally more readily accepted without the *ouch* or associated fight-or-flight response that leads to a defensive reaction in others. Therefore, whenever possible, leaders should keep in mind that employees are significantly more motivated to commit to action and improve when they see that feedback is intended to be constructive, useful, and focused more on future actions than past.

Research also suggests that investing in employees by providing feedback oriented toward the future is associated with the release of oxytocin (what is often called the "trust peptide"), thus enhancing collaborative and psychologically safe relationships (Zak 2018).

Build Rapport and Relationships to Increase Feedback Currency

Constructive feedback is frequent and specific, timely, behaviorally oriented, future-focused, and non-threatening (meaning that it doesn't judge the recipient). It includes favorable feedback as well as critical feedback the leader shares in a way that demonstrates concern and empathy for the employee, creating a psychologically safe environment for discussing job performance and interpersonal behavior in the workplace.

The more an employee trusts and values their relationships with others, the more open and receptive they will be to constructive feedback. Leaders can foster this trust with nonthreatening and empathetic language; for example, "I noticed an important omission in your PowerPoint slide you might want to correct," or "I just received this email from you about a sensitive subject, but I'm guessing it was meant for the other Sandra."

In some studies, deeper, higher-quality relationships *increased* the amount of negative feedback people sought and provided to one another (Finkelstein, Fishbach, and Tu 2017). However, the amount of positive feedback related to goal success and achievement remained the same as relationships with others deepened.

As a leader, if you make a strong investment in getting to know and genuinely appreciate your team members, you will reduce the potential for defensiveness when they respond to feedback and feedforward. The quality of relationships with others at work will also influence the extent to which each party seeks, provides, and responds to shared feedback.

Understand the Limits of Feedback

Studies tell us that leaders with higher empathy levels are more at risk of avoiding critical and necessary conversations and may be more liable to inflate their appraisals of others in an effort to be liked and minimize potential interpersonal conflict (Simon et al. 2020). However, even if the feedback is genuine and future- and growth-oriented, not all employees will welcome, accept, or act on such information. Leaders should understand and be alert for four situations in which attempts at honest and accurate feedback will likely be rejected, ignored, or even perceived to be biased:

- The employee doesn't value the leader's competency and experience or doesn't trust them.
- The employee lacks humility and is prone to entitlement or narcissistic.
- The employee is emotionally exhausted or sleep deprived (Nowack 2017).
- The employee has a low feedback orientation or a low propensity to seek and use feedback from others.

Remember, humans are biologically wired to be motivated more by losses than by gains. We mentioned earlier that a negativity bias exists around seeking pleasure and avoiding pain; this is an essential part of our survival instincts. From an evolutionary perspective, the brain acts as a cost-benefit calculator, assessing potential harm, loss, and danger as bigger motivators than pleasure. One of the ways to minimize the *ouch* in feedback is to *emphasize what might be lost* by not taking feedback seriously or not committing to changing specific behaviors. Providing constructive feedback to employees in a supportive manner but emphasizing the negative outcomes of not changing behavior (loss-framing) can be a good way to lower the cognitive and emotional barriers that can accompany unfavorable feedback (Keith et al. 2022). For example, you might take one of the following approaches to a leader who needs to increase acceptance and motivation to change behavior or take some action:

- "I've noticed that when you quickly talk over your team in staff meetings, it creates a psychologically unsafe space for them to speak up. You may come off as unwilling to truly consider the ideas and suggestions of others, making you appear overly controlling and directive." In this situation, the leader might be more motivated to change their behavior if they understand how their behavior in team meetings could limit employee involvement and participation and stifle truly creative and innovative ideas and solutions.
- "It's been noticeable lately that Sean's lack of attention to detail and missing deadlines are creating extra work and stress for the team. Your unwillingness to constructively confront and address this performance issue has already led to diminished engagement with team members. I'm afraid if you don't speak to Sean immediately, you will lose respect and trust in the eyes of your direct reports." In this situation, the leader might realize that their team members expect those in leadership roles to constructively confront weak or poor-performing team members.

Provide Informative Feedback, Even If It's Critical
Informative feedback (elaborative or evaluative) provides specific information that can be used to correct behavior or errors and serves as an emotional

regulation function to help minimize the potential *ouch* factor. Informative feedback contrasts with *confirmatory feedback*, which provides little or no useful information to help employees understand how to improve, and instead says whether a behavior or response is basically correct or not (Kim, Hwang, and Lee 2018).

Leaders must keep in mind that information shared as part of negative feedback should be less focused on evaluating past observed behavior and more on guiding specific and future-oriented behavior change. *Negative informative feedback*, although tough to deliver and accept, can still benefit learning and motivation to improve performance.

Make sure to include these three specific elements to help frame your discussion and ensure it is as informative as possible:

- **The situation.** Provide brief description of the specific incident, meeting, or event when you have observed the employee's behavior.
- **The behavior.** Detail one specific behavior you have directly observed, not information about the employee's personality or style.
- **The outcome.** Outline the reactions, feelings, and actions that occurred for you or another team member because of the employee's behavior (that is, how their behavior affected you, the team, and the organization). Provide one or more suggestions for how to act differently in the future.

These hacks won't ensure that every interpersonal interaction with employees will result in positive results or lead to a commitment on the part of the employee to change their behavior. However, they can help take the sting out of feedback meetings for both leaders and employees and create an environment of trust and perceived support.

 Key Points

Let's review a few key points from this chapter:

- Words can hurt, especially when someone is bullying, taunting, or unfairly criticizing or evaluating another person. What hurts most is not what you say, but the feelings of social rejection and exclusion that collide with our basic human drive to belong.

- Regions of the brain typically associated with physical pain and empathetic distress are also linked to the emotions associated with social rejection, perceived unfairness, bias, and social evaluation.
- We can use specific feedback strategies or hacks to take the pain out of constructive, necessary feedback for direct reports. These hacks include focusing on the ideal or future situation to highlight greater effectiveness or success and emphasizing the negative impact on the team and leader if the employee doesn't accept the feedback and take the action requested.

Tool 2-1. Tips for Creating a Supportive Feedback Climate

Set the Stage for Psychologically Safe Feedback Conversations
Welcome the employee and share the purpose of the feedback meeting.
Remember: How you share feedback can hinder or facilitate a safe conversation.

Allow the Employee to Express Emotions
Feedback can inspire both positive and negative emotions. Listen for
understanding and acknowledge the employee's emotions and feelings.
For example:
- "I understand this conversation may be difficult."
- "I can see from your reaction that the feedback I have shared with you
  is upsetting."

Consider Offering Impact Statements
Describing specific behaviors and sharing their influence on the team, and on you
as the leader, can increase the employee's awareness and minimize their emotional
reactions. By sharing that influence, you provide the employee with information
about how their actions or words are perceived by others. This can set up a safe
path toward a commitment to behavior change in the future.

**Seek to Understand Before Being Understood and Validate the
Employee's Feelings**
Listen for understanding at three levels (the content of the statement, the feelings
of the employee, and the employee's need) to validate their experience in the
conversation. Providing emotional reassurance signals support, empathy, and
caring. For example:
- Listening for content: "What I am hearing you say is . . ."
- Listening for emotion: "It sounds like you may be feeling . . ."
- Listening for need: "I'm getting a sense that you want . . ."

Check In and Follow Up
When difficult conversations are necessary and the employee expresses negative
(or even positive) emotions, it is important to have a follow-up or check-in meeting
later to acknowledge the employee's reaction and reinforce that they are not alone
and their perspective matters. This meeting can be formal or informal, but it should
occur as soon as possible after the initial feedback meeting.

Chapter 3
Feedback for a Diverse Workforce

You're reading this book because you want to provide feedback your employees understand, accept, and then follow up with a commitment to successful habits and job-specific behavior changes that have a direct impact on their overall performance. But every day you face multiple challenges and opportunities as you consider the best ways to approach feedback for each of your direct reports. Our experience tells us that challenges related to demographic factors and unconscious bias are often top of mind for leaders and employees today, so we'd like to address those issues directly in this chapter.

In Sandra's role as an organization development manager, she worked for Gino, a CEO known for his curt and blunt demeanor, assertiveness, and direct communication style. Her initial project with him set the stage for an important lesson in navigating diverse leadership styles and personalities in the workplace.

Sandra was assigned the task of presenting attrition reports, so she compiled data and analysis into a detailed 10-page report. During her presentation, she meticulously laid out attrition rates, dissecting the themes extracted from exit interviews, and elaborating on a range of recommendations aimed at steering the organization toward improvement.

A few minutes into the presentation, Gino interrupted, "Hurry up and cut to the chase!" He tossed aside the report and asked Sandra to send him a condensed version—in just five bullet points on half a page. Taken aback by his sharp tone, Sandra complied with his request but then spent the next few days reflecting on the power dynamic at play. She wanted to discover whether the people Gino regularly interrupted and ridiculed were the women on his team, new employees, or all employees below him in the hierarchy. Gino wanted succinct, action-oriented information that was presented in only a few bullet points. He wasn't interested in the data or analysis behind the bullet points. Sandra understood that she needed to change her strategy, tailoring her approach and way of communicating to her new CEO's leadership style. But she also knew she would need to push back against his harsh, dismissive tone and any demonstrations of conscious or unconscious bias.

The bigger lesson Sandra learned from that experience and applied to her work on performance feedback was the importance of demonstrating respect for all her colleagues and being mindful of any microaggressions she or others might be engaged in. Since then, as a leader herself, she's called out colleagues who ridiculed others in meetings and advised men in powerful positions on how to stop interrupting or demeaning junior employees, especially women. She has reflected on her own style and tried to consider the personalities and communication styles of clients and team members on every new project.

We believe leaders should always reflect upon and interrogate the demographic factors that influence their effectiveness in giving feedback and their employees' receptivity to that feedback. To help with this, this chapter shares recent research and offers tips for addressing the influence of personality types, the role of neurodivergence, the overall leader-employee relationship, and employees' engagement. We'll then dive into research on how culture, race, age, and gender contribute to our unconscious biases and discover ways to minimize that bias when giving feedback.

Who We Are Affects Giving and Receiving Feedback

We are all born with the same biological drive to connect with others, but a variety of factors influence the quality of our conversations, discussions, and feedback. Our ancient ancestors thrived in small, supportive communities where communication was always face-to-face. Today, our communities range from small and intimate to vast and global, and we communicate via audio and video over great distances. A host of similarities and differences in our personalities and cultures now influence how effectively we connect, but we thrive when we can communicate effectively and supportively at home and work. In the workplace, key factors that influence a leader's effectiveness in communicating feedback and an employee's receptivity to feedback include the relationship between the two, each person's personality or style, whether they are neurodivergent or neuroatypical, and the employee's level of engagement.

Good Relationships for Good Feedback

People seek feedback from those they value, trust, and perceive as true champions of their personal growth and professional development. In our workplace relationships, personality clashes, style differences, biases, and other factors contribute to how well people get along. Better relationships make us all more likely to risk sharing information, providing constructive feedback, and giving future-oriented feedforward. The quality of our relationships strongly contributes to whether our feedback will be ignored, rejected, or considered and acted upon. Most importantly, good relationships inspire us as leaders, encouraging us to be helpful and supportive in guiding employees toward future effectiveness and success on the job.

As a leader, you need trusted confidants, mentors, coaches, friends, and family members to illuminate your blind spots and let you know what you can do differently in the future to succeed. You need people who aren't afraid to let you know when you have food between your teeth or should make a radical shift in your feedback strategy.

In weak and poor-quality relationships, feedback is often received and redefined as the other person's problem; it's simply not considered seriously. In strong relationships, both parties at least try to acknowledge and accommodate the need for changes in behavior. If you regularly pause to reflect on the quality of your relationships with your direct reports and colleagues, you will gain additional insight into how to approach feedback meetings and what to expect from the people receiving your feedback message.

Empathy and Feedback

Intuitively, we all know that a leader's personality or social style plays a big role in feedback delivery, interpretation, and positive or negative responses. You might expect leaders to find it a distasteful or demanding managerial activity to give critical or negative feedback because of its ability to create interpersonal conflict and damage relationships with direct reports (Simon et al. 2022). However, in a study by leadership development firm Zenger Folkman, while 44 percent of leaders surveyed said providing negative feedback was "stressful or difficult," a healthy majority of 56 percent did not (Zenger and Folkman 2014). This led us to wonder why some leaders tend to be less comfortable providing negative feedback to improve performance in their direct reports and how to mitigate that discomfort.

In looking at recent research, we found studies suggesting that leaders who possess *high trait empathy* (saying, for example, "I feel others' emotions") were significantly more distressed after providing negative feedback. These findings provide insight into why some leaders are so reluctant to constructively confront their direct reports, provide such feedback, and offer helpful solutions (Simon et al. 2022). The authors suggest that for leaders with high trait empathy, getting off-site (if they are not working remotely already), exercising, or just taking a break might minimize the emotional downsides of providing negative feedback.

In our own research, we have found that a potential downside of having too much empathy includes compassion fatigue and burnout, which negatively affects job performance. Other researchers' findings support this conclusion. For example:

- Leaders prone to empathy are more adept at giving helpful feedback because they can anticipate others' emotional reactions. At the same time, these empathic leaders may internalize the suffering of others to a debilitating extent that reduces their attention to other leadership requirements and overall effectiveness (Simon et al. 2022).
- Empathetic leaders can more easily be deceived by manipulative emotional cues (Zloteanu et al. 2021).
- High levels of empathic concern can undermine performance in a competitive context (Longmire and Harrison 2018).

We offer the leaders we work with three suggestions for managing the potential downsides of empathy:

1. **Leader, heal thyself.**
   » Acknowledge the distress of carrying others' pain.
   » Practice self-care to detach and recover from stressful interpersonal interactions with others.
   » Ask for help when you need it.
   » Say no sometimes to avoid compassion fatigue.

2. **Learn to *tune* your caring.**
   » Depending on the employee and their circumstances, apply different "frequencies of caring"—from *healthy detachment* (letting emotionally troubling people take responsibility for their own actions) to *compassionate action* (supporting others in ways that will help reduce physical, emotional, or other kinds of suffering).
   » Keep empathic concern high and distress low.

3. **Remember that empathy is a skill.**
   » Emotionally balance your empathy, keeping in mind that caring *well* does not mean caring *more*.
   » Practice compassion-based meditation to help shift from empathetic distress to empathetic concern for your employees (Nowak and Zak 2020).

Bright and Dark: Personality and Feedback

People are complex, sometimes act in unpredictable ways, and can be hard to figure out. However, psychologists generally agree that there are six bright-side and three dark-triad factors to categorize human personalities (Table 3-1). Additional factors—including self-efficacy, self-esteem, and a sense of control—are also significant in determining the way both leaders and employees feel and behave regarding feedback.

Table 3-1. Bright-Side and Dark-Triad Personality Factors

Bright-Side Personality Factors	Dark-Triad Personality Factors
• Conscientiousness (achievement striving, drive, and self-discipline) • Agreeableness (cooperativeness, compassion, and politeness) • Extraversion (sociability, excitement, and positive emotions) • Emotional stability (anxiety, impulsivity, and negative emotions) • Openness to experience (fantasy, risk-taking, and adaptability) • Honesty-humility (integrity, humbleness, and authenticity)	• Narcissism (entitlement, self-confidence, and grandiosity) • Machiavellianism (cynical disregard, proclivity for manipulation, and deceit) • Psychopathy (lack of empathy, thrill-seeking, and impulsivity)

As a rule, the personality factors listed in Table 3-1 act interdependently and tend to be relatively stable, but they often drift or evolve over a lifetime. For our purposes, it's important to know that when it comes to performance, some personality factors have a threshold level that, when crossed, will interfere with a person's effectiveness on the job. Many studies support a U-shaped relationship between our personalities and our work–life outcomes, demonstrating that too little or too much of a particular characteristic disrupts both interpersonal relations and job performance. For example, excessively focusing on detail, "burning the midnight oil," and a relentless drive for success are not only the attributes of the conscientiousness factor, but they're also the traits that increase the risk of work stress and job burnout.

When we look at personality and feedback specifically, we see current evidence-based research pointing to a few key conclusions:

- Employees who are high in emotional stability (sensitive and nervous versus resilient and confident) are significantly more likely to *use* feedback results positively for their ongoing professional development.
- Those who are high in extraversion (outgoing and energetic versus solitary and reserved) are significantly more likely to seek additional feedback.
- Extraverted employees who also have a high level of *openness to experience* (inventive and curious versus consistent and cautious) are

more likely to view constructive feedback as valuable and more likely to seek further information to clarify which changes in their behavior would enhance performance.

- Employees who are high in conscientiousness (driven and organized versus extravagant and careless) are likely to engage in behaviors that facilitate goal setting and successful goal achievement (Nowack and Mashihi 2012).

In summary, an employee's personality or style plays an important role in their receptivity to feedback and commitment to take future development actions. While a leader can't change the basic personalities of their direct reports, they can modify their approach to feedback and communication with employees to maximize the employees' understanding and motivation to improve performance and relationships with others on the job.

Neurodivergence and Feedback

In recent years, research has shown that the inner workings of our brains vary dramatically, and there is no one way our minds are supposed to work. We see this demonstrated every day in our work with clients.

In one executive coaching session, Ken introduced a visualization and rehearsal exercise to help a leader practice before an upcoming stressful meeting. In a follow-up session, the leader said they were unable to do this exercise—not because they weren't interested and motivated but because they had *aphantasia*, an inability to create mental images. Ken had not realized that aphantasia, or "mind-blindness," was characteristic of the leader's type of neurodivergence. He learned an important lesson that day: It's essential for anyone in the role of a coach to communicate openly about any exercises and be able to suggest modifications a client or employee might require.

Recent research indicates that 15 to 20 percent of the world's population can be classified as neurodivergent (Doyle 2020). Also called neurodiversity and neuroatypicality, neurodivergence can include a variety of neurological differences, including autism, dyslexia, attention deficit hyperactivity disorder (ADHD), Tourette syndrome, and some forms of anxiety, as well as visible and invisible physical disabilities manifested through specific illnesses, diseases, and conditions such as multiple sclerosis or Parkinson's disease.

Neurodivergence is such a broad catch-all term that it includes people who consider their challenges to be disabilities as well as those who do not. In either case, leaders can put in place accommodations mandated by the Americans With Disabilities Act (ADA) to remove barriers if requested by employees, just as they would in the case of employees with physical or sensory disabilities. For example, some neurodivergent employees might struggle to make direct eye contact, regulate facial expressions, or remain still, and thus would benefit from accommodations during face-to-face discussions or the option of a communicating via telephone or email instead. Further elaboration or clarification isn't needed during most neurotypical social interactions and communication, which often depends on tonal inflections and nonverbal behavior in addition to words. However, for some neurodivergent employees, routine interpersonal interactions, formal feedback meetings, and team activities can potentially contribute to social anxiety and stress (Austin and Pisano 2017).

Leaders can look for signs of neurodivergence in their employees such as overload (confusion, distress, irritability, restlessness), sensory sensitivities (noise, light), communication and social behavior (indirect eye contact, anxiety, preference to work alone, social withdrawal, fidgeting), or work performance (poor reading comprehension, mistakes, errors, unable to meet time deadlines, hyper-focused on tasks or struggling to focus at all).

It's important to remember that you may not know whether an employee needs accommodations because only about 3.2 percent of employees choose to disclose any type of disability to their employers (Sherbin et al. 2017). Therefore, leaders should try to institute policies and practices around feedback that ensure it's always accessible to everyone. And, leaders can employ various strategies to help their neurodivergent employees thrive in the workplace.

In her book, *The Canary Code: A Guide to Neurodiversity, Dignity, and Intersectional Belonging at Work*, psychologist Ludmila Praslova reminds leaders that personality-based performance feedback is a major source of stress for neurodivergent people and can have repercussions for both engagement and talent retention. She suggests focusing feedback on skills, behaviors, and outcomes, rather than personality, and only those within the employee's control.

When a neurotypical person gives feedback to another neurotypical person, the underlying meanings of specific gestures, tonal inflections, and words are conveyed and understood without much need for additional clarification. For those who are neurodiverse, comments and feedback about personality can be missed or misunderstood. In summary, focusing feedback on behavior, instead of personality, is a recommended practice for both neurodiverse and neurotypical employees.

Praslova strongly emphasizes that leaders should not attempt to change an employee's neurodivergent characteristics or personality. Leaders should check their biases and understand that many neurodiverse employees are prosocial and quite skilled at understanding other people's perspectives. Some leaders may struggle to understand a neurodiverse perspective and some neurodivergent people might struggle to understand a neurotypical perspective—as always, communication is a two-way street (Praslova 2024). She points out, however, that it's essential to communicate as clearly and unambiguously as possible.

Here are some additional things to keep in mind when providing feedback:

- Be aware that many neurodiverse employees prefer concrete, simple communication free from jargon, idioms, metaphors, sarcasm, nuance, and irony (Goulet 2022).
- Don't hesitate to ask about and take into consideration each employee's communication preferences.
- Schedule regular check-ins to minimize anxiety associated with less frequent formal meetings.
- Try using visual aids if that helps enhance the employee's understanding.

Just as with any other employee, speak to neurodivergent employees in an honest, respectful, and constructive manner, provide clear performance expectations, and deliver messages using a direct and positive tone to build self-esteem.

Employee Engagement and Feedback

Each employee on your team maintains a certain level of engagement that determines how well they perform their job, how they interact with colleagues and leaders, and ultimately, whether they will remain with your organization.

Engagement can be steady or dynamic. It can fluctuate based on the employee's mental health, family issues, financial well-being, and other work-related factors, including workplace culture, workloads, conflict or harmony within teams, and relationships with supervisors.

But what do we really mean when we talk about *engagement?* It turns out, organizations use several definitions. Engagement can refer to:

- **A psychological state** encompassing mental health, energy, involvement, commitment, satisfaction, job burnout, perceived stress, perceived justice, and empowerment
- **A personality trait** that involves a positive mood, a negative mood, conscientiousness, resilience, hardiness, optimism, core self-evaluations, and a proactive personality
- **Behaviors,** including organizational citizenship, initiative, high performance, collaboration, teamwork, dishonesty, and theft

We've developed a tool for measuring employee engagement that can be used no matter how your organization defines the concept (Figure 3-1). The Employee Engagement Index is a simple way to quickly identify cognitive, affective, and behavioral indicators of what might be contributing to lower levels of engagement at a single point in time.

Using tools like this index, leaders should continuously monitor their employees' engagement levels and look for changes over time. Gauge how each employee's engagement might be affecting overall performance or interpersonal relationships on the job. When a *highflyer* (a high-potential employee who exhibits both a high level of performance and high interpersonal skills) experiences work or life events that temporarily affect their level of engagement, you will need to identify and address the causes as you're using our Performance Feedback Coaching Model.

Leaders can apply the *acknowledge, respond, and change* (ARC) model to acknowledge employee behavior, thoughts, and moods; appropriately respond to changes in engagement levels; and help the employee focus on addressing the specific challenges they are facing (Bhatti and Roulet 2023). When leaders meet with employees about their engagement and well-being, they can introduce techniques that facilitate and encourage changes to employees' thinking, feelings, and behavior. One proven tool for this purpose is *cognitive*

Figure 3-1. Employee Engagement Index

For each engagement factor, check the boxes that best describe your employee's current level of engagement. Follow up with those you marked as "low" to discuss further and identify possible underlying factors affecting performance and interpersonal relationships on the job. In some cases, a referral to internal employee assistance counseling or an external allied health professional might be warranted.

Engagement Factor	Low	Moderate	High
Commitment Level			
Commitment to job			
Commitment to team			
Commitment to organization (intent to stay)			
Relationships at Work			
Relationship with the team			
Relationship with customers			
Relationship with you			
Affect or Mood			
Overall mental health			
Overall physical health			
Level of energy			
Overall positive self-talk (e.g., confidence or hope)			
Engagement with social situations			
Level of enthusiasm			
Level of positivity			
Work Performance			
Timeliness or responsiveness to others			
Overall productivity			
Presence at scheduled work meetings			
Uncharacteristic behavior			
Cooperation or collaboration with others			
Attention to detail			
Focus or concentration			

Source: Mashihi and Nowack (2013)

reappraisal, which is the process of replacing unhelpful thoughts with a more realistic and balanced view of a situation. This coping technique is a major cornerstone of cognitive-behavioral therapy, but one that leaders can employ without clinical experience.

Leaders certainly are not expected to be counselors or therapists, but they should be familiar with some basic mental health first aid, as well as internal and external employee support resources, such as employee assistance counseling programs. For leaders interested in using techniques similar to cognitive reappraisal, we recommend the *Harvard Business Review* article, "Helping an Employee in Distress." The authors, Kiran Bhatti and Thomas Roulet (2023), provide additional tips and recommendations for dealing with many mental health crises that arise in the workplace.

In the next section of this chapter, we look at another challenge we all face in our more diverse and interesting workplaces today: recognizing and mitigating unconscious bias when we communicate with one another.

Unconscious Bias and Feedback

Chris, a White man in his 30s who uses he/him pronouns, is scheduled for a performance feedback meeting with his direct report Sam, who is Black, gender nonbinary (uses they/them pronouns), and in their 50s. Sam has been with the organization for more than 12 years and is a vocal LGBTQ+ activist in the community; they are warm and engaging at all-staff parties and have a reputation for getting work done efficiently and meeting high standards. Sam doesn't hesitate to criticize inequities within the company, including salary differentials, and is admired by many of their colleagues for that honesty. Sam recently had a heated confrontation with another team member about an important project deadline, which deeply upset the other employee, and Chris needs to address this issue in the meeting.

Chris also speaks out about important issues in the workplace and has always respected Sam. However, he is not looking forward to discussing this interpersonal conflict. Past performance feedback from Sam's other managers included suggestions that they could be more effective on the job if they listened more, talked less, and avoided emotional confrontations. Sam objected to some of those stereotypical characterizations of Black people, women of color, and LGBTQIA+ people, and Chris wants to listen to and validate these concerns. He worries that Sam might see this upcoming feedback conversation as an indication that the organization is silencing outspoken Black employees.

Chris and other company leaders recently attended a day-long diversity training, and he came away assessing his own unconscious biases. Now he's wondering if he should cancel the feedback meeting with Sam to minimize any possible negative consequences. Can Chris frame his feedback to take any unconscious bias into account and still help Sam improve their tense relationship with the other team member?

How we perceive and experience others consciously and unconsciously shapes the way we receive and provide feedback. Research has demonstrated that we all carry intuitive associations about various aspects of our own and others' identity—including gender, race, religion, and physical appearance—and that these unconscious biases can be different from our conscious values and beliefs. Our unconscious biases can directly influence the information we share, our approach to communicating positive and negative feedback, and our linguistic style and tone. It's important that we try to understand our biases as part of any performance feedback process.

Unconscious biases are adaptive and evolutionary cognitive shortcuts that help us navigate the interpersonal world of beliefs, prejudices, and preferences when we interact with others. Some biases may be biologically wired, such as our proclivity to feel a special bond with others who share common race, religion, language, or other features of who we are. Others are influenced by genetics, parenting, cultural norms, the media, and social experiences from an early age. For example, research shows that three-month-old infants (not newborns) demonstrate a form of racial bias by looking longer at the faces of people of their own race (Kelly et al. 2008). A study by Stanford University neuroscientist David Eagleman and colleagues found that empathic responses were stronger when participants viewed pain inflicted on a hand labeled with their own religion (their in-group) than on a hand labeled with a different religion (an out-group). In other words, greater empathy for pain occurred when participants felt an affiliation for one religious group over another. And atheists demonstrated greater neural indicators for empathy with other atheists over any religious group (Vaughn et al. 2018).

Unconscious biases explain why people often fall back on stereotyping, attributing certain qualities or characteristics to all members of a particular group. Stereotypes can apply to someone's gender identity, race, religion, sexual orientation, weight, physical disabilities, or almost any other personal characteristic, and they can be perceived as positive, neutral, or negative. Conscious biases and prejudices are intentional and controllable, but unconscious biases are less so because we're usually unaware of these cognitive shortcuts that drive our behavior.

Most of us want to believe that we are not susceptible to unconscious biases. We see ourselves as rational people with good intentions, but the truth is that we are all influenced by stereotypes and ideologies that we're not aware of in our interpersonal interactions. However, this doesn't mean we must automatically speak or behave in a prejudiced way or discriminate against others. Let's review some of the typical unconscious biases that influence leaders' feedback to employees:

- **Horns versus halo.** Leaders look for confirming evidence to justify their globally low or high overall perceptions of employees based on a single good or bad trait in others, rather than looking at the whole person.
- **Similar-to-me.** Leaders experience less fear, distress, and anxiety with their in-groups (based on race, religion, language, culture, and so on), unconsciously favoring employees who are most like them.
- **Primacy.** Leaders allow their first impression of an employee to dictate inaccurate or incorrect evaluations of the employee's true skills, abilities, and performance.
- **Recency.** Leaders place more emphasis on recent events and behaviors than older ones, ignoring an employee's earlier accomplishments and actions.
- **Leniency.** Leaders inflate the overall evaluation of an employee's skills, abilities, and behavior. As a result, they find it difficult to provide constructive or negative feedback because they are blinded by the employee's strengths.
- **Strictness.** Leaders have elevated standards that lead them to focus primarily on development areas, rather than emphasizing the employee's strengths in feedback.

- **Contrast.** Leaders use specific employees as "standards" against which to judge and evaluate others. This leads to an underestimation or overestimation of each employee's true skills and abilities.
- **Attribution.** Leaders incorrectly interpret the skills and performance of others based on the leader's own personality or background, which causes them to overestimate the weight of someone's personality traits and underestimate the influence of their individual circumstances.
- **Confirmatory.** Leaders tend to seek evidence that supports their specific points of view about others or a topic.
- **Stereotype.** Leaders tend to put employees into specific groups, which limits recognition and acceptance of individual differences.

If we look back at the case of the feedback conversation that needed to happen between Chris and his employee Sam, you might recommend that Chris review this list of common unconscious biases before the meeting. This could guard against any biases that might interfere with their conversation and to help alleviate any short- or longer-term influences on Sam's level of engagement, commitment to the organization, and working relationship with Chris.

Our Survival Brains Wired for Bias
- Brains are cost-benefit calculators that, from an evolutionary perspective, emphasize avoiding pain and seeking pleasure, which contributes to our being more comfortable with in-groups and more threatened by out-groups.
- Brains conserve energy by searching for and recognizing patterns, while simultaneously running complex biological systems to ensure our safety and well-being.
- Biologically, we're all wired to have biases. And sometimes our unconscious biases don't line up with our conscious beliefs.
- Both conscious and unconscious biases can negatively affect our decision-making and interpersonal behaviors toward others.
- Biases cannot be eliminated, but they can be mitigated by being self-aware and creating new habits and associations to overcome them:
  - Bias awareness and training tends to be ineffective—only developing new habits can help address biases.
  - Positive experiences with people who are different from ourselves in any way can help mitigate biases (Paolini et al. 2021).

Race and Feedback

Research suggests that humans are wired to feel safer and less threatened when surrounded by others who share a common history, values, and background. In many cases, this means feeling more comfortable with those of the same race or ethnicity, a form of *in-group bias.* This bias can begin at a young age, even before interacting with individuals of other races and ethnicities (Kelly et al. 2008).

In three experiments, five- and six-year-old Canadian children looked at photos of two other children and listened to recordings of them speaking. One of the recorded voices had a Canadian English accent and the other had either a British English accent or a Korean accent. The subjects of the experiment were asked, "Which one would you like to be friends with?" The children consistently selected the photo associated with the child who spoke with a familiar Canadian English accent (Pacquettte-Smith et al. 2019). In another study, six-to-eight-month-old infants were shown videos of people and animals; they followed the gaze of members of their own race more often than they followed the gaze of individuals of other races, suggesting that infants are inherently biased to learn information from adults of their own race (Xiao et al. 2017).

As we mentioned briefly already, researchers have been able to use fMRI to demonstrate and replicate experiments showing the activation of the emotional areas of the brain associated with empathy when participants observed videos of people of their own race in pain. When observing the same painful situations for people outside their race group, those areas of the brain were not activated (Cao et al. 2015). These findings did not depend on the closeness of contact or personal relationships, but simply on the overall level of experience with people of the other race in the subjects' everyday environment. In other words, this study showed that people feel greater concern and compassion for those who are most like them in terms of race.

What lessons can we learn from this research and apply to performance feedback? Recent analyses by Textio (2022, 2024) identified some key racial differences in workplace feedback that may be attributed partially to leaders' in-group biases, which they may or may not be aware of. Here are some of the workplace feedback biases revealed in the research:

- Asian employees received more feedback than people of any other race—25 percent more than White employees. Black men received the least feedback.
- Only 8 percent of Black employees and 14 percent of Latino employees received feedback describing them as ambitious, compared to 39 percent of White employees and 57 percent of Asian employees.
- Just 12 percent of Black employees received feedback that they were easy to work with, compared to 41 percent of White employees.
- Black and Latino employees received 2.4 times more unactionable feedback than White and Asian employees.
- Black women received nearly nine times as much unactionable feedback as White men under 40 received.

Let's look at these findings in the context of Chris and Sam's feedback conversation. As a White male, Chris might have an unconscious bias that orients his feedback more toward personality, rather than actionable behaviors that Sam might be able to address and modify. Now, take a moment to consider how *your* racial and ethnic identity might affect the frequency and type of feedback you tend to give to employees who are most and least like you.

Remember that Chris was considering whether he should cancel his feedback meeting with Sam to avoid any potential harm based on his unconscious bias. Many leaders, educators, and executive coaches are tempted to hold back their feedback or become extremely cautious for fear of saying something to an employee that reveals an unconscious bias. In fact, some studies have shown that teachers don't give non-White students as much valuable critical feedback as White students because teachers are concerned about appearing to show unconscious bias or racism (Croft and Schmader 2012). Similarly, leaders who are unknowingly influenced by a desire to connect more supportively with people of color may avoid giving negative feedback (Dupree and Fiske 2019). One study found that even well-trained White executive coaches were less comfortable offering developmental feedback to Black clients and engaging in diversity-based conversations than doing the same with White clients (Bernstein 2023).

Tough feedback conversations are already challenging, but they become even more difficult when the racial identities of leaders and team members are different. Leaders like Chris often find it easier to say as little as possible to avoid generating conflict, being accused of being racially biased, or creating a hostile work environment. But it's never enough for leaders to emphasize only positive feedback or stay silent. All feedback should be specific and actionable for everyone on your team so each employee can benefit and improve.

Five Ways to Help Minimize Racial Bias in Your Feedback

1. Reflect on the unconscious racial biases and stereotypes you might have. What do you see as threatening in those different from you? Name examples of people who defy those biases and break those stereotypes. Focus on people for whom you are preparing feedback as individuals rather than as members of a group.
2. Seek positive interactions and connections with people outside your racial, ethnic, or religious network (your in-group identity) to expand your comfort level.
3. Provide both critical and constructive feedback with specific and actionable information.
4. Reflect on and monitor the quantity and type of feedback you provide to each member of your team. Do you provide more or different types of feedback (constructive versus recognition or praise) to individuals in one group over another?
5. Seek feedback from your team about your performance feedback and coaching skills, and then use internal or external mentors or coaches to improve those skills.

Gender and Feedback

Three studies in the past few years tested whether expressing anger in court made attorneys more effective and whether that effectiveness depended on their gender. The studies confirmed that male attorneys who expressed anger in court were seen as powerful and driven by their convictions, while the same behavior in female attorneys was seen as being obnoxious and shrill (Salerno et al. 2018). In two other studies, men who spoke up to share ideas in workgroups were seen as having higher status and more likely to emerge as leaders than women who did the same (Martin 2017). Additionally, research has shown that men are three times more likely than women to report being described as confident and 3.7 times more likely to report being described as ambitious (Textio 2022, 2024).

Gender bias against women still permeates organizations around the world (although it is diminishing in some industries as more women enter leadership roles). According to the 2023 UNDP Gender Social Norms Index, nine out of 10 people, regardless of their gender, hold some biases against women. Bias against women has remained stable over the past decade and continues to create barriers in business, politics, and the workplace. The UNDP report points to the following statistics:

- 40 percent of those surveyed believed men were better executives and business leaders.
- 50 percent of citizens in 80 countries believed men were better political leaders.
- In the 59 countries where women are now more educated than men, the average gender income gap remains a staggering 39 percent in favor of men.
- 28 percent of those surveyed believed a university education was more important for men than for women.
- Only 27 percent believed women should have the same rights as men in a democracy.

The research we've examined over many years illustrates the power of stereotypes about men's and women's behavior. In general, men are seen as more agentic (authoritative and directive), while women are seen as more communal (empathetic, warm, and supportive). But a study conducted from 1946 to 2018 (using data from 16 nationally representative public opinion polls involving more than 30,000 US adults) found an important shift in the period after World War II. According to this data, by 2018, Americans viewed women as *equally competent* or even *more competent* than men in the workplace (Eagly et al. 2020). However, the stereotype of women as more compassionate and sensitive than men has also strengthened over time. This shift appears to mitigate the traditional views of women lacking valued stereotypical male agentic qualities in leadership roles.

Stereotypes about women vary by race and ethnicity in ways that are relevant to leaders who must give feedback in a way that accounts for *intersectionality*, or how multiple forms of discrimination overlap and intersect in people's lives. Three powerful, common stereotypes in the United States are that White women are supportive and caring, Black women have notable agency, and Asian women are highly intelligent (Eagly 2023). Equally important to point out is the stereotype of East Asian and South Asian women as part of a "model minority." These stereotypes are problematic even if on the surface they paint these women in a "positive" light because they restrict people to a narrow set of preconceived characteristics instead of allowing them to be seen as individuals. We should also note that when women behave in ways that don't align with the majority culture's expectations, they are often punished.

What about our own research in this area? A few years ago, we used a validated, behaviorally based emotional intelligence (EI) measure to compare the way people rated themselves with how others rated them in 17 categories, which we organized into three larger topics: self-management, relationship management, and communication skills. In a comparison of 671 men and 674 women randomly selected from diverse companies and industries, the women rated themselves significantly higher than men on an overall measure of EI, communication skills, and relationship management (Nowack and Munro 2019). And managers, direct reports, and peers rated women significantly higher in communication, relationship skills, and overall, EI than men.

The Neurobiology of Leadership Differences in Men and Women

When neuroscientists examine gender differences, they see small but significant distinctions between men's and women's leadership behaviors, most of which can result in advantages for women as leaders because:

- Women often have a more transformational, participative, and involvement-oriented leadership style. This may indicate that women have an evolutionary, neuroscience-based advantage in possessing and expressing communal leadership approaches (Nowack and Zak 2020).

- Women tend to be significantly better than men at judging the emotions and mental states of others (Kirkland et al. 2013).
- Women are significantly more sensitive to perceptions of injustice and unfairness than men, as observed in fMRI activation of empathy neural networks (Dulebohn et al. 2016).
- When seeing others in pain, women showed relatively higher fMRI activation in a sensory area of the brain associated with pain than did their male counterparts, demonstrating greater caring and empathy (Christov-Moore et al. 2020).

Leaders of any gender should recognize that persistent gender-based biases continue to shape how women employees are perceived and the feedback they receive. For example, an analysis of performance evaluations of people across three high-tech companies and a professional services firm found that women consistently received less feedback tied to business outcomes and career advancement than men (Correll and Simard 2016). When women received specific developmental feedback, it tended to be overly focused on their communication style rather than their technical skills. Additionally, feedback providers who feel social pressure to avoid being seen as biased and prejudiced overcorrect when giving women performance feedback. This leads them to handle women with "velvet gloves" and deliver inflated and inaccurate performance feedback (Sheppard, Trzebiatowski, and Prasad 2024).

In general, men tend to receive more *actionable* feedback than their female counterparts, both formally (in written performance evaluations) and informally (in individual meetings). When compared with younger White men, all women over 40 receive more than four times the amount of *unactionable* feedback (Textio 2022). And about 88 percent of outstanding women workers receive feedback on their personalities, while the same is true for only 12 percent of their male counterparts (Textio 2024).

An analysis of written feedback for 146 mid-career leaders provided anonymously by more than 1,000 of their peers and managers, identified several important trends and highlighted different aspects of gender bias in feedback (Table 3-2; Doldor, Wyatt, and Sylvester 2021).

Gender and the Science Behind Empathetic Leadership

We all constantly seek the right balance between interacting with others and being wary of those who pose a possible threat at home, in our communities, and in the workplace. Research over the past two decades by Claremont University neuroscientist Paul Zak and his colleagues has established that the biological basis for psychological safety, empathy, and interpersonal trust is the hormone and peptide *oxytocin*. Their studies found that oxytocin, testosterone, and stress-related neurotransmitters compete for the same receptor sites in the brain and heart to enhance emotional awareness and collaborative behavior.

Even before their research clarified the role of oxytocin in supporting a sense of safety and empathy, UCLA Professor Shelly Taylor (2006) hypothesized that the release of oxytocin in women under stress played a role in what she called their "tend and befriend" pro-social behaviors toward others. Men under stress, on the other hand, produce about five to 10 times more testosterone than women, which may explain their higher levels of competitiveness and aggression.

We believe that many of the gender differences associated with emotional intelligence—especially women's tendency toward empathy and involvement-oriented leadership styles—may be attributed to the prevalence of pro-social oxytocin, which provides women with a *slight* evolutionary advantage over men in getting along with others. In practice, however, studies of contemporary organizations show that women's success in leadership roles is often attributed to luck rather than inherent ability, while their leadership failures tend to be ascribed to a lack of ability (Carlin et al. 2018).

Table 3-2. The Focus of Feedback to Men and Women

Topic	Men are encouraged to:	Women are encouraged to:
Vision	Create and deliver the vision.	Emphasize impact and delivery.
Political skills	Make use of politics.	Manage politics.
Assertiveness	Get ahead.	Get along.
Confidence	Express confidence.	Develop confidence.

Bias and Transgender and Nonbinary Employees

Transgender and nonbinary employees face significant challenges in the workplace, including discrimination, bias, and harassment. One recent study found that 30 percent of transgender individuals reported experiencing harassment in the workplace and 26 percent said they had been fired or denied promotions because of their gender (Humiston 2023). Some studies of biases around transgender and nonbinary people suggest that these stereotypes can affect recruitment, promotion, and hiring practices, as well as perpetuate widespread prejudice, discrimination, violence, and other forms of stigma (Gibson and Fernandez 2018; White Hughto, Reisner, and Pachankis 2015).

In providing feedback of any kind, leaders should always use the names and pronouns their employees choose to share. Some employees will feel comfortable sharing their trans or nonbinary identities while others won't. It is also important for leaders to reflect on the existing biases they and others in the organization may hold around gender and recognize that gender is *not binary* but a complex function of genetics, anatomical and hormonal differences, and social identity.

Four Ways to Help Minimize Gender Bias in Feedback

1. Reflect on any conscious or unconscious gender biases and stereotypes that you may personally have that influence your feedback. Do you evaluate assertiveness in men, women, and nonbinary employees differently?
2. Pay attention to the language you and your colleagues use related to gender identity. Are you speaking about women, men, and nonbinary people in the same way? Are you unintentionally excluding nonbinary and transgender employees? Strive to write performance reviews and evaluations of the same length, the same level of specificity, and similar language for all employees.
3. Ask about, learn, and use employees' stated gender pronouns in written and oral feedback and all other communication. Using a person's name and pronouns is a form of respect and courtesy. Intentional refusal to use someone's stated name and pronouns is a form of harassment and a violation of their civil rights.
4. Tie your feedback for all employees—positive or developmental—to business goals and outcomes, with no differences based on gender.

Microaggressions in the Workplace

Some leaders hesitate to provide feedback for fear that an employee will accuse them of *microaggressions*, which are intentional or unintentional statements, interactions, or behaviors that subtly communicate bias against historically marginalized or nondominant groups or emphasize a stereotype related to any aspect of someone's identity.

Let's think about microaggressions in the context of this chapter's running example with Chris and Sam. If Chris told Sam, "You're more diplomatic than the other Black managers in the company," he would be demonstrating that he harbored a stereotype about Black managers. Sam might find the comment hurtful and offensive, even though Chris might have thought he was framing the comment as a compliment.

Another example of a microaggression would be if a Jewish employee was asked to bring in a menorah to add to a "winter celebration" display full of Christmas trees and Santas—they may feel their religion was being diminished or tokenized.

The important thing for leaders to remember is that microaggressions can negatively affect employees in a variety of ways, including prompting some to leave their jobs. We've discussed them here in the context of race and religion, but they can focus on any kind of bias, from disabilities, body size, age, or sensory ability to ethnicity, gender, sexuality, or language.

Fortunately, as a leader, you can use two types of countermeasures to help neutralize microaggressive comments and behaviors. You can illuminate the invisible by drawing attention to comments and interactions that might otherwise go unnoticed. And you can educate employees and other leaders about why their comments are harmful.

Let's review a few counter measures that leaders can take against microaggressions:

- **Label what you hear.** "That's a biased and insensitive comment that shows disrespect to our Spanish-speaking employees."
- **Provide feedback to expand categorizations.** "What you're describing is not true of our Black team members. They're no more likely to be difficult to work with than our White, Asian, or Latino employees."
- **Provide feedback that challenges the stereotype.** "You seem to be assuming all our Asian interns have an affinity for science and math, but I know that is not the case."

- **Provide feedback that appeals to the employee's core values.** "Your actions undermine your expressed desire to treat everyone on the team equally and fairly."
- **Reappraise the meaning of the idea expressed or the action observed.** "Can you think of another possible explanation for your team member's behavior?"
- **Provide feedback that examines intent versus impact.** "Your colleagues generally appreciate your humor, but sometimes it can be interpreted as hurtful or mean-spirited."

Cultural Differences and Feedback

When you have team members who currently live in or have grown up in cultures different from yours, misunderstandings will always occur—even when everyone speaks the same language! Ken manages employees working in the United Kingdom, and, on many occasions, while conducting webinars or classes or holding staff meetings, he has heard participants respond to his remarks by saying simply, "That's very interesting." He used to assume that was a positive, intellectually curious response. Eventually, however, Ken's managing partner, Matt, set him straight and explained that some members of his British audience were *challenging* his statements with that remark but were too polite to openly disagree.

After spending a great deal of time with the team in the UK, Ken began to realize that English isn't the same everywhere. By extension, Spanish in Lima, Peru, or Mexico City will differ from Spanish in Madrid, Spain, and so on. Every country (and even region) has its own cultural overlay on language that includes vocabulary, intonation, and things that commonly go unsaid, but that anyone leading globally needs to grasp if they want to be understood and effective. For example, "Perhaps you should consider . . ." may really mean, "This isn't a suggestion; it's a strong request," but it could also mean, "Please reflect on this idea and decide if you wish to change it." Similarly, "That is a very original point of view" might mean, "Your concept is truly stupid," or "What a brilliant idea!" The statement, "It was my fault" might mean, "It was not entirely all my fault," or be understood in another culture as, "Indeed, it was certainly *your* fault."

As a leader, you must study cultural variations; talk with as many diverse colleagues, employees, and friends as possible; and apply cultural intelligence to every situation. Try to understand how your feedback might be interpreted by those who are from a cultural background different from yours.

Culture Models That Strengthen Communication and Feedback

How should leaders understand and categorize differences among and between various cultures to improve performance feedback for all employees? Two of the most recognized and well-established models of culture are:

- The theory of cultural dimensions from Dutch management researcher Geert Hofstede.
- The culture map from Erin Meyer, an American international business expert and professor at INSEAD Business School.

From 1967 to 1973, Hofstede conducted a large survey that examined value differences across the divisions of the corporate giant IBM. He collected data from 117,000 employees across 50 countries in three regions. After two additional studies using factor analytic statistics, Hofstede created a framework to describe the effects of culture on the values of its members and—most importantly for leaders who must communicate with employees—how these values relate to behavior. Today, we apply Hofstede's framework to understand differences in the way business is done in different cultures. His theory identifies *six dimensions* that define culture, which leaders can use to understand similarities and differences among their international employees. (For a full tour of Hofstede's work, go to hofstede-insights.com/country-comparison-tool.)

Meyer's culture map allows global leaders to pinpoint their leadership preferences and compare their methods to the management styles of other cultures. Her 2014 book, *The Culture Map*, looks at how individuals communicate, lead, approach time, and make decisions. Her framework is independent of the country's politics, religion, or worldview and identifies *eight dimensions* that allow a leader to compare how two or more cultures build trust, give positive and negative feedback, and make decisions.

We've briefly summarized each of these cultural models in Table 3-3. Each one is rich in research and insights that can guide leaders who are working in multinational and global organizations or remotely managing international teams. The goal of using tools like these is to learn to avoid missteps and mistakes in giving feedback to team members.

Table 3-3. Feedback and Culture Through Two Lenses

Hofstede's 6 Cultural Dimensions	Meyer's 8 Culture Map Dimensions
1. Power distance (extent to which power is distributed) 2. Individualism vs. collectivism (degree to which individuals are integrated into groups) 3. Uncertainty avoidance (preference for collective tolerance for ambiguity) 4. Motivation toward achievement and success (preference for being competitive, driven by individual striving, and material reward and winning) 5. Long-term vs. short-term orientation (preference for a focus on shorter- or longer-term actions) 6. Indulgence vs. restraint (degree of societal freedoms to seek gratification of needs)	1. Communicating (low to high context) 2. Evaluating feedback (direct to indirect) 3. Persuading (principles-first to applications-first) 4. Leading (egalitarian to hierarchical) 5. Deciding (consensual to top-down) 6. Trustworthiness (task-based to relationship-based) 7. Disagreeing (confrontational to avoidance) 8. Scheduling (linear time to flexible time)

A New Anti-Racist, Person-Centered Cultural Competence Framework

In his book, *Developing Anti-Racist Cultural Competence*, Rehman Abdulrehman (2024) of the University of Manitoba offers a fresh perspective and a new model of race and culture that resists placing individuals into categories or viewing others as part of what he calls a "cultural zoo." Using research experience and expertise in mental health, leadership, bias, and DEI (diversity, equity, and inclusion), he developed a person-centered model that goes beyond the popular "categorization" models of race and culture. Adbulrehman advocates for focusing on cultural intersectionality, fluidity, and individual identities to allow leaders to better understand and define each person they work with.

Abdulrehman says we can define culture and race more accurately and with less bias by focusing on the whole person—their life experiences, view of the world, heritage, rituals, and values—rather than only categorizing them by race, ethnicity, or culture. He also says it's important to consider the impact of politics, racism, and immigration on a person's cultural identity. This means that leaders should actively attempt to understand each employee more fully based on their life story, rather than the categorizations that so often perpetuate bias, disrupt trust, and even perpetuate unintended racism. He explains further, using his own life story as an example:

> If I think of myself as an example of a client, at what intersection would I want to be viewed, or what would be the most accurate cultural intersection of my identity to be understood by any professional working with me? Zanzibar [his home] is a mixture of different cultures and ethnicities and, as a result of that, has developed its own unique culture. Should such a professional fall back on the cultures that made up Zanzibar? But I was born in Dar es Salaam, a mainland city in Tanzania, which also has its own unique culture—a mainland rather than an island culture (such as that in Zanzibar). Would that be the cultural perspective a professional should adopt when working with me? Or should they approach me as a Muslim? And Muslims themselves have a diverse perspective of experiences and values, depending on the region of the world they grew up in or where their families originated. But then I moved to Canada. I consider myself a Canadian, and I have lived here most of my life.
>
> At which point do we need to be an expert on another culture to be well-informed enough to work with people from diverse backgrounds? It becomes a ridiculous exercise in trying to learn about other people. So, what would be helpful? For me, it is important to be seen as a part of a society, to have similarities noted, and not be seen as a foreigner. But it is also important for me to retain my cultural and ethnic identity and see myself as distinct. The challenge for any practitioner is to be able not to make any assumptions on either, and recognize that the challenge with me would remain the challenge with any other White client; only the variables that made them distinct might

differ. What would also need to be recognized for me, particularly in a therapy or health setting, would be the barriers I have experienced as a result of who I am. (Abdulrehman 2024)

A person-centered framework requires leaders be motivated to take risks and make the necessary effort. They need to be aware of and try to discard their biases and authentically listen and learn more about each employee, their life journey, and their intersecting identities. The result of such an anti-racist review of cultural competence will be more effective communication and a truer understanding of each employee with less bias based on gender, age, and culture. Abdulrehman's model acknowledges and supports the observation that greater intersectionality and differences exist *within* cultures than *between* cultures, allowing us all to be more effective not only in multicultural workplaces, but also our own communities.

Tips to Help Minimize Cultural Bias in Your Feedback

1. Reflect on conscious or unconscious cultural biases and stereotypes you might have. What about your employees' cultural biases or stereotypes? What is threatening to them? Who might break the stereotypes your employees harbor about other cultures? Think about each employee as an individual rather than as a group.
2. Remember that differences within your own culture might be as important as differences between cultures, so always keep the individual factors governing each employee's needs and responses in mind.
3. Expand your cultural awareness and intelligence by reading, interacting with a variety of people, and consuming art, music, films, and other aspects of culture from outside your own cultural heritage.
4. Find an internal or external culture coach who can help illuminate your unconscious biases and stereotypical thinking about other cultures.
5. Identify cultural preferences for feedback on your team. Do they prefer direct or indirect feedback? Do they respond best to more emotional expressions? What is their approach to time management? How do they respond to a focus on trustworthiness?
6. Express your desire to understand and work with each employee's preferences. For example, say, "I want to make sure we work well together and don't miscommunicate. Would you share how you prefer to give and receive feedback?"

7. If you're working with people from more indirect cultures than your own, don't reiterate the same points in writing that you've already mentioned orally (for example, don't email them a recap of your meeting). Soften feedback, but don't avoid it. Some examples of more indirect phrases are:
   - "It's just my opinion . . ."
   - "One idea you might consider is . . ."
   - "Have you thought about . . ."
   - "Maybe, this could be considered . . ."
   - "Just about all of these things worked very well."
   - "Perhaps just a little more (or less) would make it even better."

Age and Feedback

Differences in age between leaders and their direct reports can play an important role in giving and receiving feedback, employee engagement, and even overall company performance related to what is called "status incongruence" (Kunze and Menges 2017). For example, in a study of 61 companies and 8,000 workers in Germany, the discrepancy in age between a younger manager and an older employee had significant negative effects. In this study, the average age difference was 7.15 years, and the larger the age gap between manager and employee, the more negative emotions the employees experienced.

Let's examine some conventional wisdom about generational divides today. Are younger employees *really* demanding more feedback than more tenured and older workers? Do older and more experienced employees *really* need extra performance reviews and feedback to keep them motivated and engaged? These questions are leaving a lot of leaders scratching their heads. In 2023, one researcher declared: "There are no meaningful differences in personality traits for job applicants between Generations X, Y, and Z based on a large sample of applicants within a large industry" (Stelling 2023).

The truth is that each employee is different but stereotypes and biases about baby boomers, Gen Xers, millennials, and Gen Zers are now pervasive and can certainly shape the frequency, content, and type of feedback leaders think they should provide.

By 2025, millennials (born between 1981 and 1996) will make up a large part of the global workforce. This age cohort was raised on social media in an era when texting and posting to Twitter, Facebook, and other platforms was commonplace. More than any other age group, this generation tends to expect instant communication—they do not want to wait 12 months for a performance review or even 24 hours for an email reply. A 2019 study suggests that contrary to popular belief, millennials aren't more sensitive than baby boomers (born between 1946 and 1964). In fact, millennials tended to be less sensitive and defensive when receiving feedback (Meyer 2023).

Old Dogs, New Tricks: What About Generations in the Workplace?

Researchers Zenger and Folkman explored generational differences in feedback leaders received. They analyzed 899 individuals, 40 percent of whom were US-based. For this study, they categorized congratulatory comments, praise, and reinforcement as *positive feedback* and constructive criticism, suggestions for improvement on the job, and ways to be more efficient as *corrective feedback*. One valuable general finding was that independent of age, employees wanted corrective feedback more than praise, by about a three-to-one ratio if it was delivered sincerely and constructively. In addition, the study found that employees with the strongest self-esteem and confidence were significantly more open to receiving negative feedback.

In the study, 12 percent of respondents were categorized as baby boomers (average age of 57), 50 percent as Generation X (average age of 42), and 38 percent as Generation Y or millennials (average age of 28). Independent of age, almost everyone in the study had a strong aversion to providing negative feedback to employees, even when warranted. Based on a scale from tend to avoid (-5.0) to tend to prefer (5.0), clear differences were observed, as shown in Table 3-4.

Table 3-4. Feedback Tendencies Across Generations

	Receiving Positive Feedback *Scale: -5 (avoid) to +5 (prefer)*	**Receiving Negative Feedback** *Scale: -5 (avoid) to +5 (prefer)*
Generation Y	1.88	4.18
Generation X	2.38	4.81
Baby Boomers	2.80	6.11

Contrary to the popular stereotype that younger workers expect and demand more feedback overall, this study found that the older the employees were, the more feedback they wanted of both kinds. Baby boomers showed a stronger preference for receiving negative feedback than the other age cohorts. Although this is only a single study, the sample size was large and broad enough that leaders should take note of it. It seems that employees, across age cohorts, want constructive criticism delivered in the spirit of development, and they see it as essential to their career development even if they have been in the workforce for a long time.

Generations in the Workplace

- Employees over 40 are far more likely to be called "responsible" and "unselfish" than younger workers.
- Employees under 40 are described as "ambitious" 2.5 times more often than people who are 40 and older (Textio 2022).

To date, most research on generational differences in values and beliefs has found that the differences are quite negligible, and far more diversity typically exists *within* than between these cohorts (Ravid, Costanza, and Romero 2024). It is easy for leaders to assume that baby boomers don't text or use social media as frequently as millennials or that millennials are more likely to demand flexible work schedules to remain with an organization. However, there is little consistent evidence to back up these stereotypes. In fact, recent academic researchers like Stelling have challenged the existing discussions, and comparisons based on generational differences might need to be revised despite their popularity.

It is important to emphasize recent findings suggesting that historical periods and an individual's life course explain work motivation, attitudes, and behavior better than generational membership (Schröder 2023). Additionally, we recognize that *generationalized thinking* is often exclusive, in that it encourages a focus on groups and group differences by overemphasizing the role of cohorts in determining individual attitudes and behaviors at work.

Some academics prefer to replace generational thinking with a *lifespan lens*, emphasizing developmental trajectories and individual change at different ages to explain the greater differences *within* generations than between them

(Rudolph, Rauvola, and Zacher 2018). On the other hand, it is important to note that the workplace is one setting where generations usually are not segregated. In most organizations, young adults in their 20s interact daily with other age cohorts.

Tips to Help Minimize Age Bias in Feedback

1. Reflect on your age-related biases and stereotypes and how these might shape the type of feedback you provide, how often you provide feedback, and the emotional impact that feedback creates.
2. Create the norm that "feedback is a way of life in our team culture."
3. Explain the why behind all your recommendations and requests to employees of all age groups.
4. Define what excellence in performance looks like by clarifying evaluative standards and outcomes.
5. Frequently check in with millennials to ask about the progress they have made on the job (Amabile and Kramer 2011). Remember that millennials tend to prefer future-oriented feedback to sharpen their skills and behaviors related to their careers, but that preferences always vary within each generation.

Megan Gerhardt, a professor at Miami University, views the intergenerational workforce as a profound business opportunity. In her book, *Gentelligence: The Revolutionary Approach to Leading an Intergenerational Workforce* (published in 2021 with co-authors Josephine Nachemson-Ekwall and Brandon Fogel), Gerhardt rejects common stereotypes assigned to different generations and replaces them with a more nuanced understanding of why those who grew up in different times may act and behave in different, equally valuable ways (Gerhardt, Nachemson-Ekwall, and Fogel 2021).

Now, after all these perspectives and some caution, we do offer generational observations throughout this book that can be useful if carefully weighed and considered in light of your own experience. We agree with Gerhardt when she argues that leaders need to identify and reflect on their biases about younger and older workers and always be curious to learn, rather than judgmental.

Resisting Stereotypes in Practice

The stereotypes leaders and employees have internalized about age differences can and do persist and influence workplace interactions. For example, when corporate training and development specialists believe they are training an older employee on some new computer-related task, they report lower expectations and less instruction than when they believe the employee they are training is younger (Finkelstein et al. 2020).

The takeaway for leaders is simple: Check your age-based stereotypes and assumptions at the door when providing feedback across your diverse workforce.

Reflect on whether the popular heuristics in Table 3-5 hold true for each employee working for you, or whether your employees defy the categories. Undoubtedly, as technology evolves and generative AI and alternative feedback platforms are created, different feedback approaches may need to be tailored to the age diversity within organizations.

Table 3-5. Cross-Generational Feedback Guidelines

Generation	Development Approach	Feedback Preferences
Generation Z (born 1997–2012)	"Connect Me" blended learning, social platforms, and experience with AI	Based on social media experiences, Gen Zers expect and are open to immediate and real-time feedback from all directions (boss, colleagues, and friends).
Millennials or Generation Y (born 1981–1996)	"Network Me" e-learning and coaching	Millennials are less sensitive and defensive when receiving feedback compared with Gen Xers and baby boomers. They expect recognition and praise but are tolerant of negative feedback despite the stereotype that "everyone gets a trophy."
Generation X (born 1965–1980)	"Show Me" workshops and on-the-job experiences	Gen Xers, the independent "latchkey kids," will provide upward feedback to their bosses and prefer not to wait for an annual performance review for project-based feedback.
Baby Boomers (born 1946–1964)	"Teach Me" classroom lectures and manuals	Baby boomers use and prefer formal oral and written feedback processes, such as annual performance reviews or in-person meetings with their bosses or peers.

Sources: Meyer (2023) and Wisdom and Brancu (2021)

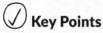 **Key Points**

Let's review a few key points from this chapter:

- We all hold unconscious biases or prejudices about various groups of people because our brains are built to organize the world into categories. Some unconscious biases exist even in infancy and develop further in childhood and beyond. Leaders need to know that unconscious biases have a proven influence on hiring, feedback, and mentoring of employees and can be modified through reflection and deliberate behavior change.
- Leaders should reflect on their communication and feedback style with each team member, paying special attention to differences based on gender, culture, race, age, and other demographic characteristics to ensure they are providing equality and fairness in specific, actionable, and constructive feedback.
- Leaders can use specific exercises, tips, and suggestions to minimize potential bias in feedback and tailor feedback strategies to be sensitive to individual differences, preferences, and values.

Tool 3-1. Unconscious Bias Exercise: My Trust Circle

Write down the initials of five people in your life you most trust and feel comfortable with in the top row of the table. Don't include family members. Look at the descriptors in the table and check the box if the person's characteristic and yours are similar. (For example, if you and person 1 are both introverted, you'd check that box. But if person 2 is extroverted, you wouldn't check that box in their column.) Then answer the reflection questions.

My Trusted Five	1	2	3	4	5
Introvert or extrovert					
Age					
Gender					
Education					
Religion					
Disability					
Sexual preference					
Ethnicity					
Income or wealth					
Political orientation					

Reflection questions:
1. What does this information illustrate about those you most trust and why?
2. What opportunities do you have in your workplace to interact with and listen to others whose experiences, backgrounds, and opinions are different from your own?

Tool 3-2. Unconscious Bias Exercise: Reflecting on Stereotypes

As you read across each row in this table, think about how you naturally react to each phrase. Note whatever comes to mind. Be honest and try to bring to the surface any biases you might be aware of. Then answer the reflection questions.

Column A	Column B	Column C
Is very slender	Is very short	Is overweight
Is ultrareligious	Is agnostic	Is spiritual
Likes rap or hip-hop music	Likes classical music	Likes heavy-metal music
Owns a dog	Owns a cat	Owns a snake
Women with many visible tattoos	Men with many visible body piercings	People with unusual hair colors
52-year-old unmarried woman	52-year-old married woman	52-year-old unmarried man
Is under 25	Is middle-aged	Is over 65
Resides in a large city	Resides on a farm	Resides on a ranch
Female CEO	Male nurse	Female police chief
Is LGBTQ+	Is transgender	Is a nonbinary
Men who get manicures	Women who drink beer	Women who shave their heads
Elderly drivers	Teenage drivers	Truck drivers
Has an eating disorder	Has a mental illness	Has a drug addiction
Owns firearms	Doesn't own firearms	Supports the NRA
Drives an electric vehicle	Drives a gas vehicle	Drives a hybrid vehicle
Shares conservative political beliefs	Shares liberal political beliefs	Shares conspiracy theories
Did not attend college	Attended an elite university	Has a PhD
Couples with large families	Couples with small families	Couples with no children
Never divorced	Divorced once	Divorced several times
Speaks with an accent	Speaks multiple languages	Lived in several countries
Immigrated to this country	First-generation American	Multigenerational American
Has strong pro-life beliefs	Supports capital punishment	Supports legalizing assisted suicide
Avid adult skateboarder	Avid deer hunter	Avid pickleball player

Reflection questions:

1. **Recognize bias:** Select several of the categories and note what classifications, judgments, and stereotypes emerged from your reflections.
2. **Challenge bias:** Is it possible that some people who fit into each box might not fit the stereotypes your bias led you to note? Can you put yourself into the shoes of a person that fits the description in one of the boxes to better understand their experiences in life?
3. **Modify bias:** What initial impressions, judgments, and biases can you set aside in the social interactions you have with others? How could you go about doing that?

Tool 3-3. Checklist for Giving and Receiving Feedback in Diverse Teams

☐ When giving feedback, focus on observable facts; avoid evaluation ("That wasn't very motivating") and expressing emotions ("The team was bored with your slides").

☐ When expressing an opinion, use "I" statements rather than "we" or "you" statements.

☐ Manage diverse expectations around giving and receiving feedback by defining and agreeing upon specific norms for how and when it will be provided to the team.

☐ Use check-in meetings to solicit input from direct reports; use a "start doing," "stop doing," and "do differently" structure to elicit specific behaviors you can work on.

☐ Use 360-degree feedback assessments for each team member to compare self-impressions of behavior to those of their teammates. Compile results for all team members that can be used to highlight team strengths and possible blind spots to improve team functioning.

☐ Encourage team members to meet individually with one another and use the "start, stop, and continue" structure to share impressions of one another confidentially, openly, and candidly.

☐ Use "feedback dating" sessions in team development meetings to enhance openness and trust. Team members are paired together to give and receive feedback (three minutes each) and then rotate in pairs to give everyone a chance to share with each other.

☐ Use the 3A's method to minimize power discrepancies in relationships (Meyer 2023):

    ○ **Assist.** The message should be feedforward with the genuine desire to help the other individual improve and grow.

    ○ **Actionable.** The message should be specific about behaviors to do more, do less, or do differently that is observable and measurable.

    ○ **Asking first.** Power discrepancies often lead to entitlement or the belief that those in power (such as, men in leadership positions) have a right to share and give feedback even if it's not solicited or wanted. Unless someone has asked for direct feedback from you, *ask first* what feedback the other person might have for you *before* sharing your feedback (even if it's well-intentioned).

Chapter 4
Feedback
The Prerequisite for Successful Behavior Change

Ken has a secret running club. He lives about five blocks from the beach, and part of his morning routine is to get out for an early run on the bike path. He's kept this up since 1994—same direction, same distance, and same time each day. Although to be honest, the overall time seems to get longer each year!

To keep their routine interesting, Ken and his wife initiated a secret club of "regulars": the people they saw walking, cycling, running, skateboarding, roller skating, or rollerblading along the path almost every day. They nominated members, gave them names, and even held mock club initiation meetings to discuss who should or shouldn't be granted membership. The one common denominator was and still is that members had to work out at least three days each week and stick with their physical activity for at least three months in a row.

As you might predict, a surge of potential new members shows up every January during New Year's resolution season. Each New Year's Day, Ken goes for a run to celebrate the beginning of another year and sees crowds of people in new workout clothes with the latest brands of bikes (now mostly electric), rollerblades, and skateboards (now mostly motorized). By April, only a couple of the newbies are still showing up.

For Ken, 20 years of people-watching on the bike path have reinforced basic principles about how we establish new routines and convert them into lasting habits: It's easy to start committing to a new habit, but it's *a lot* harder to keep it up over time. Without plenty of support, most people—including your employees—simply won't succeed in maintaining their new behaviors.

In this chapter, we will review some of the research on why behavior change is so hard and explore two key neurological pathways—one associated with goal setting (*the will*) and another associated with goal flourishing (*the way*). Then we'll explain what we call the 3E Model of Successful Individual Behavior Change—our formula for helping your employees, colleagues, and even family members change their habits over time—which is based on what we now know about how our brain works when goal setting and goal striving.

The Neuroscience of Goal Setting and Goal Striving

We are all creatures of habit. Based on several studies of student and community diaries, a stunning 45 percent of our everyday behaviors tend to be repeated in the same location almost every day (Neal, Wood, and Quinn 2006). Despite our habit-loving nature, initiating and maintaining new habits is notoriously difficult, which is why so many of us abandon new resolutions within a few weeks.

Recent neuroscience research provides a framework for understanding our resistance to initiating new habits and other challenges. Research by professor Elliot Berkman (2018) at the University of Oregon suggests that behavior change and habit formation are heavily influenced by two separate areas of the brain; one (the will) affects how we get started on our goal setting and the other (the way) affects how successfully we accomplish our goal and ultimately create a new habit. The *will*, also known as the default mode network (DMN), relates to the emotional and motivational aspects of behavior change or why a goal or new habit is important to us. In contrast, the *way*, also known as the task-positive network (TPN) or executive function, refers to the informational aspects of habit change related to a specific plan, rewards, and measurements to ensure goal success.

Goal Setting and the Will

The "will" is what Berkman (2018) calls the network of areas in the brain that are activated when we get started on our goals (Table 4-1).

Table 4-1. Parts of the Brain Activated by Goal Setting

Default Mode Network (DMN): The Will	
Ventromedial prefrontal cortex (vmPFC)	• Daydreaming and rumination • Self-reflection • Introspection • Social and emotional understanding • Emotion regulation (fear and anxiety processing) • Engagement and openness to ideas • Emotional reappraisal • Evaluation of fairness • Intuitive-experiential thinking style
Posterior cingulate cortex	
Ventral striatum	
Nucleus accumbens	
Parasympathetic activation (relaxation response)	

Let's review several neuroscience-based strategies and hacks, focused on the will, that leaders can use to help set meaningful goals for employees and themselves.

Goal-Setting Strategy 1. Enhance Intrinsic Motivation

People are more likely to focus on behaviors when they are intrinsically motivated for intentional change. The brain is a cost-benefit calculator and reacts more strongly to penalties, punishment, and loss than to other external motivators. In one study, participants who were offered a monetary reward for achieving a goal of walking 7,000 steps a day were 50 percent *less* successful than those who had the same amount taken away from their bank account each day they failed to meet the goal (Patel et al. 2016).

Goal-setting hack: Clarify exactly what your employee is most interested in focusing on at a behavioral level. Do they want to stop doing something, start doing something, do less, do more, or do something differently? Define whether the desire is to change this behavior once, sometimes, or all the time. For example, do they want to run one marathon, enter a 10K four times a year, or run three miles every day? Ask the employee to define where they are now (What is their current self doing?) and where they want to be (What will their future self be doing?). Current studies suggest that developing this kind of clarity early in coaching meetings facilitates greater acceptance of goals and the desire to work on them.

Goal-Setting Strategy 2. Break Down Goals Into Tiny Subgoals

A goal that is overly complicated or too difficult will impede success. Helping people redefine their goals into tiny habits increases motivation and the belief they can be successful (Fogg 2020). Employees usually start new habit-change efforts with great enthusiasm and excitement but often slack off or lose motivation around the middle of the project.

Goal-setting hack: Try to assess the difficulty level of the desired goal or behavior with the employee and then make it easier to do. Create shorter "middles" by having the employee break their goals into much smaller chunks to maintain stamina until they achieve success.

Goal-Setting Strategy 3. Use Uncertain, Not Certain Rewards

Everyone is motivated by internal and external rewards when keeping up new behaviors and making them automatic. Research suggests that *uncertain rewards* are more motivating because they are more challenging and exciting than certain rewards; this enhances the activation of reward circuits in the brain (Shen, Fishbach, and Hsee 2015).

Goal-setting hack: Instead of just defining a set reward, consider introducing more variability in the rewards you are providing. For example, if you're using a monetary reward, offer a 50 percent chance of getting a $50 or $100 gift card versus a 100 percent chance of winning $75. This small difference can increase motivation substantially.

Goal-Setting Strategy 4. Focus on What's Completed, Not What's Left to Do

Research suggests that people experience greater motivation when they focus on completed progress at the beginning of pursuing a goal and then concentrate on lack of progress toward the end (Bonezzi, Brendl, and De Angelis 2011).

Goal-setting hack: At the beginning of a goal pursuit, encourage employees to pay attention to and measure completed progress. For example, they can track what they are doing daily or weekly toward the goal and reward themselves for what they have already done. Toward the end of the goal pursuit, as they get closer to completion, encourage them to pay attention to the remaining progress they need to make. This hack can maximize motivation.

Goal Striving and the Way

The network of related areas in the brain that are activated during goal striving is also known as the "way" (Table 4-2).

Table 4-2. Parts of the Brain Activated by Goal Striving

Task-Positive Network and Executive Functioning (TPN): The Way	
Ventrolateral prefrontal cortex (vmPFC)	• Decision making • Problem solving
Dorsal anterior cingulate cortex (dACC)	• Judgment • Working memory
Parietal cortex	• Attentional control • Emotional regulation (suppression, distancing, cognitive reappraisal)
Temporoparietal junction (TPJ)	• Emotional distress or pain • Goal setting or goal striving • Perceptual or analytical thinking style
Sympathetic activation ("fight or flight" response)	

Goal striving typically includes the implementation of specific behaviors based on initial goal setting, redefining goals during their pursuit, managing lapses caused by distractions, and losing energy or resources, which interferes with successful accomplishment. Some important aspects of successful goal setting or planning revolve around five contrasting pairs of characteristics:

- Easy goals versus challenging or stretch goals
- Short-term goal focus versus long-term goal focus
- Initiation of single goals versus multiple goals
- Learning goals versus performance goals
- Avoidance goals versus approach goals (Nowack 2019)

Many people express a strong desire or intention to become more effective and to try new behaviors but often don't initiate or sustain the new behaviors for very long. Like the new January joggers Ken sees on his path along the beach, they quickly relapse into old behaviors. Some research suggests that the perceived importance and benefits of our goals, or our degree of concern for the endpoint of the desired behavioral change, might be the best predictor of who will initiate new behaviors and whether they will keep them going (Woolley and Fischbach 2017).

On the other hand, individual factors such as achievement motivation, self-efficacy, perceived control, and clarity about the disadvantages of behavioral change generally are stronger predictors of employees who successfully maintain new behaviors over time. Motivation to set goals (intentions) is a poor predictor of actual goal success and long-term habit change. Motivation will get us started but habits keep us going (Nowack 2017a).

Let's review several neuroscience-based strategies and hacks leaders can use to help employees (and themselves) successfully create new and lasting habits.

Goal-Striving Strategy 1. Use If/Then Practice Plans

Just defining a desired future behavior is unlikely to result in successful behavior change (Nowack 2015). In fact, some approaches to goal setting, including creating SMART goals, aren't very smart. Instead, it's better to use implementation plans that incorporate if/then statements, which have been shown to double the likelihood of goal success (Gollwitzer and Sheeran 2006).

Goal-striving hack: If/then goals have two components. The first (the "if") is a situation, time, or trigger like a weekly staff meeting that cues up a desired behavior for the employee to practice. The second component (the "then") is a statement of the specific behavior the employee wants to implement, such as doing something more, less, or differently. For example, instead of creating a goal intention such as, "I want to be a better active listener," help your employee translate this desire into an implementation intention using an if/then approach: "*If* I am leading my weekly team meeting, *then* I will solicit input from other team members and summarize what I hear before sharing my point of view."

Goal-Striving Strategy 2. Neurons That Wire Together Fire Together

In general, it takes approximately six to eight (closely spaced) repetitions of a new behavior to begin the formation of new neural habit pathways (Grill-Spector, Henson, and Martin 2006). Phillippa Lally and her colleagues (2009) from the University College London suggested that new behaviors could become automatic, on average, in 66 days (the range was 18 to 254 days), but this would also depend on the complexity of the behavior the person was trying to put into place and their personality (such as conscientiousness). It takes more than a one-shot training program or brief coaching engagement to ensure someone has adequate practice to create the automaticity we associate with new habits that can be sustained over time (Nowack 2024; Nowack 2017a).

Anastasia Buyalskaya, professor of marketing at HEC, Paris, and her colleagues (2023) used a machine learning approach to infer how quickly habits formed concerning gym attendance (four to seven months) and hand washing (several weeks). Their findings supported earlier research by Lally and her colleagues (2009) that, contrary to the idea of a "magic number" of days in which habits form, developing a handwashing habit takes weeks, while developing a gym habit takes months.

Goal-striving hack: Build in adequate nudges or reminders to keep the goal visible and use a full range of rewards and social support to ensure continuous practice and facilitate habit formation. Tracking and monitoring progress also helps reinforce the desired behavior and provides a metric of success for continuing—even when people hit those inevitable bumps in the road that might lead to a lapse in behavior or a full-blown relapse.

For both learning and performance-based goals, lifestyle habits can either facilitate or interfere with goal success. For example, physical activity increases a brain fertilizer known as brain-derived neurotrophic factor (BDNF), which enhances memory and learning as well as exercise after learning. Research suggests that memory and learning are optimized four hours after a person is physically active (von Donge et al. 2016). And lack of quality sleep, even for one night, interferes with psychomotor functioning, memory, and performance on new tasks to an extent equivalent to the effect of being legally drunk in most countries (Nowack 2017b).

Goal Striving Strategy 3. Practice Makes Better, Not Perfect

There is little evidence to support the "rule," popularized by journalist Malcolm Gladwell, that it takes 10,000 hours of practice to become an expert at any endeavor. We do know that the sheer number of hours of practice is not as important as the quality of deliberate practice, which suggests that expert performance varies among individuals and domains. However, a meta-analysis and a follow-up study by Brooke McNamara and her colleagues at Case Western Reserve University also showed that deliberate practice explains only a tiny fraction of what constitutes successful performance, whether in music, sports, education, or a chosen profession (McNamara, Hambrick, and Oswald 2014). In addition, we still don't know how much heritability explains, but we do know genetics plays a role.

Goal-striving hack: Schedule deliberate, challenging, and varied practice over an extended period (65 to 90 days for complicated behaviors) to help employees become better. However, note that this only works up to some finite genetic set point for each person. Success and expertise in one's field lie at the intersection between deliberate practice and innate ability. Unfortunately, coaching and leadership development programs that focus only on learning transfer are unlikely to convert "competent jerks" into "lovable stars," regardless of how much they practice.

Goal-Striving Strategy 4. Know When to Hold 'Em and When to Fold 'Em

Many of us heard the advice "Never quit, never give up!" from parents, educators, and colleagues. However, current research suggests that individuals who do not persist in obtaining hard-to-reach goals have significantly lower inflammation (caused by C-reactive protein), decreased cortisol secretion, and decreased emotional distress. It's important to know when it's healthier to walk away from overly difficult, complex, or unattainable goals (Miller and Wrosch 2007).

Ken Gets Thrown a Curve Ball

Ken learned firsthand about "ability set points" and overcoming setbacks and challenges when he was in college trying to realize his dream of becoming a great baseball player. He recalls going to practice early and staying late, taking as many grounders at second base and as much batting practice as he could get.

"I spent every waking minute I wasn't in class at the gym or batting cages trying to improve my biggest weakness—hitting curve balls," Ken recalls. "I knew I was improving and was sure I would be able to compete at the collegiate level. When the day of final cuts for the team roster came up, the coach called me into his office, and I had high expectations.

"He said, 'Ken, we love your effort, and frankly, not many kids I've coached have shown your dedication to practice. You've listened to the feedback from all of us, and you've shown great improvement. I think you'll be able to enjoy the game and demonstrate your baseball skills on campus in intramurals.'"

Naturally, Ken was crushed. But after a few weeks, he had to admit that his coach was right.

"Long before I began researching leadership and relationships between managers and employees, I learned that we all have ability set points. I was never going to make the varsity team. But all my baseball skills and hard work helped me excel when I found my ideal spot at second base on several intramural teams. The lesson I share with the leaders I work with is that coaching and determination can strongly influence employees who have natural abilities and are willing to put in the effort. But all of us have distinct performance ceilings, and even with hours of practice, we might never reach every one of our goals."

Goal-striving hack: It may be prudent for employees to cut their losses in the face of insurmountable obstacles to remain healthy. To achieve long-term success, help them redefine, simplify, and create goals that are easier to obtain.

People should make sure their goals are more specific and carved into bite-size chunks to ensure success. For example, you would start training for a marathon by working on a 5K walk or a one-mile run, which is much less physically challenging and more likely to lead to goal success.

By adopting one or more of these hacks related to motivated goal setting, planning, and execution, leaders are more likely to shift employees from goal setting to goal accomplishment and successful behavior change. By following a few basic principles grounded in neuroscience, you can help translate your feedback into deliberate practice long enough to establish the new behaviors that lead to the enhanced effectiveness you're looking for in your employees.

Neuroscience Insights for Increasing Feedback Acceptance

The two neural networks we've just discussed suggest fundamentally different components of habit change. We now dive a little deeper into what neuroscience can teach us about increasing employees' acceptance of feedback. The *will* (default mode network) is more intuitive and experiential, and it stimulates a relaxation response in the body. On the other hand, the *way* (our task-positive executive function) is much more analytical and rational. The way takes a lot of our energy to identify goals, solve problems, and plan activities, activating the sympathetic fight-or-flight response.

Recent neuroscience research suggests that most leaders, coaches, therapists, and parents employ a problem-solving or solution-focused mode with their employees, athletes, clients, and children—particularly those who are performing poorly. Some new evidence is emerging that indicates using a *compassion-based approach*, which emphasizes listening and identifying someone's vision for how they want to behave, leads to stronger acceptance of behavior change. However, it is still necessary to confront poor performance constructively and address the root causes with a plan to improve.

Research by Richard Boyatzis of Case Western University focused on executive coaches and the latest neuroscience measurements of the brain (using fMRI). The study found that the employee's parasympathetic default mode network was activated when coaches started meetings with a set of questions that reflectively set a tone encouraging them to compare their future or ideal selves as seen by others with their current selves (Boyatzis and Jack 2018). As a result, employees were more self-reflective and open to considering and implementing future-oriented goals. In several separate studies, Boyatzis's team showed that coaches who started meetings with a set of reflective questions—rather than jumping immediately into providing feedback on current performance issues and problems or reviewing feedback reports (personality inventory or 360-degree data)—were rated significantly more inspirational, empathetic, and trustworthy. The employees in the study were also significantly more reflective and receptive to feedback, and more frequently set specific development goals to work on.

Starting your feedback meetings by first asking about the employee's ideal self activates the same default mode network Boyatzis and his colleagues explored. Because this network is associated with openness to consider future options, motivation to change, and goal setting, its activation can facilitate greater acceptance of feedback. A bonus of this approach is that it minimizes the sympathetic stress response often associated with anxiety, fear, and defensiveness that often gets in the way of accepting the messages leaders are delivering.

Of course, it's always difficult to resist quickly getting to the point and focusing on finding a solution when you are pressed for time, anxious about providing constructive or negative feedback, or dealing with a frustrating employee. There are several exercises at the end of this chapter that can help.

Although you can't place your employee into an fMRI machine to observe which areas of their brain are activated in feedback meetings, as a leader you can do a few things to increase openness and acceptance of feedback by activating their default mode network. The neuroscience research by Boyatzis and his colleagues suggests that to maximize success during a feedback meeting, you should encourage employees to share their story and their perspective and explain how they would like to be seen by others. Doing this *before* trying to address the performance problem at hand will increase your likelihood of arriving at a mutually acceptable solution and increasing motivation to change.

Now take a look at how our model of successful behavior change works.

The 3E Model of Successful Individual Behavior Change

The first thing to understand about behavior change is that *goal intentions* are weak predictors of actual behavior change, but people who create *implementation intentions* are significantly more likely to complete their goals (Gollwitzer and Sheeran 2006). For example, someone who opens a calendar on New Year's Day and simply writes down the goal of cycling along the beach every day is highly likely to abandon this intention before long. As we describe in one stage of our model, people who use implementation intentions with a trigger, cue, or existing routine with a specific desired behavior are more likely to successfully achieve their goal. For example: "Before dropping the kids off at school at 8:30 a.m. on Mondays, Wednesdays, and Fridays, I'll ride my bike along the bike path past the pier and then back home."

In chapter 1, we described three results of effective feedback: *understanding, accepting,* and *commitment to action.* Each outcome maps back to a model we have researched, developed, and written about (Nowack 2019). If leaders understand this model of individual behavior change, it can help them translate feedback into behavior change in employees more effectively. The 3E Model of Successful Individual Behavior Change is derived from theories based on organizational psychology, health psychology, and behavioral medicine. It provides helpful context for leaders who want to understand the dynamics of behavioral change and the special role feedback plays in ensuring employees are ready and have the confidence to begin a developmental journey.

Initiating and successfully maintaining new habits and behaviors over time requires three stages. Figure 4-1 shows simple definitions of each stage.

Figure 4-1. The 3E Model of Successful Individual Behavior Change

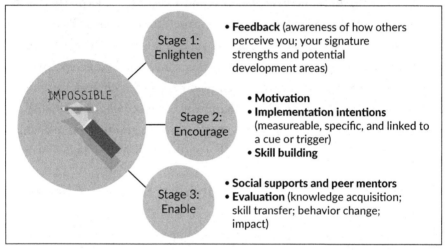

Stage 1. Enlighten

During the *enlighten stage*, an employee uses feedback from the leader (from interviews, personality inventories, or 360-degree assessments) to gain a more accurate understanding of how their performance and personality are being experienced and evaluated. Leaders must be strategic in how they craft feedback to ensure the employee fully understands—whether or not they agree with the details.

Employee reactions to the feedback or meeting with a leader can range from pleasant surprise to hurt, anger, or even depression, with predictable consequences for performance, engagement, and psychological well-being. Many factors influence whether an employee will listen and understand based on the information, data, and observations presented to them. Those factors include the level of trust the employee has with the leader, the level of empathy or compassion the leader expresses, whether the feedback comes across as constructive and helpful or evaluative and punishing, and, as we discussed in chapter 3, the personality characteristics of the employee and leader.

The enlighten stage is necessary, but it's not sufficient to get the employee to see the world through the eyes of others, despite their own filters and biases. An employee might entirely accept the information, data, and perceptions leaders share or outright reject them. After a leader tests their employee's understanding of the feedback, it then becomes a question of how motivated the employee is to act on the information and do things more, less, or differently to achieve the behavior change the leader wants.

Stage 2. Encourage

The *encourage stage* involves what we call "finding the crease" with employees. That is, a leader tries to help the employee accept feedback, see the positive value in committing to behavior change, and finally translate motivation into specific goals and plans to implement that change back on the job. This stage requires leaders to get a commitment from the employee to get on board for a collaborative and explicit behavior change plan.

The leader can begin (as we discussed in the section on neuroscience earlier in this chapter) by asking the employee to share their perspective and how they want to be seen by others. Then, the leader can explore any signs of defensiveness and resistance (for example, identifying hidden competing commitments to change) before actively strengthening the clarity of the employee's action-plan goals and commitment to help implement them on behalf of the employee. In fact, research suggests that this less-direct coaching style, as opposed to a direct and clear but blunt performance feedback conversation, results in employees who are significantly more likely (22.8 percent) to feel accountable for achieving their individual goals (Elfer and Belovai 2024).

When an employee expresses a desire to make a change or behave differently, the leader should help them determine whether their goal is *realistic*. Enthusiasm and motivation to change are not always associated with the *ability* to change and, even if you observe *some* change, the magnitude of that change may not be meaningful. For example, we have seen employees who are authoritative project managers continue to dominate meetings, talk over others, and micromanage team members, despite having a strong motivation to modify their style.

After feedback, it is rare for employees to spontaneously announce that they "get it" and share their motivation to make immediate behavior changes back on the job. With any commitment to a new behavior or habit, people inevitably move through several levels of motivation (Prochaska and Velicer 1997):

1. *Precontemplation* (no real intention to change)
2. *Contemplation* (intention to change in the future)
3. *Preparation* (intention to change now)
4. *Action* (translation of intention to specific goals).
5. *Maintenance* (plans to deal with lapses or relapses back to the old behavior)

In the next section, we will share some approaches, based on recent neuroscience research, that leaders can use to enable employees to move through those final stages following feedback.

Research suggests that using implementation intentions is far superior to using SMART goals to ensure achievement and create habits that sustain over time (Nowack 2015, 2019). An *implementation intention* is a habit change strategy in the form of if/then plans, which can lead to better goal attainment and create useful habits and modify problematic behaviors. We often ask our coaching clients to write out a sentence using the if/then goal-setting approach to help them become more successful in developing a new habit, such as actively listening for understanding before responding to team members in a meeting.

Stage 3. Enable

Motivation only takes an employee so far in establishing new habits. The translation of commitments into change must be concrete, specific, observable, and measurable if the employee wants to form and maintain habits successfully over time. The *enable stage* of behavior change is all about leaders and employees mutually agreeing on clear and realistic key performance indicators around the change. In general, employees are more likely to try new behaviors if they are confident of a successful outcome and create a sense of mastery over time, despite possible setbacks and challenges.

During this stage, leaders need to schedule check-in meetings with employees to monitor and track their progress and discuss potential roadblocks and barriers. They should look for opportunities to catch employees doing things right and provide positive reinforcement and praise to maintain a high level of motivation. These positive nudges help maintain the momentum of behavior-change efforts, minimizing any lapses that occur during the change journey. Of course, changing behavior can be a daunting and lonely experience without a support network to encourage, champion, and keep the goals in front of the employee. Encouraging them to identify and engage with what we call *goal mentors* (supportive peers, mentors, and coaches) along the way can truly be helpful, particularly if their motivation wanes or barriers to change occur.

This stage is all about monitoring, practicing, rewarding, and using one's support network. Is also about getting employees to find specific times, situations, and cues to experiment with, and express changes in their behavior with others. Most employees, whatever their level of motivation, typically underestimate how long it takes to change behavior and form new habits. One exercise we encourage people to try is to write their signature, first with their dominant hand and then with their nondominant hand, and to reflect on how much time and concentration it takes to change that habit. Then, compare the quality (legibility) of the two signatures. It's not easy to change deeply ingrained habits!

Yet, with practice, most people can begin to create neural pathways that lead to automatic behavior. Figure 4-2 shows how we move through the four stages of developing new habits—from becoming aware of what *needs* to change (unconscious to conscious incompetence), to committing to what the person *wants* to change, to doing things over and over until they become second nature as *a habit* (conscious competence), and finally to a state of joy often referred to as a *flow state* (unconscious competence).

Figure 4-2 builds on the four stages of competence, or the process of progressing from incompetence to competence in a specific skill (De Phillips, Berliner, and Cribbin 1960). It also nicely captures what occurs at a neural and behavioral level as new habits become automatic.

Figure 4-2. The Four Stages of Developing Habits

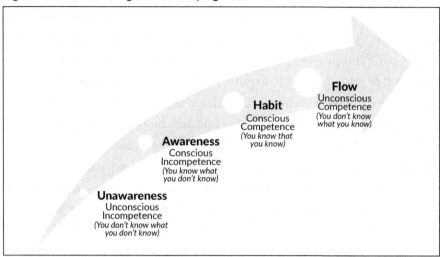

 Key Points

Let's review a few key points from this chapter:

- The 3E Model of Successful Individual Behavior Change (*enlighten*, *encourage*, and *enable*) can help leaders understand how to successfully translate feedback from employee understanding to motivated acceptance, resulting in a commitment to change and deliberate practice over time.
- Initiation of goals and implementing plans for deliberate practice until goals are successfully accomplished are related to two separate neural networks known as the will and the way. Each can be employed successfully with specific evidence-based hacks and strategies, increasing intrinsic motivation and successful habit change.
- Leaders can enhance understanding and acceptance of their feedback by holding back from a problem-solving and solution-focused approach at the beginning of their feedback and coaching meetings, and instead encouraging the employee to share how they would like to be seen by others and how their current self might differ from their future or ideal self. This approach will activate the default neural network associated with self-reflection, motivation, and greater openness to goal setting and successful behavior change.

Tool 4-1. Habit Change Exercise 1

Practice Your Signature With Your Nondominant Hand

Ask the employee to write their name with their *dominant* hand. Then ask them to write it with their *nondominant* hand.

Reflection Questions
1. How much time did it take you to write your name with your nondominant hand compared with your dominant hand?
2. How much thinking did you have to do and how difficult was it for you to write your name using your nondominant hand?
3. What was the quality and clarity of your name written with your nondominant hand compared with your normal signature?
4. How long do you estimate you would need to practice writing your name with your nondominant hand to make it as easy to do as with your dominant hand? And with the same quality? (Days? Weeks? Months?)
5. What does this exercise suggest about concentration, effort, and competence for a behavior-change journey you might make in the future?

Tool 4-2. Habit Change Exercise 2

Creating Goal Intentions and Practice Plans

Goal intentions are general statements about what a person wants to achieve in developing one or more competencies at a behavioral level (goal). In the first box, have the employee write down what they are trying to achieve and the key outcome. Ask them to be specific—a goal to be a better leader is too broad, but improving strategic-thinking skills is more actionable.

Goal practice plans have two parts. The first is a time, situation, or opportunity that triggers a desired behavior—a cue. The second describes the specific behavior a person will be doing more, less, or differently to develop into an ongoing habit.

Use the second and third boxes to consider the "if" (cue or trigger) and "when" (behavior) of your employee's desired behavior. Using practice plans following this approach has been shown to be two to three times more effective in translating insight from goal intentions to deliberate practice and successful behavior change.

Goal
(Intention or outcome)

Cue
("If or when . . .")

Behavior
(What I will be doing more, less, or differently)

Tool 4-3. Habit Change Exercise 3

Questions to Ask Employees to Enhance Openness to Behavior Change

Leaders typically activate either a task-positive network (TPN; problem-oriented and solution-focused) or default mode network (DMN; listening and seeking vision or positive forward-looking emotion) in employees, depending on their communication and feedback style preferences.

When employees have activation in the DMN, they evaluate the interpersonal interaction as more pleasant, are more receptive to feedback, and are more motivated to translate insight into deliberate practice to change behavior.

Here are five questions that leaders can ask employees when they are having difficult discussions around performance and when negative feedback needs to be shared to decrease defensiveness and potentially negative emotional reactions:

1. Describe a situation when you were at your very best. What did you do? What were your thoughts and feelings?
2. What do you want out of life? What are your vision and dreams of your ideal life?
3. What are your passions and loves in life? How do you strive for these?
4. Who is the person you want to become? What legacy do you want to create for your life?
5. How are you currently seen by others, and what are your signature strengths? How can you leverage and put your signature strengths to work more in the future?
6. What changes would you want to make to realize your ideal self, based on your current self?

Tool 4-4. Checklist for Creating a Supportive Interpersonal Climate for Feedback Coaching Meetings Leading to Successful Behavior Change

☐ **Set the stage for safe feedback conversations.** Welcome the employee and share the purpose of the feedback meeting. How you share the feedback can either hinder or facilitate a safe conversation.

☐ **Allow them to express emotions.** Feedback can create both positive and negative emotions. Listen for understanding, acknowledging emotions and feelings in the employee you are speaking to. (For example, "I understand this conversation can be difficult" or "I can see from your reaction that the feedback I have shared with you seems to be upsetting.")

☐ **Consider offering impact statements instead of feedback.** Describing their behavior specifically and sharing the influence it has on you and the team can increase awareness and minimize emotional reactions. By sharing impact, you provide the employee with information about how their actions or words are perceived by others, which can prepare the way for a safe path for a commitment to change behavior in the future.

☐ **Seek to understand (before being understood) and validate feelings.** Listen for understanding at all three levels (content, feeling, and need) to validate your employee's experience in the feedback conversation. Providing emotional reassurance can signal support, empathy, and caring.

    ○ *Content example:* "What I am hearing you say is . . ."

    ○ *Emotion example:* "It sounds to me like you may be feeling . . ."

    ○ *Need example:* "I'm getting a sense you are wanting . . ."

☐ **Check in and follow up.** When difficult conversations are necessary and when negative (or even positive) emotions are expressed by the employee, it is important to have a follow-up or check-in meeting to acknowledge the reaction of the employee and to reinforce that they are not alone and that their perspective matters. This meeting can be formal or informal, but it should occur as soon as possible after the feedback meeting.

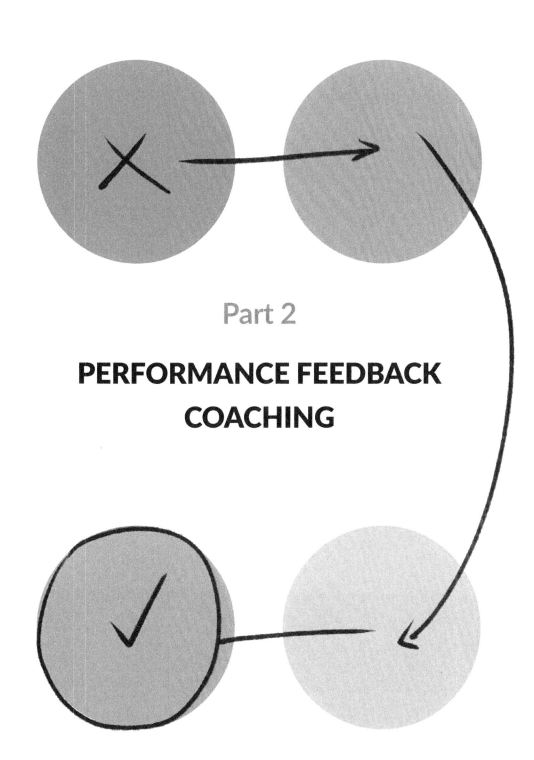

Part 2

PERFORMANCE FEEDBACK COACHING

Chapter 5
The Performance Feedback Coaching Model

In the first half of this book, we discussed the essential elements of constructive feedback, its impact on employees on a psychological and biological level, and the way that influence can vary depending on an employee's culture, gender, race, age, and other individual variables. We explored our 3E Model of Successful Individual Behavior Change for effective feedback and the science behind the model. In the following chapters, we present a proven model for performance feedback coaching that can support employees at all levels. We'll include a variety of practical tips, strategies, and techniques to keep each employee engaged and improving on the job.

We've worked with a variety of large and small organizations and diverse industries around the world for more than two decades. The biggest challenges we've run into are ineffective performance feedback coaching and poor communication skills. We see leaders at every level up and down the corporate hierarchy struggle to communicate effectively with their teams. Most don't fully realize that employees must:

- Understand the feedback.
- Accept the feedback.
- Use the feedback to enhance their commitment to changing a specific behavior.

Some of the most common feedback mistakes leaders make include:

- Providing too little feedback

- Providing too much feedback (which can be perceived to be micromanaging)
- Providing feedback in a one-way direction, without giving the employee a chance to respond
- Not acknowledging an employee's strengths and positive performance
- Presuming that a one-size-fits-all approach will work for everyone, rather than tailoring feedback to each employee's situation and needs
- Not supporting the employee's career goals and aspirations through feedback
- Not considering each employee's unique personality, interpersonal style, and level of engagement when developing an approach to feedback
- Providing feedback that is too direct, blunt, or evaluative
- Only giving feedback when something goes wrong
- Providing feedback that elicits an extreme emotional response or defensiveness
- Providing feedback that is condescending, too critical, or biased
- Providing no feedback at all, whether positive or critical

Feedback research over the last 25 years often falls short of providing a clear definition of feedback or a picture of why, when, and how people learn from it; thus it doesn't offer a clear and meaningful guide for how to manage the complexities of feedback conversations in everyday work life (Anseel and Sherf 2024).

Ineffective feedback directly affects every employee's level of engagement, cooperation, success, and productivity, and there is rarely a single approach to improve feedback for everyone. Each employee has different needs, motivational drivers, career aspirations, and personalities. Given all these variables, we've created a practical approach that leaders can use and tailor to each employee.

We define our Performance Feedback Coaching Model as one that helps employees feel understood, respected, and valued and allows leaders to grasp the needs of their employees and communicate feedback accordingly. It focuses on feedback that is based on each employee's unique circumstances, signature strengths, level of engagement, and personality. It helps leaders accurately categorize employees along two dimensions and use the right communication and feedback strategies for addressing individual performance issues and interpersonal challenges that commonly arise in teams. Let's briefly review how we derived our model before diving deeper into how it works in practice.

Universal Dimensions of How We Are Perceived by Others

According to psychologist Amy Cuddy and her colleagues (2008), people evaluate and judge others based on two global personality attributes:

- Competence necessary for performance on the job (Can I respect this person's knowledge, skills, and abilities?)
- Warmth (Can I trust and cooperatively work with this person?)

As a leader, you probably have employees who are kind, easy to get along with, team players, approachable, and highly trusted by others. At the same time, you probably have other employees who are highly competent, experienced, knowledgeable, diligent, and high performers (Note: It seems obvious, but competence alone does not always guarantee high performance). These people get things done and are highly respected by others for their technical capabilities. We suspect you also have employees who are warm and competent and others who, unfortunately, are neither!

We would all love all our team members to be highly competent as well as warm and friendly, but it just doesn't always happen. Both leaders and employees instinctively understand the concept of arranged marriages in the workplace—we usually don't get a chance to choose the people we work with on our teams.

From your point of view as a leader, delivering feedback to an employee who is warm, open, and receptive is nothing like giving feedback to someone who is competent but lacks friendliness, empathy, and kindness. A likable and caring employee may appreciate your expression of empathy, and as a leader, you are probably able to help them develop further. On the other hand, a competent employee who lacks warmth may require you to be a bit more direct, specific, neutral, and factual in communicating feedback. Research shows that we are hard-wired to seek out people who are warm and have social and emotional competence because they can have a positive impact on our relationships. In choosing people to collaborate with, our ancient ancestors enjoyed a greater benefit from their partner's warmth than from their competence, and those same ancestors could face significant negative consequences from a lack of warmth. Overall, someone else's competence varies from situation to situation and thus has a less dramatic impact on our relationships (Eisenbruch and Krasnow 2022).

Likable Fool or Competent Jerk?

Put yourself in the shoes of your employees. What type of boss do most people want to work with? Someone with the necessary knowledge, skills, and abilities to make informed decisions, solve problems, and execute strategies effectively? Or someone who is less talented and has more limited knowledge and skills, but is approachable, kind, caring, and likable?

In today's competitive global economy, your first reaction is likely that employees would overwhelmingly prefer someone who demonstrates *competence*—including the technical knowledge, experience, and skills necessary to accomplish key objectives. However, an older but still classic study of about 10,000 workplace relationships found that employees prefer to work with someone less skilled and more approachable rather than someone very skilled but challenging to interact with on a personal level (Casciaro and Lobo 2005). The researchers created a typology for categorizing people in the workplace into four archetypes—lovable stars, likable fools, competent jerks, and incompetent jerks—and it's still in use today.

It's no surprise that the researchers concluded most people prefer to work for a likable fool rather than a competent jerk! More importantly, their study helps us better understand and apply different approaches to providing feedback and coaching for each archetype. Better feedback and coaching can then lead to enhanced engagement and performance for all employees.

How Do You Coach a Likable Fool?

Likable fools possess excellent interpersonal and social skills; they can be tremendous assets to most organizations because they are perceived to be relationship builders, team players, and easy to work with. However, if not managed correctly, likable fools can also fail in the workplace because of their deficits in knowledge or skills. Leaders address these deficits, focusing on the employees' knowledge and job-related skill sets to enhance overall performance and contributions to the team. For these types of employees, ongoing feedback and performance coaching are keys to enhancing their success and ensuring career growth within the organization.

What Do You Do With a Competent Jerk?

Companies often reward their competent jerks because they are good at what they do and typically deliver high performance and outstanding results. If not managed correctly, however, these employees can pose long-term liabilities for organizations. Interpersonal skill deficits can negatively affect other team members and customers, leading to a potentially hostile work environment and higher voluntary turnover.

If there are competent jerks on your team, you will need to communicate in a specific way to help build their awareness of how much their poor interpersonal skills adversely affect others. If the employee's interpersonal skills cannot be addressed or corrected, you must analyze the long-term cost-benefit ratio of keeping a potentially toxic employee who possesses strong skills and a solid performance record.

Admittedly, we have both worked with leaders who fell into the competent jerk category. From surgeons to CEOs, CROs, CFOs, and CIOs; from leaders in entertainment and hospitality to manufacturing, biotech, and agriculture, they are everywhere. Some of these leaders possess a sense of authority that comes with their feeling of superiority, and they behave condescendingly toward others. In other cases, these problem leaders just don't know better. They were probably led by similar competent jerks in the past and are simply continuing a "my way or the highway" legacy. In some instances, the "jerk" aspect of their behavior can be traced to personality traits such as narcissism, perfectionism, or neuroticism. But no matter the reason for their behavior, thousands of organizations are challenged every day to come up with the best way to manage these employees. Are there underlying individual problems interfering with their interpersonal interactions? Should they seek coaching? Are they even coachable? What is the liability of keeping them? What is the cost of losing them?

We believe it is possible to give interpersonally challenged leaders and employees feedback in such a way that they receive it with less defensiveness and a bit more openness. We also have ways to assess their motivational drivers and key needs and align their needs with the strategic objectives of your department. You'll have to make some decisions and choices, but you can keep them engaged and performing well.

> Research has shown that warmth is rated higher than competence in people's overall evaluation of individuals and groups. In other words, when evaluating potential relationships, people tend to appraise a warm, incompetent person more positively than a cold, competent one (Cuddy, Fiske, and Glick 2008).

Diving Deeper Into the Performance Feedback Coaching Model

We believe that our Performance Feedback Coaching Model can serve as a framework to enhance the skills and productivity of employees at all levels of the organization. It provides leaders with tailored feedback conversations that increase acceptance and motivation to perform.

Our model is based on the two global capability and personality attributes we've mentioned earlier in this chapter: competence and warmth. It is also important to note that this model is based on more than 80 years of research, which supports the importance (and consistent recurrence) of the warmth and competence dimensions under diverse and various labels (Fiske et al. 2002). We conceptualize these two attributes as overall employee job performance based on mutually agreed upon expectations and standards, social skills, and interpersonal competence. Building on the four archetypes developed by Casciaro and Lobo, we created our own typology of four performance coaching approaches:

- Performance management
- Performance acceleration
- Performance improvement
- Performance enhancement

Each approach targets specific goals with methods aimed at facilitating both *what* gets done based on existing knowledge, skills, abilities, and experiences (performance) and *how* things get done (social, emotional, and interpersonal skills) for all employees within organizations (Figure 5-1). You can use the model to quickly identify the best approach for facilitating employee development at all levels by plotting each employee's levels of overall performance and interpersonal competence on the chart. For example, if an employee demonstrates high performance as a result of their skills and abilities but lacks emotional and social competence, they will benefit from performance management feedback coaching strategies, which address important interpersonal challenges and development opportunities.

Figure 5-1. Performance Feedback Coaching Model

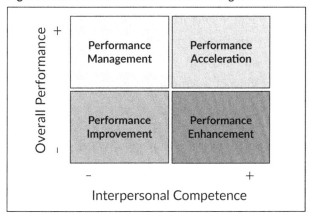

An important reminder: As a leader, you should always consider the intersectionality of factors such as personality, style, age, tenure, culture, gender, race, ethnicity, well-being, and your own relationship with an employee to monitor how they might be influencing your performance feedback and coaching strategies.

How to Use Our Model for Performance Feedback Coaching

In the following sections, we offer brief descriptions of the characteristics and challenges specific to employees in each of the four quadrants of our model. We also touch on specific techniques and strategies to guide successful performance feedback coaching conversations. In subsequent chapters, we will explore the performance feedback coaching quadrants in-depth and share ways to troubleshoot for specific knowledge, skills, and motivations that might hinder employee performance. For each coaching strategy, we will provide examples of feedback tips, suggestions, and techniques to address employees' deficits.

What Do We Mean by Overall Performance?

Whenever possible, appraisal of overall performance should be based on achievement (falling short of, meeting, or exceeding goals) of mutually agreed on key performance indicators (KPIs). In practice, evaluations of overall performance also involve subjective perceptions, observations, and biases. While there is no general consensus about the definition of performance, people are often tempted to measure it only from a task or in-role perspective. We conceive performance as a multidimensional construct comprising task performance, organizational and co-worker support, teamwork, and cognitive and motivational effectiveness. Performance can also be considered as a byproduct of an employee's experience, knowledge, attention, and abilities.

Performance Management Feedback Coaching

The people who fall into the performance management quadrant are highly competent, respected for their abilities, highly achievement oriented, and typically successful, despite deficiencies in some specific social and interpersonal skills. These employees are at risk of potential derailment at some point in their careers and might be described as consistent performers but somewhat difficult to deal with. In other words, these are the *competent jerks.*

These individuals are an asset in terms of their performance outcomes but can quickly become a serious liability if their interpersonal deficits are not addressed. These leaders and employees are excellent performers but struggle to build strong relationships with their teams and internal and external stakeholders, which inevitably can lead to a lack of engagement, low morale, high turnover, customer dissatisfaction, and loss of productivity on the part of their team members and peers. These employees may struggle to manage their own emotions and reactions under stress, behaving impulsively, which can lead to poor decision making and volatile interpersonal interactions. Their behavior can result in conflicts, misunderstandings, and damaged relationships. Others may find collaborating or simply interacting with these individuals challenging and may attempt to avoid them as much as possible.

In our model, the focus of improvement for leaders who are designated competent jerks is enhancing their social, interpersonal, and communication skills. If you're a leader dealing with employees in this category, you need to make sure they see their interpersonal blind spots accurately and give them specific feedback to better understand how they are perceived by others. Explain the potential negative influence their leadership, communication skills, and interpersonal style is having on others. One of the primary challenges in providing feedback to these individuals is that it is likely to generate defensiveness due to their lack of self-awareness about how others perceive, experience, and interpret their behavior.

Performance Acceleration Feedback Coaching

In the performance acceleration quadrant, you'll find high-performing employees and leaders who also demonstrate excellent interpersonal skills and competence. For these *lovable stars*, we often find the problem to be that they are not challenged enough or not receiving enough meaningful feedback. Organizations want to retain these high-potential employees over time and need ways to accelerate their professional growth and development.

Lovable stars are the most likely to seek employment elsewhere if their organization's leadership and culture do not meet their needs. What are their needs? They thrive on challenges and opportunities to learn and grow in their roles. When not sufficiently challenged, they may feel disengaged. They seek ongoing and specific feedback and appreciate recognition for their efforts and accomplishments. Lovable stars often go underrecognized by the organization because they perform so strongly and don't create friction.

Organizations need to provide their lovable stars with plenty of opportunities for career and professional growth, development, and challenge. This can include offering stretch assignments and encouraging leaders to take on new responsibilities or projects. If these stars stay engaged and challenged, you will help them continue to develop their skills even further and contribute to the organization's long-term success. Sometimes, you might notice a change in performance levels with lovable stars due to issues outside work, such as health or other temporary personal situations. It is important for leaders to identify and address any personal barriers and challenges to help these employees return to their high levels of performance.

Performance Enhancement Feedback Coaching

In the performance enhancement quadrant are the employees and leaders who have good interpersonal skills but lack specific knowledge or job-related skills that interfere with higher levels of performance. They are often labeled *likable fools* because they struggle to meet the everyday demands of their roles and may not achieve their individual and team goals. While being friendly and approachable is important for building positive relationships with others, it is not enough to be effective. Almost all employees and leaders have some knowledge, skills, and abilities they can improve to enhance their overall performance. For example, leaders and employees at all levels can demonstrate deficiencies in areas such as planning, problem solving, delegation, time management, or technical knowledge or skills specific to their jobs.

The goal with these employees is to identify knowledge and skill areas that might be hindering higher performance and then implement a personal development plan to address one or more of them. It is all about finding ways to help them become their best selves. Employees and leaders within this quadrant typically have high emotional intelligence and respond to specific instruction and more pragmatic coaching, training, and mentoring techniques, and tools. This could include offering additional support, providing an external coach, reassigning the leader to a different role, or formalizing a mentor relationship. Most coaching assignments with these individuals will be task-focused and can be done in a shorter timeframe, based on a demonstration of skill acquisition by the employee to key stakeholders within the organization.

Performance Improvement Feedback Coaching

In the fourth quadrant of our model, performance improvement, we find leaders and employees who are performing poorly and neither fully competent in terms of their job-related skills and knowledge nor gifted with people skills. The deficits of the people Casciaro and Lobo labeled *incompetent jerks* will have a significant negative impact on your organization, including reduced productivity, disengagement, and high turnover. Consistently poor-performing and low-potential employees can interfere with team functioning and take tremendous management time away from high performers.

Determining when a leader or employee belongs in this category can be difficult, but signs include poor performance, low employee satisfaction, employee complaints to your HR team, other team members requesting stress-related leave, and a pervasive lack of trust and respect among team members.

In our model, the focus of feedback coaching for these employees is on immediate and significant performance improvement or deciding to remove them from the organization. These employees are often the lowest performing members of a team and many organizations will try to eliminate them by offering outplacement and severance packages.

Using the Performance Feedback Coaching Model

Let's take a minute to review two recent coaching scenarios with common themes. Read them and consider how you might address the performance issues presented. As you reflect on these scenarios, think about how you might modify your communication and feedback approach to maximize employee understanding, acceptance, and commitment to action.

Two Performance Feedback Coaching Scenarios

Scenario #1: Performance Management

Erin is perceived by others as an experienced technical expert but is often too authoritative, dismissive of other employees' ideas and suggestions, and monopolizes team meetings and discussions without involving others. Her team members say they don't feel psychologically safe enough to challenge Erin or participate openly in meetings. Many revealed privately to HR that they were considering leaving the company because of Erin's disengaging, authoritative, toxic leadership practices.

Packaging and delivering feedback to Erin based on your confidential team interviews and a recent 360-degree feedback assessment will be a challenge. You must ensure Erin understands, is willing to accept your feedback, and is motivated to make specific changes in her behavior.

Scenario #2: Performance Acceleration

Ali has been with your organization for more than 13 years and has advanced through several ranks. He is seen by everyone as a strong performer, is very independent, and gets his work done without requesting support from you or relying on other team members to a large extent. He gets along extremely well with other team members and is perceived as a trusted and respected colleague. Lately, however, Ali has been less vocal in meetings and hasn't attended company events. His team's performance is starting to decline after many years of consistent success. When you asked about the noticeable decline in performance, Ali said it was because employees were not as collaborative when working virtually and he was struggling with work-life scheduling as a single parent. You have observed a noticeable decline in follow up on projects, less timely responses, and a decrease in his overall level of engagement.

In analyzing the scenarios with Erin and Ali, ask yourself:

- How would you prepare feedback for each person to minimize defensiveness and increase motivation to address the performance and interpersonal relationship issues you've observed?
- What individual characteristics (such as personality, style, and experience) may influence how your feedback is be received and interpreted by each person or become a barrier to their acceptance of that feedback?
- How can you manage potential stereotypes and biases (conscious or unconscious) you may harbor based on age, gender, race, culture, and the strength of your relationship with each person in your coaching conversations to ensure they are as productive, constructive, and positive as possible?

Our Advice

You should take a much more directive approach with Erin. Make sure to address one or more aspects of her current performance that, if not corrected, could lead to eventual derailment and even failure. With Ali, you will need to diagnose and understand his current level of engagement and explore what specific kind of support and mutually agreeable steps forward will help shift him back to being the star performer he once was.

We have faced many scenarios like these. In coaching leaders to address their own unique situations, we provide specific feedback techniques and strategies to enhance employees' acceptance and increase their commitment to specific development action plans for performance improvement.

In the next four chapters, we will explore more specific issues, techniques, and strategies to effectively manage an employee's performance within each category of our performance feedback model. While some of your employees might straddle a few quadrants, most will land squarely in one of the four.

Key Points

Let's review a few key points from this chapter:

- How you give effective feedback will vary from one individual to another. Our Performance Feedback Coaching Model includes feedback strategies, tips, tools, and suggestions for leading and supporting everyone on your team according to their unique personality, skills, level of engagement, well-being, and other relevant characteristics.
- People are generally perceived and evaluated according to two universal dimensions: competence and warmth. Our coaching model is derived from those universal dimensions and from the observation that most people prefer to work with considerate, supportive, and friendly people rather than more competent people who lack core warmth and empathy.
- Our coaching model helps categorize employees into four types, each of which needs a different approach to performance feedback:
  - Performance acceleration: High performance and high interpersonal skills
  - Performance management: High performance and low interpersonal skills
  - Performance enhancement: Low performance and high interpersonal skills
  - Performance improvement: Low performance and low interpersonal skills

Tool 5-1. Performance Feedback Coaching Model Exercise 1

Categorizing Your Direct Reports

Write the initials of your direct reports in the appropriate quadrant based on a relative comparison of their *overall performance* (that is, their skill level and performance) and their *interpersonal competence* (or their emotional and social intelligence).

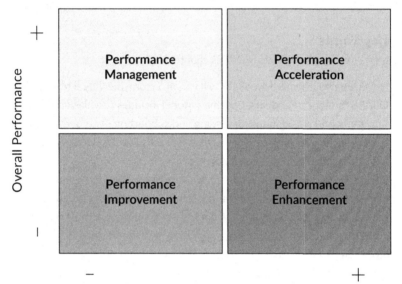

After categorizing each direct report, use the strategies, techniques, and methods of the Performance Feedback Coaching Model to more effectively provide feedback that will be understood, accepted, and will increase employees' motivation to change their behavior on the job.

Tool 5-2. Performance Feedback Coaching Model Exercise 2

Identify Which Performance Feedback Coaching Model to Use

The following situations describe two different employees, each of whom falls within a different quadrant of the Performance Feedback Coaching Model. As you read through them, decide which coaching approach you would use and check the box indicating your choice.

Meet Chris

Chris is a 54-year-old pediatric surgical oncologist at St. Peter's Hospital. They have been working there for about 14 years. As a well-known oncologist, they have achieved outstanding results with patients, established an international reputation in research, and been recognized for innovations in surgical procedures by their peers. Chris currently supervises seven surgical oncology residents and oversees six staff members within the oncology department.

Recently, some of the staff and residents have complained about the way Chris leads them. They don't feel empowered or motivated. They claim that Chris does not listen to them and is constantly criticizing them. These complaints have led to diminished performance for the team. While everyone on the team respects Chris for their knowledge and surgical skills, most complain that Chris's feedback style and temper are belittling and personal. The team also says Chris comes across as extremely arrogant and disrespectful to those who are less experienced.

Chris needs:
- ☐ Performance acceleration
- ☐ Performance improvement
- ☐ Performance management
- ☐ Performance enhancement

Tool 5-2. (cont.)

Meet Aaron

Aaron is a 38-year-old manager of financial services at NationCorp Financial. He has an MBA from a prestigious school and has worked for four years in financial services.

Recently, individual and team performance in Aaron's department has declined due to a lack of individual coaching and team development on Aaron's part. He has great relationships with the team members but is not perceived as a strong influencer and communicator. Aaron struggles with time management, team presentations, and capturing his team's attention during group meetings. He claims to be overwhelmed and does not have time to fulfill his own assigned tasks and manage the tasks of others. Aaron needs:

☐ Performance acceleration
☐ Performance improvement
☐ Performance management
☐ Performance enhancement

Answers to Performance Feedback Coaching Model Exercise 2:

- *Chris needs performance management feedback coaching strategies.*
- *Aaron needs performance enhancement feedback coaching strategies.*

Chapter 6
Performance Management
How to Coach High Performers
With Low Interpersonal Skills

As leadership coaches, we often find that the most brilliant, talented people—including surgeons, engineers, finance leaders, and C-suite executives—lack the ability to maintain positive working relationships. Despite being highly accomplished in terms of their technical skills, knowledge, and experience, these people struggle to connect with others on a personal level; Casciaro and Lobo (2005) would call them "competent jerks." If one of your direct reports is a high performer with low interpersonal skills, you need to learn to communicate with them appropriately because their behavior can be costly. In this chapter, we explore some of the factors to consider when dealing with these individuals and share our proven techniques for coaching them.

Working alongside or for a competent jerk can be exhausting. They lack consideration for others and treat colleagues in ways they would hate to be treated themselves. Sandra remembers an executive she knew early in her career working as an organization development manager. They were especially arrogant, condescending, and completely unpredictable. They said "hello" only to employees who were high performers for the company and used humiliation tactics to motivate employees by publicly announcing performance results, including those of the poorest performers. This executive expected employees to work long hours, weekends, and holidays, demonstrating zero empathy or interest in supporting a healthy work-life balance.

Because the company was performing well at the time, no one questioned the executive's harsh interactions, and everyone conformed. Eventually, however, luck ran out and the executive's behavior caught up with them. Employee morale and engagement decreased, turnover increased, and company revenue declined.

We highlight this as a perfect example of the kinds of mistakes many organizations make when they avoid challenging the disagreeable or downright hostile behaviors of those who are high performers with low interpersonal skills. We encourage you to ask yourself some important questions as you think about how best to handle your organization's version of the competent jerk:

- Can your company continue to be successful if someone with low interpersonal skills remains in a key leadership role?
- Consider leaders you have known who fit the description of a competent jerk. Can such a leader ever change?
- At what cost should your organization keep such individuals, especially if they are extremely high performers?
- Can a leader succeed in the long term without fostering positive relationships with their team?
- When a leader creates a toxic working environment, why do some companies not only keep them but reward them?

All too often we are called in to coach a leader with a record of multiple lawsuits for bullying employees and numerous complaints about rude and condescending behavior around team members creating a hostile work environment. We usually shake our heads and ask each other, "What is this organization thinking? Why keep a leader who has caused so much anguish among employees?"

When we pose these questions to people within the company, we hear a variety of responses, including:

- "He's our best performer!"
- "She is a master surgeon!"
- "They regularly bring in too much new business and revenue to let them go!"

But while they are clearly successful in the work they do, these toxic leaders create unhappy, stressful work environments that can have profound consequences for the entire organization. Unfortunately, many organizations don't account for the costs in terms of low morale, disengagement, and turnover—not to mention, ultimately, the bottom line.

Time and again, companies promote and reward people solely based on performance when they should also acknowledge interpersonal skills. In fact, according to a 2019 McKinsey survey, jobs that require technical skills (often called "hard skills") pay more than twice as much as jobs requiring "soft skills" like teamwork and effective communication (Avrane-Chopard and Potter 2019). Most organizations claim they value empathy, communication, leadership, and compassion in their leaders; if so, these skills must be rewarded in accordance with their value. The primary focus of behaviors for both leaders and employees will almost always be on whatever is rewarded.

Promoting an employee for performance alone can lead to workplace disasters that have lingering consequences for your company, including employee dissatisfaction and high turnover. In fact, according to a 2022 employee survey, 82 percent of employees quit their jobs because of bad managers (Korolevich 2022).

Interpersonal Disorders and the Competent Jerks

Individuals who lack interpersonal skills are often hard-wired with these characteristics, and the same goes for people with strong social skills. For example, one study looked at 1,300 healthy young adults with higher expressions of the genes that regulate the release of the prosocial peptide oxytocin (CD38 and CD157). These individuals reported significantly better social functioning, warmth, and empathy, and the genetic factor accounted for about 14 percent of the variance in social functioning in the group (Chong et al. 2017).

Someone who seems confident and charming but has an exploitative and overbearing sense of entitlement may have a clinically defined condition known as *narcissistic personality disorder* (American Psychiatric Association DSM-5). If one of your colleagues or employees exhibits this behavior and causes frequent disruption in the workplace, you may need to seek the consultation of a clinician or employee assistance program (EAP) representative if your company offers this service.

However, not all people who demonstrate narcissistic traits are hopeless cases, create interpersonal distress, or are resistant to performance feedback coaching. You may be surprised to learn that studies have found a positive relationship between slight or moderate levels of narcissism and leadership effectiveness (Grijalva et al. 2010). Narcissistic leaders are more likely to be seen as charismatic because they often have the skills to communicate bold and daring visions and act in a forward-driven way (Galvin, Waldman, and Balthazard 2010). Some research even suggests that they are more likely to initiate the mergers and acquisitions that can expand and enrich their organizations (Braun 2017).

As a leader, you need to distinguish between extreme cases of individuals with true personality disorders and those who simply have some social deficits and are motivated and able to learn and improve their skills. The first step when examining those who are interested in learning and changing is to gauge the person's strengths and the costs of their behaviors—especially if they are in a leadership position. Do aspects of their behavior positively influence the people they work with? Can you help develop those aspects further?

The good news is that with the right feedback and communication approach, most people can improve their behavior. The magnitude of change will depend on how extreme their behaviors are, how aware they are of the influence of their behavior, and their motivation to make a change.

Why Do Emotional and Social Competence Matter?

Studies have confirmed that leaders who are *emotionally and socially competent* (or what has until recently been called *emotionally intelligent*) are much better equipped to lead because they are highly self-aware, can tune in to others, and can express empathy (Nowack and Munro 2019). What recent research has confirmed is that employees also consider emotional and social competence to be a key factor in their leaders and a reason to remain with their organizations.

In a 2021 article on what people need to perform at an elevated level, researchers Zorana Ivcevic, Robin Stern, and Andrew Faas described the key role that emotional and social competence plays in the workforce. "In our survey of 14,500 US workers," they wrote:

We learned that employees report working to their full potential when they are clear about what they are expected to do; they are willing to ask questions and feel safe doing so; they are not overwhelmed with rules about how the work must be done or with unproductive meetings; their organization supports creative problem-solving (e.g., implementing employee suggestions for improvements) and provides rewards and recognition for jobs well done; supervisors notice and acknowledge employees' feelings, understand how their decisions will impact employees, and help them manage their emotions; [and] they see purpose and meaning in their work and are committed to their organization.

Part of their survey also included interviews with nurses who worked during the COVID-19 pandemic. The researchers got valuable answers when asking what led to improvements or declines in the nurses' performance under peak stress conditions.

As a leader, you can also solicit input from employees at every level in your organization. Acknowledge their ideas and always consider how top-level decisions affect their experiences on the job. If you don't accept employees' ideas, make sure to communicate why. Ivcevic, Stern, and Faas (2021) concluded that, "During the COVID-19 pandemic, acting in emotionally intelligent ways means acknowledging employees' heightened anxiety and assuring them that being overwhelmed under these circumstances is not a sign of poor skills. Supervisors who act in emotionally intelligent ways will create a more positive work climate, have employees who can grow in their jobs, and be more effective."

Another post-pandemic survey revealed the importance of managers turning toward their employees on a personal level, confirming that psychological well-being was an extremely high priority for workers themselves (APA 2024). Here are a few other highlights from this survey:

- 61 percent of those experiencing lower psychological safety felt tense or stressed out in a typical workday versus 27 percent of those experiencing higher psychological safety.

- 92 percent of workers said it was important to work for an organization that valued their emotional and psychological well-being.
- 92 percent said it was important to work for an organization that provided support for employees' mental health.
- 95 percent said it was important to feel respected at work.
- 95 percent said it was important to work for an organization that respected the boundaries between work and nonwork time.

The World Economic Forum's *The Future of Jobs Report 2020* predicted that by 2025, emotional intelligence would be among the top 10 workplace skills in demand in the United States. In addition, a 2020 survey from the Society for Human Resource Management found that 84 percent of American workers said poorly trained managers created unnecessary work and stress, and half of those surveyed said their performance would improve if their manager received additional training in skills like communication and building company culture. In other words, the majority of employees clearly care about their leader's people skills. If you are a leader who cannot empathize with your employees and their emotional needs, you run the risk of disengagement and turnover.

One critical area every leader should pay attention to is the increased rate of depression among employees as reported in the wake of workplace changes in 2020 and afterward. A fifth of those surveyed in the APA's *Work in America Survey* experienced harm to their mental health at work. Unfortunately, only 29 percent of employees reported working in a culture in which leaders encouraged employees to take care of their mental health. We believe the need for leaders to enhance their own emotional and social competence is demonstrably urgent. Some of the strategies and tools in this chapter are designed to address this need.

Performance Management Feedback Coaching

Most of those who lack social and emotional competence but tend to demonstrate high performance on assigned tasks and projects can be coached using our performance management feedback strategies and techniques (Figure 6-1). We begin by identifying the specific knowledge, skills, or abilities that might be interfering with higher interpersonal performance and creating a mutually acceptable development plan to address some or all the deficits. You will be able to enhance individuals' people skills with training, coaching, mentoring, and on-the-job instruction. Let's now review some strategies and tools for managing the interpersonal deficits of these employees.

Figure 6-1. Performance Management Feedback Coaching Quadrant

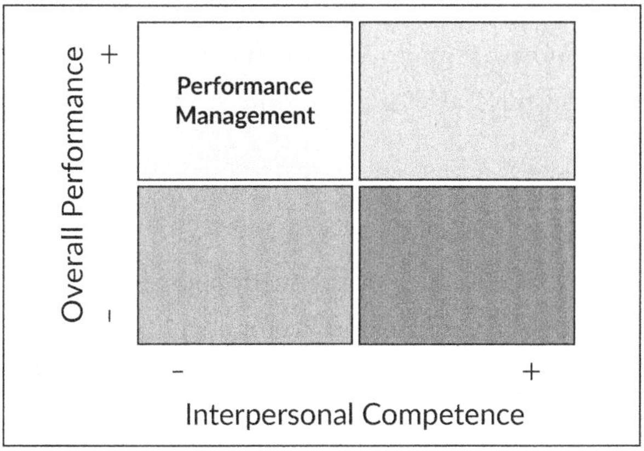

Overall Performance (+ / –)

Performance Management

Interpersonal Competence (– / +)

Find Motivational Drivers

In any feedback conversation, it is important to figure out what motivates your direct reports. Our listening filters lead us to pay more attention to certain things and ignore others. Depending on those filters, one person might laugh and another might cry while hearing the same story. If we understand what motivates people at work, we can ensure they pay attention and receive our messages.

When we coach employees, the first step is figure out their personalities and motivational styles. Here is one framework we use when looking for motivational drivers:

- Is the person driven by achieving results?
- Is the person driven by maintaining harmony with people?
- Is the person driven by being correct all the time?

Once you identify their motivations, you can tailor your feedback accordingly to ensure they understand and accept it. For instance, suppose you are giving feedback to a leader who is driven by results. In that case, you probably don't need to explain a lot of details; instead, you should ensure your message is succinct, to the point, and links to the bottom line. On the other hand, when you are giving feedback to someone who is driven by being correct, you should ensure they hear all the information necessary to support your point, including data, examples, and patterns. In that situation, elaborate and be meticulous to match their motivational filter. If you are communicating with someone driven by maintaining harmony with people, you should ensure they feel accepted and liked by others. Connecting to an employee's motivational drivers is beneficial not only for feedback conversations but also for any conversation in which you want to delegate or influence.

Communicate What's in It for Them

People often want to see the personal benefit before they're willing to try to make a change—and this is even more true for people with weak interpersonal skills, who are often strongly motivated by their own interests. Frame your requests or proposals to these individuals in a way that highlights how the outcome benefits them or aligns with their goals.

When we first begin a coaching process, we always try to identify our clients' self-interests and clearly communicate them back to the client. We might ask about their goals with the company or what would entice them to work on new projects. Are they looking for the next promotion? Are they motivated to earn an outstanding reputation and gain formal recognition? Are they looking for power and authority? We then use that information to tailor our feedback. For example, imagine you are communicating feedback to a leader who lacks tact and empathy in all conversations with their employees. You could frame your feedback conversation as suggesting incentives for the leader to change to enhance *their* career rather than as a means of improving their employee's well-being.

Help Them See Their Blind Spots

It is not unusual for employees to have distorted or inaccurate views about themselves. According to the Dunning-Kruger effect, most people tend to overestimate their own abilities, particularly for those who are less competent and skilled (Kruger and Dunning 1999). For instance, studies have found that less experienced and older automobile drivers in the US tend to overestimate their driving skills and take risks that a more experienced driver would typically avoid. Narcissists may exhibit and express a more extreme version of the Dunning-Kruger effect because of their limited ability to understand their shortcomings and reticence to receiving feedback or criticism.

So, how can you help someone see their blind spots? First, it is important to accurately identify the blind spots, clarify how others are experiencing the person's behavior negatively, and find out whether the person is aware of this. Let's put that important point another way: When giving feedback about interpersonal behavior, it is imperative to identify how the employee's behaviors are *affecting others* they work with and ensure the employee is aware of this. Many companies regularly put employees through a 360-degree feedback assessment process to continue to leverage their strengths and illuminate their blind spots (Nowack and Mashihi 2012).

Defuse Employees' Defensiveness

When receiving feedback, it is not unusual for an employee's defenses to rise. Research shows that receiving feedback creates physical stress responses, including an increased heart rate, an adrenaline rush, and even physical pain (Eisenberger, Lieberman, and Williams 2003). Let's look at a few ways to manage inevitable defensive reactions in most employees, but particularly for strong performers who don't necessarily see the need for social competence based on their contributions and accomplishments.

Remain Calm

Preparing to give someone else feedback can add a layer of stress to your day because you don't know how they will react. However, your fight-or-flight response as the feedback giver could also trigger the other person to become stressed and lead to an uncomfortable situation for everyone. Approaching a potentially stressful conversation with a calm and mindful demeanor will lower the tension and communicate to the other person that you are not a threat. Always begin by ensuring you have a relaxed facial expression.

Listen and Demonstrate Your Understanding

Show that you are actively listening to the person's concerns and ideas by reflecting on their statements before responding. This will help them feel heard. Sometimes, we advise our clients to pause for a few seconds before responding to make sure they clearly understand the point of view of the person they are speaking with. You can verify your understanding by paraphrasing and repeating their ideas back to them.

Even if someone says something you don't agree with, you can still show that you understand their feelings and perspective; acknowledging does not mean agreeing. For example, you could say something like, "I understand that you feel that way, and I have a different perspective." The mere act of acknowledgment goes a long way toward helping lower an employee's defenses so they can receive your message.

You might even want to relate a similar personal experience you've had that links to their perspective. For example, you could say something like, "I understand how you feel about ensuring your team is performing at their best. I experience the same urge to get involved with the details of what my team does. But there may be ways to manage without making your team feel micromanaged or think that you don't trust them. I have learned to empower my team and it has worked to keep them more engaged and productive."

Recognize Your Employee's Strengths . . . But Not Too Much!

Just as negative feedback or criticism activates our fight-or-flight response, positive feedback activates our brain's reward circuits, which encourages us to repeat those behaviors so we can keep feeling that rewarding dopamine high. If you are working with someone who displays deficits in interpersonal communication and behavior, compliment them on what they are doing well. They will respond well to the praise.

However, while recognizing that an employee's strengths is a great way to disarm them in a feedback conversation, you don't want to overdo the praise because people with more arrogant, less emotionally intelligent personalities might accept only the positive and ignore anything constructive. Strike a balance in each conversation between recognizing someone's strengths and addressing problematic behavior.

Communicate the Impact of Behaviors Instead of Intent

When you discuss the impact of someone's behavior you can defuse their defensiveness because your focus is on observable facts rather than their motives or your assumptions. When sharing feedback, always give people the benefit of the doubt when it comes to their intentions and direct the focus toward what they can do more, less, or differently based on their behaviors.

For example, instead of saying, "You were trying to put Peter down in the meeting last week," you could say, "During the meeting, I noticed that when Peter was sharing his perspective, you criticized him. He said this made him feel like his ideas were not valued. It has also made it harder for Peter to share anything during subsequent meetings."

With this approach, you are describing the behavior (criticizing) and its impact (someone thinking their ideas are not valued or accepted and being silent going forward) without making assumptions about the intentions behind the criticism.

Give Candid and Specific Feedback

Because many employees in this quadrant tend to push boundaries and exploit others, it is important to communicate candidly and directly to set clear boundaries around any unacceptable behaviors. It's not uncommon for leaders to avoid providing feedback to narcissistic employees or those who lack social and emotional competence because they are afraid of their reactions. These leaders don't want to "rock the boat" with one of the company's high performers. We suggest following several helpful feedback guidelines with such employees.

Use "I" Statements Instead of "You" Statements

Framing your feedback using "I" statements allows you to own them without making the other person feel attacked or blamed. This strategy defuses defensiveness and allows people to listen more deeply to your feedback. Avoid using statements like, "you always" or "you never." These accusations typically don't sit well with employees, especially those who react to constructive criticism and negative feedback with a defensive posture.

Be Clear and Concise

Keep your communication simple and to the point. Narcissists and those with poor interpersonal skills may try to derail the conversation or manipulate it to their advantage, so make sure to stay on topic.

Focus on a Recent and Specific Event

Ensure your feedback isn't about an incident that happened a year ago, but rather something recent and easy to remember. Communicating the need for change about an event that happened a long time ago can set you up for backlash and argument.

Focus on Behavior, Not Personality

Make sure your feedback isn't about your direct report's personality; that can be seen as a personal attack. Instead, focus on a single behavior that they can change.

Do Not Argue About Past Events; Instead, Discuss Present-Day Solutions

Resistant employees may argue about exactly what happened and provide excuses to justify their stance. There is no point in arguing about the details, so divert the conversation toward a solution for the future, even if you have not agreed about what occurred in the past. You can agree to disagree about past details but reiterate the behavior you expect to see going forward.

Try the DESC Feedback Technique

Using a proven feedback model can give leaders more confidence and a road map for holding conversations with direct reports. Some of the most well-known models are:

- SBI (situation, behavior, impact)
- SOAR (situation, observations, association, assessment)
- STAR (situation, task, action, result)
- CRAVE (context, review, action, viewpoint, encourage)

One communication approach we often employ when providing direct feedback to a defensive employee is the DESC technique (Tool 6-1). This technique allows you to rehearse and prepare to fully communicate what behaviors need to change and the consequences and advantages of doing so. The DESC technique also helps the employee better understand how their interpersonal actions and behaviors can undermine their overall competence, skills, and experience.

The suggestions, techniques, and strategies outlined in this chapter aren't always 100 percent effective when working with the "competent jerks" on your team, but when used wisely, they can help these individuals hear and accept performance feedback.

Social and emotional competence can be among the most challenging issues to address with feedback, even when employees are motivated to change. Helping them understand the value of being aware of how they interact with others and the impact of poor interpersonal skills is a crucial step toward motivating them to enhance their emotional and social competence.

Performance Management Feedback Coaching: A Case Study

Alex Williams is a 46-year-old vice president of finance at Treasure Corporation Worldwide. He plays a key role in managing the firm's treasury and tax functions and is responsible for overseeing 57 employees. Alex is an expert finance officer with 22 years of experience, is a licensed CPA, and holds an MBA from Harvard University. He has managed the company's funds and taxes and allocated resources effectively throughout his career. Alex has also attracted important clients to the firm because of his financial services skills.

Recently, Executive Vice President Lee Nguyen called Alex in to a meeting to discuss a series of complaints about him and his leadership style, but the situation did not improve. Alex's team leads believe he is still more focused on reprimanding them than developing their potential. They say they don't have leeway to make their own decisions even though they are in management positions and feel entitled to do so. Alex is typically boastful about his accomplishments, has an air of superiority, expresses defensiveness when challenged by others, and can be manipulative and deceiving when those tactics are in his best interest.

Every time members of his team try to talk with Alex, he reminds them that he has years more experience and expertise. They say that even when they try their best and do good work, Alex never recognizes or acknowledges them; he only points out what they have done wrong. Several of Alex's team members have been subjected to his condescending behavior in staff meetings and are now afraid to speak up and contribute. Overall, they are losing motivation to be productive in their jobs.

EVP Nguyen and others on the senior leadership team now have a dilemma. How do they appease one of their most high-profile leaders—who contributes significantly to the firm's return on investment (ROI)—while also addressing his team's concerns about toxic leadership practices and interpersonal behavior?

Imagine you are Alex's supervisor and answer the following questions:

- What key issues related to Alex's behavior must you address?
- How will you communicate with Alex about your concerns?
- What techniques can you use to defuse his defensiveness?

 Key Points

Let's review a few key points from this chapter:

- People in the performance management feedback coaching quadrant have weak interpersonal skills but tend to be high performers due to their technical knowledge and skills that lead to successful outcomes (such as exceeding sales goals, securing large research grants, and generating breakthrough laboratory discoveries). These individuals rarely change their interpersonal behavior without strong motivation to do so.
- Emotionally and socially competent leaders tend to do much better in the workplace than those with poor interpersonal skills. Recent post-pandemic studies point to a growing need for leaders to tune in to employees on a personal level as workplace depression hits an all-time high.
- The best way to communicate with a competent jerk is to identify their motivational drivers, blind spots, and personal incentives to change. It's valuable to provide direct and candid feedback to these individuals and disarm them in conversation.

Tool 6-1. Performance Management Feedback Coaching: Providing Feedback Using the DESC Technique

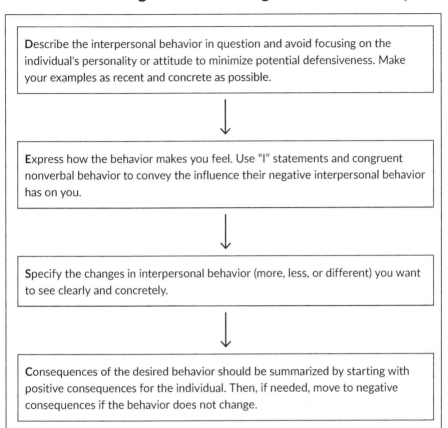

Describe the interpersonal behavior in question and avoid focusing on the individual's personality or attitude to minimize potential defensiveness. Make your examples as recent and concrete as possible.

↓

Express how the behavior makes you feel. Use "I" statements and congruent nonverbal behavior to convey the influence their negative interpersonal behavior has on you.

↓

Specify the changes in interpersonal behavior (more, less, or different) you want to see clearly and concretely.

↓

Consequences of the desired behavior should be summarized by starting with positive consequences for the individual. Then, if needed, move to negative consequences if the behavior does not change.

Tool 6-2. Dos and Don'ts for Communicating With an Interpersonally Challenging Employee

What to Do to Enhance Understanding and Acceptance	What Not to Do to Maximize Defensiveness and Conflict
Do remain calm and collected even when the employee deflects blame onto you. Always pause before you respond.	Do not become overly emotional and reactive to the employee's statements.
Do frame your feedback in a way that motivates the employee to see what's in it for them.	Do not frame your feedback in a way that makes it about your needs.
Do praise the employee when they behave correctly.	Do not only focus entirely on what the employee is doing wrong.
Do use "I" statements or ownership statements that do not put blame on another person.	Do not use "you" statements because they can be interpreted as an attack.
Do give feedback on the specific behavior you want to see change.	Do not give feedback about the employee's personality, style, or character.
Do focus your feedback on the impact of the behaviors.	Do not use the "sandwich technique" (starting and ending with what the employee does exceptionally well, and explaining how this could be compromised by interpersonal deficits in the middle).

Tool 6-3. Tips for Performance Management Feedback Coaching

- ☑ Focus on developing the employee's social, interpersonal, and communication skills, improving overall emotional and social competence, and helping them eliminate interpersonal blind spots.
- ☑ Keep in mind that this group believes their "competence" is more important than their influence and social skills. In other words, getting things done and getting ahead are far more important than getting along with others.
- ☑ Expect this type of employee to be somewhat defensive and challenging because they tend to lack self-awareness about how their behavior is perceived and experienced by others. Be concrete and specific about what behaviors should be done more, less, or differently.
- ☑ Frame the feedback dialogue so your employee can see what's in it for them. They need to believe the feedback is for their benefit.
- ☑ Let them know you can help make them successful and that you are a champion working on their behalf to ensure they are valued for their competence, expertise, and skills, as well as their ability to work well with others.
- ☑ Use a developmental 360-degree feedback process and other tools, together with a five-factor personality inventory, to help the employee discover their strengths and potential interpersonal areas for development.
- ☑ Explore whether the employee is open to working with an external executive coach to increase their insight about interpersonal deficits and challenges.
- ☑ Encourage the employee to work with an internal or external mentor who can serve as an objective sounding board for discussing challenging issues that could derail their career despite strong technical skills and abilities.
- ☑ Create, communicate, and stand behind norms, policies, and values focused on civility, inclusivity, and a culture that doesn't tolerate bullying. Calling out such negative interpersonal behavior and microaggressions will be valued by other team members. Communicate that "jerk" behavior is not tolerated in the team or organization.

Chapter 7
Performance Acceleration
How to Coach High Performers With High Interpersonal Skills

Maria, a 53-year-old executive at a midsize company, recently came to Sandra as a client. Maria said that while her performance as a manager and her department's metrics have been solid over the past 25 years, her team had recently come under intense pressure to not just meet but exceed their quarterly goals. She said she was willing to do anything she could to hit the targets but admitted that many of the goals seemed unattainable because it was difficult to motivate and manage her very best employees. In addition, she said that ramping up new hires' skills while keeping veteran employees engaged and committed had started feeling like a high-stakes juggling act. And she worried that she was dropping too many balls.

Maria wanted help because she was overwhelmed and frustrated that her current team members—all of whom are millennials or Gen Zers—expected so much from the organization to remain motivated. She asked Sandra for practical advice for communicating with and developing her team of bright, talented, and likable young top performers.

"I don't know how to have effective, motivational conversations with them," explained Maria. "I sometimes think the gap between our generations is too wide—we don't speak the same language. At the same time, they're all incredibly talented and supportive of me, and I don't want to lose them. I want to help these stars on my team grow and excel but I don't know how."

Sandra told Maria she wasn't alone in facing these challenges. It's relatively easy to hire and initially support high-potential and high-performing employees, but it's much harder to hold onto them and ensure they are contributing to the organization's future. These high performers bring exceptional skills, exceed expectations, and deliver outstanding results; when they also demonstrate strong interpersonal skills, they become true superstars. Simply put, in today's constantly changing, competitive global work environment, high performers with emotional intelligence are among the most valued employees.

You must learn to identify the needs of each employee and communicate in ways that recognize those needs. As a leader, you not only have to see and harness each team member's potential, but you also must provide enough guidance, support, and tangible benefits to ensure they stay engaged, committed, and thriving for the long haul. As coaches, we help leaders like Maria analyze the factors that influence overall engagement, well-being, and development. Then, we create a plan for motivating each employee according to specific career drivers, personality, and personal needs.

The ability to develop your best employees so they become even better and grow with your company is a skill leaders can't take for granted. All too often, leaders assume that high performers don't need special attention if they're doing their work and meeting their goals. But time after time, we've seen this behavior result in high performers losing interest in their work or leaving for a better opportunity. Remember, the best of the best employees are often highly mobile—free agents who can go on the open market to negotiate better salaries, demand bigger roles and responsibilities, and seek out companies that align with their values and lifestyle needs. And these are the people you simply can't afford to lose.

This chapter focuses on how to develop effective feedback coaching specifically for high performers who possess high emotional and social competence.

The Challenge: Major Shifts in Workplace Culture

Let's go back to Maria's team for just a moment. Why is she facing more challenges now than she did 10 or 15 years ago? It's because the world of work has changed. Career paradigms have shifted from the 20th-century expectation of lifetime employment to the 21st-century necessity for employability security. Our parents and grandparents were often grateful to find a steady job with a chance to advance slowly through the ranks. They typically stayed with the same organization for decades until they retired with a pension and some good friends.

Today's employees expect meaning out of their jobs, not just a paycheck. They want their employers to have a positive influence on society and want their company to align with their core values, provide meaningful work, and be committed to their professional development and mental health. And, according to Deloitte's new *Well-Being at Work Survey*, 59 percent of employees are seriously considering quitting their job for one that better supports their well-being (Fisher et al. 2024). Table 7-1 shows some of the most notable shifts and changes in careers in the past century.

Table 7-1. Major 21st-Century Workplace Paradigm Shifts

Old Paradigms	New Paradigms
Traditional families	Nontraditional families
Job security	Employability security
Longitudinal career paths	Alternate career paths
Job or person fit	Person or organization fit
Work is where you go	Work is what you do
Hierarchical structure	Flat or matrix structure
Organizational loyalty	Job or task loyalty
Career success	Work-life integration
Academic degree	Continuous relearning
Position and title	Competencies and development
Full-time employment	Contract employment
Retirement	Encore careers
Single jobs or careers	Multiple jobs or careers
Change in jobs based on fear	Change in jobs based on growth
Promotion is tenure based	Promotion is performance based
Many workers are smarter	Many workers are different
Career paths	Career patterns
Informational interviewing	Networking
Performance evaluation and reviews	Continuous performance check-in discussions
Boss	Performance coach

Today's workforce is more diverse than ever by many measures, including age. In 2023, the US workforce was made up of baby boomers (19 percent),

Gen Xers (35.5 percent), millennials (39.4 percent), and Gen Zers (6.1 percent). Currently, more than 10,000 baby boomers per day are reaching the traditional retirement age of 65, and researchers project that by 2030, we'll see Generation Z constitute about 30 percent of the workforce (Lee 2023). Young workers' fresh perspectives on work and technology will soon influence workplaces on a deeper level.

As Maria and other leaders we've worked with have learned, each generation has different needs, values, and motivational drivers, all of which add new challenges and complexity to the task of leading across so much diversity. For example, many young millennials and Gen Zers in your workforce might express a strong desire for personal attention as do employees from other generations. They are entrepreneurial, independent, and competitive, which means they thrive in companies with socially responsible practices. At the same time, baby boomers and older Gen Xers may be trying to slow down while keeping their jobs as supplemental retirement income. The youngest workers are dealing with constant change while older workers are experiencing the perks of stability. Table 7-2 outlines other generational differences that sometimes appear in the workplace.

Table 7-2. Generational Differences That May Appear in the Workplace

Generation	Important Values at Work	How to Engage and Retain Them
Gen Z (Born 1997–2012)	• Personal connection • Attention to mental health • Attention to personal values • Fairness and equity • Pay and benefits	• Mentoring • Wellness cultures • Remote work opportunities • Career development • Corporate social responsibility
Millennials (Born 1981–1996)	• Career growth opportunities • Professional development • Promotion opportunities • Team building initiatives	• Financial security • Autonomy • Flexible work schedules
Gen X (Born 1965–1980)	• Clear goals and specific deadlines • Social connection • Loyalty to the company • Mentoring and developing others	• Personal and professional development
Baby boomers (Born 1946–1964)	• Recognition of their work • Retirement plans	• Clear career paths • Job security

Our clients often complain about the sense of entitlement felt among their millennial and Gen Z employees. They resist these young workers' need for flexibility and the way they question the traditional nine-to-five work schedule. We've heard baby boomer executives say things like, "Those millennials are so demanding! That's not the way I was led back in the day. They're going to have to learn to get what they want the hard way."

Yes, young workers may seem demanding, but organizations must find a way to meet their needs. As we go through 360-degree feedback reviews from Gen Z employees, a lack of flexible work schedules, which they believe should be the post-COVID-19 pandemic norm, is a common thread we see. These same young employees are known for leaving organizations because of poor working conditions, insufficient growth opportunities, and lack of connection to the company's mission or purpose. To attract and retain Gen Z workers, organizations big and small must consider corporate social responsibility (CSR) initiatives centered on sustainability; diversity, equity, inclusion, and belonging (DEIB); pay equity; employee rights; access to healthcare; and philanthropy. This may be a challenge for many companies, but it can be a great opportunity as well.

For instance, Alphabet, the parent company of Google, devotes a great deal of energy to social issues, strives to reduce its environmental impact through sustainability programs, and contributes to global projects focused on encouraging economic development. These initiatives are taken seriously across all divisions and levels. Media giants Netflix and Spotify offer strong benefits to support employees' families, including 52 weeks of paid paternal leave. Shoe manufacturer TOMS declares its mission is to donate a pair of shoes for every pair it sells, which has resulted in the donation of more than 100 million pairs to children in need (Digital Marketing Institute 2022).

According to a study by Johns Hopkins University (Lee 2023), the workplace changes most likely to accompany the wave of Gen Z and younger employees (the iPad Generation or Generation Alpha) include:

- **A greater emphasis on DEIB and accessibility hiring and training at all levels.** For example, the World Economic Forum says more than 40 percent of Gen Zers, compared with 24 percent of earlier generations, reported they would debate sexism in the workplace (Kreacic, Romeo, and Uribe 2023). Companies not actively and sincerely supporting DEIB, increasing inclusivity and accessibility, and recognizing neurodiversity in their policies and programs may find fewer employees eager to come on board.

- **Greater autonomy on the job and flexibility in schedules.** Remote and hybrid work has become more prevalent post-COVID-19, and many companies realize they must provide flexible and part-time schedules and remote work to recruit and retain employees.

- **Greater emphasis on supporting mental health and well-being.** Although most companies have offered wellness and health programs for many years, the emphasis has expanded to encompass employee mental health, work-life integration, and well-being. In 2019, the 11th Revision of the International Classification of Diseases (ICD-11) and the World Health Organization recognized job burnout as an occupational phenomenon rather than a medical condition. Heavy workloads, unrealistic expectations, and lack of autonomy and control over decision making all contribute to significant negative health consequences for employees at all levels.

- **Greater focus on corporate social awareness and ethics.** Today's young employees care more about the environment, sustainability, and social justice than ever before. Research by Deloitte reported that nearly half (46 percent) of Gen Z respondents said it was vital to work for a company whose values aligned with their own (Deloitte 2022).

A Warning About Generational Comparisons

As we pointed out in chapter 3, although generational comparisons are still popular, they may reinforce some outdated stereotypes. Some differences between generational cohorts do appear in academic research, but we again encourage leaders to explore and interrogate their understanding of why people who grew up in different eras might think and behave in different but equally valuable ways. In working with diverse age groups on your teams, consider differences *between* and *within* each cohort.

As a leader, you will find that it is critical to identify each employee's specific needs. When we coach our clients, we help them identify the different factors that influence overall employee engagement, well-being, and development. Our goal is to help them create a plan for motivating each person according to their unique and specific career drivers, personality needs, and personal values (rather than overarching categories like older millennials or younger Gen Xers).

Performance Acceleration Feedback Coaching

When Maria sought out Sandra's help in motivating her high-potential team, Sandra viewed her challenges through the lens of the Performance Feedback Coaching Model (Figure 7-1). As a reminder, this model is designed to accelerate and enhance the aspects of an employee's working life that are going well and create a developmental plan to improve their performance and commitment going forward.

Figure 7-1. Performance Acceleration Feedback Coaching Quadrant

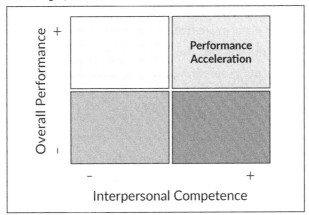

When dealing with high performers, performance feedback is about identifying the employee's talents, leveraging their signature strengths, and providing opportunities that match those strengths and their career ambitions. Our approach is to use a variety of communication and feedback tools to

understand exactly what motivates each type of employee to thrive and engage on a high level—and to understand and address any changes in performance due to external factors (such as family challenges). We explore this communication for high engagement throughout the rest of the chapter.

When we're called in by companies to coach high performers, we often hear (within the confidentiality of our sessions) that these employees are looking for new opportunities because they are no longer inspired or excited by their jobs.

Let's consider the example of Joe, another one of Sandra's clients. Joe is an outstanding performer, working above and beyond the call of duty as a senior marketing manager to achieve the best results for his entertainment company. He is kind, empathetic, and easy to get along with. Recently, he stopped attending nonmandatory company events and no longer demonstrates his usual level of initiative in generating ideas and guiding projects. He admitted to Sandra that he knows his performance has slipped a bit, but his colleagues say he is still an invaluable member of the marketing team and the organization.

During one of his coaching sessions with Sandra, Joe admitted, "I'm frustrated in my current situation—I really would like to grow in my career and have greater levels of responsibility than I have now."

Sandra tried to elicit more details about the situation: "You sound a bit stuck in your current position, and I am hearing that professional growth in terms of advancement is something that resonates with you."

"Yes," said Joe. "I would like more autonomy, a bigger budget than I have now, and the resources I need to show what I can really do. I'm not being used to my full capacity or recognized for the skills and experience I can offer. To be honest, I'd like to be seen as a 'marketing expert' for the company."

As the discussion continued, Sandra gained more valuable insights and ended the session with a plan. "Thank you for sharing all this information with me, Joe," she said. "Let's continue our coaching meetings to explore political strategies to gain greater attention and recognition for your signature strengths. We can also create greater awareness of your current accomplishments and your vision for the future of the organization."

Although the details are different, the cases of Maria and Joe inspire many of the same questions—all of which need to be answered as part of a productive performance acceleration feedback coaching plan:

- What career drivers are most significant for Joe? Which drivers are most important for each of Maria's team members? Do they want to lead? Do they want to master their craft? Do they want to do both?
- What specific changes in their division or organization will make Joe and members of Maria's team feel engaged and appreciated?
- What kind of conversation should Joe's manager have with him? Which one of Joe's signature strengths can be defined and leveraged best? What kind of conversation should Maria have with her team members? What can she discuss with them about their needs for flexibility, autonomy, and control over their work, as well as some mutually agreed upon key performance metrics?
- What is Joe's manager doing or saying to support and enhance his strengths? What is Maria doing or saying to support or enhance her team members' strengths?

In each case—and in scenarios other managers face every day—we recommend five specific steps for effectively communicating with high-potential, high-performing employees like Joe and other members of Maria's team. We'll go over each of these five steps in more detail in the sections that follow:

1. Use a separate stay interview to enhance engagement and commitment to the organization through a focused conversation.
2. Identify specific career drivers, motives, interests, and values to leverage signature strengths.
3. Commit to matching motivational drivers with opportunities at work.
4. Create, implement, and monitor career and professional development plans.

Use Stay Interviews

One thing we recommend all leaders do with high-performing and high-potential employees is to conduct a *stay interview* (Kaye and Jordan-Evans 2015).

Before becoming an external executive coach and consultant, Sandra worked for a nationwide firm as an organization development manager. As part of her responsibilities, she presented quarterly attrition reports to the executive board and made recommendations based on themes she observed and analyzed through exit interviews. The organization continually lost successful, high-potential employees, and through her analysis, Sandra discovered that their complaints were remarkably consistent. They all said:

- "My leader doesn't support me."
- "My leader doesn't care about my career."
- "I'm bored."
- "I'm not challenged."
- "No one is talking about my career trajectory."
- "I want a higher salary."

Although the organization conducted exit interviews consistently, it did very little with the valuable data they collected. Sandra wondered if there was a way to use this information to prevent the loss of high-potential talent. She suggested that rather than examining their needs through exit interviews (when it was too late to retain them), the company should use stay interviews to identify what could keep high performers engaged and reduce attrition. Sandra uses the following set of questions in her stay interviews:

- What aspects of your job are most energizing? What is most draining?
- Are you satisfied with your work-life balance?
- Do you feel heard and valued as part of your team?
- If you won the lottery and resigned tomorrow, what would you miss about your job or the company?
- What one thing did you love about a prior job?
- What can I do to keep you engaged and happy at your job?
- What might entice you to leave?

Keep in mind that stay interviews are designed for difficult-to-replace high performers that you are most concerned about seeking employment elsewhere. Ideally, they're used separately from other performance-based discussions or individual meetings. But they can be deployed annually for high-flying employees.

Performance Feedback How-To: Holding a Stay Interview

1. Greet the employee. Mention they are a valued member of the team and company, and you want to make sure you are doing everything you can to ensure they are satisfied and productive, so the purpose of the meeting is to talk about that.
2. Use stay questions to uncover what keeps them engaged and committed to the company. Try to understand what factors would lead them to work elsewhere.
3. Discuss what is meaningful to the employee and what other tasks, projects, or assignments would facilitate their ongoing professional growth and career development. What brings them joy and satisfaction? And what kinds of things would they like to be doing more of on the job?
4. Ask the employee to create a development plan focusing on their specific strengths, skills, and experiences to enhance current performance and achieve future career goals.
5. Schedule a date to review and finalize the development plan, discuss specific on-the-job challenges and assignments, and agree on a follow-up date to track and monitor progress.

Identify Career Drivers, Motives, Interests, and Values to Leverage Signature Strengths

Ask a high-performing employee to share an appraisal of their *signature strengths*—the ones that make them the most energized and fulfilled on the job. Research by Martin Seligman, who heads the Penn Positive Psychology Center, has demonstrated that identifying and implementing one's signature strength was significantly associated with enhanced well-being and satisfaction when compared with a control group for about six months (Seligman, Rashid, and Parks 2006). It's important to explore these strengths, how they relate to both short- and long-term career goals, and how they drive your career. Most people want to advance in their careers and to know they are doing the things they are good at and care about.

When you think about motivating your staff, put yourself in their shoes. What would make them feel more excited to do their work? What would make them feel trusted and recognized? What would make them want to stay at the organization for years to come? Your team members want to work on projects that lead toward their career goals. A feeling of purpose and looking toward the future will encourage them to work above and beyond the call of duty.

For example, you might have discovered in a stay interview with Joe that he could leverage some of his untapped marketing skills on current and future projects. Or you may have uncovered hidden analytical skills and an interest in generative AI that the organization could use in new and creative ways.

Understanding the Career Path Preferences of Employees

We've conceptualized four main career path preferences and some blends based on clusters of employee motives, values, personalities, and personal drivers:

- **The leadership career path.** Do your employees want to supervise and manage others?
- **The specialist or independent contributor career path.** Do your employees want to pursue their craft, stay in place, or enhance their knowledge, competence, and expertise?
- **The generalist or project manager career path.** Do your employees enjoy ongoing development and like project management and diverse assignments?
- **The entrepreneurial career path.** Do your employees like to create, develop, innovate, and implement products and services? Do they want to be their own boss?

With these career path preferences in mind, you can better understand how to provide employees with specific tasks that align with their preferences. And you can also reward them accordingly. Let's take a closer look at each path.

The Leadership Career Path

Employees with a leadership career path are driven toward positions that allow them to exert authority and take control of tasks and assignments (Table 7-3). They are typically results oriented and enjoy the ability to influence others. If you want to motivate these members of your staff, consider their titles. People pursuing a leadership career path feel a sense of authority and enjoy the status conferred with the title of executive, senior manager, or director.

Table 7-3. The Leadership Career Path

Common Career Drivers	Preferred Rewards
Power and influence	Upward mobility
Goal oriented	Promotion
Leadership competence	Perks
Control	Titles
Task accomplishment and results oriented	Benefits
Status	Increased span of control
Influencing and directing others	Decision latitude
Improving profitability and increasing growth	Incentive or bonus program

If you are leading employees with a leadership path preference, you should think about the best way to help them become more effective in these future roles. This means you should be strategic about placing them in assignments or tasks in which they can lead and supervise others. Consider the following ways to achieve this:

1. **Facilitate cross-functional versatility.** By making sure your employee is exposed to a variety of functions within the organization, you can ensure they are better equipped to lead because they have a better understanding of the organization.

2. **Provide job or developmental challenges.** By challenging your employees with strategic assignments and responsibilities, you empower them to take on some additional leadership duties.

3. **Develop core competencies.** Train employees in specific competencies that correlate with leadership and effectiveness in their jobs.

4. **Address potential derailment factors.** Derailment happens to those who are at risk of being fired, demoted, or held on a career plateau. These factors can be addressed with mentoring, coaching, and ensuring effective promotion and selection systems. Some of the more common reasons for derailment in jobs at any level include:
   » Difficulty building and leading a team
   » Failure to deliver business results

» Lack of a broad, strategic orientation

» Problems with interpersonal relationships

5. **Consider job and developmental challenges.** Employees with a leadership career path preference will thrive if they have the competencies and skill sets to exert their ability to lead. Here are some common ways of getting them the practice they need to be leaders:

» Have them carry an assignment from beginning to end.

» Involve them in a merger, acquisition, strategic alliance, or partnership opportunity.

» Ask them to implement an organization-wide change initiative.

» Allow them to negotiate agreements with external organizations.

» Have them operate in a high-pressure or high-visibility situation.

» Ask them to head a visible committee or organization-wide task force.

» Suggest they look for relevant volunteer opportunities outside the organization for further development.

» Engineer stretch assignments and developmental activities.

» Suggest they use an executive coach to enhance their signature strengths.

» Look for opportunities to provide more specific feedback.

» Encourage them to improve their work-life balance.

» Champion their future career potential with other senior managers.

The Specialist or Independent Contributor Career Path

People who are ideal for this path are driven by a passion for their chosen area of specialization and excel in their roles based on dedication (Table 7-4). These are your organization's lawyers, accountants, technology specialists, marketing specialists, designers, and other specialist individual contributors. Their expertise and dedication are an asset to the organization or industry because they often play a pivotal role in solving complex problems and driving innovation within their domains.

Typically, these specialist types remain in one occupational field for most of their careers. They're either economically anchored to one occupational area or explore further specialized education, knowledge, and credentials. Some dual-career paths allow them to hold an independent contributor role. In general, specialists love their autonomy and the freedom to master their craft, so micromanaging and strict oversight does not work for them. Specialists often seek recognition and respect from their peers and colleagues within their niche. Always ensure they have the best equipment and supplies to get the job done.

Table 7-4. The Specialist or Independent Contributor Career Path

Common Career Drivers	Preferred Rewards
Technical or functional competence	Job enrichment
Expertise or skill mastery	Continuing education and professional associations
Independence	Job security
Achievement	Benefits
Refining quality	Budget authority
Curiosity and being the best at their craft	Latest equipment and supplies

The Generalist or Project Manager Career Path

Generalists are often known for their adaptability, versatility, and ability to perform a variety of tasks. They tend to move from one task to another, work well across departments, and have a variety of skills. Generalists also have spiral career movements based on related experiences, knowledge, and skills. Thanks to the variety of career moves they tend to make, these individuals also have an array of skills and experiences. They might also work in positions that require a mix of skills, such as project management or general management roles. Generalists focus on developing a wide array of transferable skills, including communication, problem solving, adaptability, project management, and teamwork (Table 7-5).

Table 7-5. The Generalist Career Path

Common Career Drivers	Preferred Rewards
Professional growth	Job rotation
Variety	Coaching and mentoring assignments
Change	Leading problem-solving teams
Broadening competencies and knowledge	Cross-functional teamwork experiences
Innovation	Sabbaticals and personal projects
Project and program management	Lateral assignments

The Entrepreneur Career Path

Employees with an entrepreneurial spirit are innovative, self-motivated, proactive, resourceful, adaptive, creative, and visionary (Table 7-6). They can be invaluable assets because they bring fresh perspectives, drive innovation, take risks, and contribute to the growth and success of the company. They are often instrumental in identifying and capitalizing on new opportunities for the organization. These individuals may make frequent career or job changes because their curiosity and desire to be innovative keeps them moving until they can come up with cutting edge ideas. They need to be aware that this could cause them to come across as unreliable or unstable.

The entrepreneurial is the fastest-growing path among women. While they may work within a larger organization, they exhibit traits commonly associated with individuals who start and run their own businesses.

Table 7-6. The Entrepreneur Career Path

Common Career Drivers	Preferred Rewards
Taking risks and trying new things	Independent contracts
Challenge	Bonuses
Creativity	Autonomy and managing oneself
Autonomy	Job sharing
Freedom from politics	Profit sharing
Drive	Pay for results

Career Path Blends

Career path preferences can also be blended. In fact, many people represent blends of several career paths, so it is important to keep in mind the primary aspect of their preference. Table 7-7 outlines some common career path blends.

Figure 7-7. Blended Career Paths

Common Career Path Blends	Typical Roles
Specialist + entrepreneurial	External or independent consultant
Specialist + generalist	Internal consultant or general consultant
Specialist + leadership	Technology leader or functional manager
Entrepreneurial + leadership	Program manager, startup or fix-it leader, or intrapreneur
Entrepreneurial + generalist	Entrepreneur or independent business owner
Generalist + leadership	Project manager or general manager

Commit to Matching Motivational Drivers With Opportunities at Work

Once you have identified your employees' career drivers, it is time to communicate how they match opportunities on the job. It's important to have a constructive conversation about each employee's career drivers and potential opportunities within the organization. You and your employees should reach a level of alignment about their drivers and the opportunities for building them up at work.

Let's look at a typical discussion you might have with one of your high-performing employees. The two of you are meeting to explore professional growth and career development opportunities. You've watched them show initiative and take charge of new ways to enhance the company's processes and solicit input from other team members to implement improvements.

- **Leader:** "Let's explore some opportunities within the company that align with these drivers. I see you are driven by leading projects and would like the opportunity to do more leading. We have several options available, including roles in project management, for you to take the lead on a challenging project. Or we could explore training and development programs to further enhance your skills. Additionally, there are cross-functional teams in which you could have a broader organizational influence."

- **Employee:** "Those options sound promising. I'm particularly interested in the project management role and the training programs. How can we proceed to explore these opportunities further?"

- **Leader:** "Let's create a development plan to help you bridge any gaps and prepare for these roles. Does that sound like a good next step?"

- **Employee:** "Yes, I like the sound of that."
- **Leader:** "Glad you're up for the challenge. Let's plan another meeting to discuss this again in more detail."

A Word of Caution: The Strengths-Weakness Balance in Leaders

It's common sense that leaders should leverage and capitalize on their strengths. Conventional wisdom and strength-based coaching approaches emphasize focusing on what leaders naturally do well and finding others on a team to compensate for any weaknesses or missing strengths.

However, research also cautions that overusing a leader's strengths can become a liability or weakness (Kaiser and Overfield 2011). It's not difficult to see how some strengths, such as being direct, are easily interpreted by employees as too authoritative. Sometimes empathy is seen as "soft" or even "weak" when dealing with difficult interpersonal situations. For decisive leaders, taking in available information and quickly coming to a rapid decision might be seen as overly impulsive.

When talking with your most competent and high-performing employees, you should encourage their strengths but also point out how overusing them could get in the way of effectiveness. Helping high performers wisely manage their strengths so they do not become weaknesses is another important aspect of performance acceleration feedback coaching.

Create, Implement, and Monitor Career and Professional Development Plans

Today's high-performing employees are seeking continuing career growth and development opportunities to remain engaged and willing to stay with their current employer. Performance acceleration feedback coaching is designed to identify key motivators and drivers and to match these employees' signature strengths with the best ways to help them grow. The investment you make in understanding an employee's unique talents, skills, and interests will pay dividends by reinforcing their outstanding performance and preventing them from rushing to explore outside career opportunities.

 **Key Points**

Let's review a few key points from this chapter:

- Performance acceleration feedback coaching addresses the need to keep high-potential talent by identifying and leveraging the strengths of those employees and accelerating their engagement and performance on the job. As a leader, you can identify the motivational needs of high performers through stay interviews and then match their needs with those of the organization.
- With so many generations now vying for attention in the workforce, understanding the needs of different types of employees is more important than ever. For younger employees, work-life balance, virtual work options, and career path guidance are often critical.
- Identifying the career motives, values, and drivers of high-potential and high-performing employees can help leaders assess how to position them to do their best work and stay engaged. Once you identify the primary career drivers of your high performers, conversations can focus on matching individual drivers with current opportunities on the job and career planning within the organization. Understanding and addressing temporary changes in high performance due to personal, family, and external factors are also important to retain these valued employees.

Tool 7-1. Five Steps for Holding a Signature Strengths Conversation

1. Greet the employee. Let them know they are a valued member of the team and company, and you want to make sure you are doing everything you can to help them stay satisfied and productive. That's the purpose of the meeting.

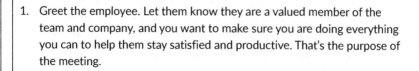

2. Ask questions to discover what tasks and assignments are the most meaningful and what keeps them engaged and committed to the company, as well as what factors could lead them to look elsewhere.

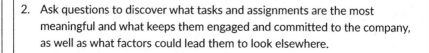

3. Discuss the employee's signature strengths and how they can deploy those strengths more often on the job. Provide specific feedforward (as opposed to traditional feedback) about how they can become even more effective.

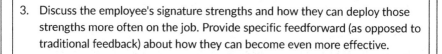

4. Ask your high performer to create a development plan focusing on specific strengths, skills, and experiences that can enhance their current performance and help them achieve future career goals.

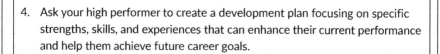

5. Schedule a date to review and finalize the development plan, discuss specific on-the-job challenges and assignments, and agree on a follow-up date to track and monitor progress.

Tool 7-2. Performance Acceleration Coaching Role Play

Using the following scenario, you will play the role of a supervisor in your organization tasked with conducting a performance acceleration coaching meeting with a high-potential employee named Julio O'Brien. Julio is already an effective and valued team member within his department and the organization.

Purpose

The purpose of the performance acceleration coaching meeting will be to:
1. Explore what aspects of work are engaging to Julio.
2. Provide candid feedback about Julio's current strengths, development areas, and potential to the organization.
3. Identify Julio's personal career goals and development plans.
4. Initiate a professional development plan.

Situation

You believe that Julio is a high-potential talent who the organization should invest in and develop further. Your own manager wants to know what you know about Julio's career goals and potential. You mention he has been a tremendous performer—highly motivated and committed to the organization—in the year you've been directly supervising him.

Your manager asks whether Julio has any leadership development plans in place. You mention that you just scheduled a developmental discussion meeting and will be focusing on goals for the future. Most recently, Julio has been serving in an independent contributor or specialist staff role for the organization, and you don't know if he wants to stay in a leadership role. In the upcoming conversation, you plan to explore Julio's leadership career goals and initiate a formal professional development plan.

Expectations

Your purpose in this 20-minute meeting is to begin a discussion that results in a development plan to enhance one or more critical competencies for Julio's successful performance now and in the future. You also want to discover Julio's leadership goals and how he believes the organization can best employ his experience, skills, and knowledge.

Meeting Prep

Take five minutes to prepare and plan your approach to this developmental coaching meeting. If you have a partner available, role-play the scenario with them and ask them to provide feedback about:
- What you could do more, less, or differently to clarify specific development goals
- How to reach commitments around the resources needed to achieve those goals
- How to get commitment for follow-up

Tool 7-3. Performance Acceleration Coaching Activities, Tasks, and Assignments to Support Employee Development

Activity, Task, Project, or Assignment	Examples
Startup Experiences These assignments emphasize starting new departmental and organizational programs, processes, or projects from start to finish.	1. Chair a taskforce on a business problem. 2. Go off-site to troubleshoot problems or improve processes. 3. Install a new system, program, or procedure. 4. Initiate a large-scale change project within the organization. 5. Plan an off-site meeting, conference, or major event. 6. Serve on a new project or product review committee. 7. Work on a short-term international startup initiative.
Fix-It Experiences These assignments emphasize team building and dealing with a specific crisis or problem in which high conflict is likely. These might involve dealing with emotionally charged situations that require motivating and developing others or addressing task, people, and process challenges in a team or organization.	1. Manage an inexperienced project team. 2. Manage a dysfunctional team. 3. Resolve conflict among direct reports. 4. Manage a group of low-competence or low-performing employees. 5. Assign a challenging project that failed previously. 6. Close a department, unit, or failing business.
Development Experiences These assignments emphasize stretch assignments that expand and develop existing knowledge, skills, abilities, and experiences.	1. Conduct a competitive SWOT analysis. 2. Create a strategic plan for a department. 3. Conduct a market analysis with recommendations for gaining market share. 4. Coordinate a process improvement initiative. 5. Chair or participate in a cross-functional team.

Tool 7-3. (cont.)

Activity, Task, Project, or Assignment	Examples
Coaching or Mentoring Others These tasks emphasize something an employee needs to know or intellectual pressure, either of which can lead to heightened self-awareness.	1. Teach someone how to do something they are not an expert in. 2. Serve as an external executive coach. 3. Serve as an internal or external mentor. 4. Identify a senior leader sponsor and champion who is respected and successful.
Outside Work Activities These activities take place away from work and emphasize individual leadership and working with new people. They may also involve learning to influence, communicate more effectively, and persuade others.	1. Join a community or governmental board. 2. Become active in a local volunteer or charitable organization. 3. Become active in a professional association in a leadership role. 4. Use your experience, knowledge, and skills to offer pro-bono work to schools, groups, and others.

Tool 7-4. Tips for Performance Acceleration Feedback Coaching

☑ One of the best predictors for enhancing continued engagement, commitment, and satisfaction in high-potential and high-performing leaders is the perception of making progress in meaningful work (Amabile and Kramer 2011). Because high-performing leaders are often viewed as less needy than others, it is important to schedule regular check-ins to explore and discuss barriers to performance.

☑ For high-potential and high-performing leaders, it is important to observe and point out how the overuse of their skills and style may get in the way of their ongoing performance.

☑ Moving leaders from good to great requires more specific, timely, and concrete feedback to share what they already are doing very well. It's the little pointers, suggestions, and tips that such high performers crave to become even better over time.

☑ As the old saying goes, "catch them doing things right" and reinforce and recognize both their outstanding efforts and accomplishments. Feeling ignored or not noticed can erode both engagement and commitment to the organization.

☑ Define and discuss career trajectories and ongoing professional development on a regular basis. Explore and encourage such leaders to seek internal and external champions, mentors, and coaches to continue their ongoing growth. Such investments in these leaders result in high ROI for the organization.

☑ Explore, discuss, and create meaningful work assignments and tasks that use their signature strengths and capabilities. Refrain from just adding more tasks and projects that you know they will do well just because they are strong performers. Make sure new assignments and projects are well-suited to their career strengths, interests, and goals.

☑ Demonstrate trust and psychological safety by providing these leaders with flexibility and autonomy to decide where, when, and how their work gets done based on agreed-upon performance goals and standards. With such leaders, perceptions of micromanaging create mistrust and a lack of commitment to team goals.

Chapter 8

Performance Enhancement
How to Coach Poor Performers With High Interpersonal Skills

When Sandra worked as an adjunct professor, she conducted an exercise in one of her leadership courses in which she asked students to share all the traits they loved and hated most about their past bosses. In every class, their responses about the bosses they loved looked something like this:

- "My boss was always supportive."
- "My boss respected my work-life balance."
- "My boss was approachable and friendly."
- "My boss empowered me."

Their remarks about the bosses they didn't like were equally unambiguous:

- "My boss didn't motivate me to excel."
- "My boss never gave me feedback."
- "My boss didn't care about me or my colleagues."
- "My boss looked down on me."
- "My boss was a total jerk."

Very few students said they were affected by their bosses' success in their industry or technical skills and talents. In the vast majority of responses, they pointed to one thing—people skills. For us, these casual surveys crystallized a surprising truth: the importance of likability in the workplace, even at the cost of performance.

Three Feedback Scenarios

To demonstrate a few ways that workplace performance and interpersonal skills are juxtaposed, let's take a look at three hypothetical scenarios based on common performance feedback coaching challenges we have seen among our clients.

Scenario 1. Elena Has Charm, but Where Are the Sales?

Elena is a sales representative for the Edgeway Corporation, a gardening equipment manufacturer. She is known throughout the company for her captivating charm and finesse in handling interpersonal relationships. Clients adore her warm and engaging demeanor, making her a key asset in managing client relationships.

Elena's challenge is that she often fumbles with product specifications and pricing details during her sales presentations. Her mistakes sometimes result in clients receiving inaccurate information and returning merchandise. When complex customer requests that demand a deep understanding of the company's products arise, Elena frequently must call for assistance from another sales representatives. For the past three quarters, she has failed to achieve her sales quotas.

Scenario 2. Henry's Team Doesn't Respect Him

Henry is the manager of consumer services at NationCorp Financial. Recently, his performance and his team's metrics have declined because of poor project management and missed deadlines. Henry has good relationships with his direct reports but is not a strong influencer and communicator. He tries to support and please all the members of his team, and they say they like him—but they rarely follow through on his initiatives and don't take his advice seriously.

Henry's challenges include time management, formal presentations, clear communication, and capturing his team's attention during group meetings. The executive team members at NationCorp see potential in Henry and appreciate his hard work and aspirations, but they are concerned about his and his team's recent decline in new and returning customers. In conversations with leaders, Henry says he is overwhelmed and does not have time to complete all his tasks and manage the tasks of others. He has also shared that he is socially anxious when speaking in front of a group.

Scenario 3. Blake Is Weak on the Details

Blake is a charismatic project manager at SLC Entertainment. They have an uncanny ability to build loyalty and rapport with cross-functional team members and stakeholders throughout the organization. Their energetic leadership style fosters collaboration, cooperation, and enthusiasm.

Unfortunately, when it comes to understanding and managing the intricacies of project timelines, budgets, and financial analyses, Blake's weaknesses are undeniable. They consistently show they do not understand technical details about the business, which leads to project delays, frustrated clients, and budget overruns.

Responding to the Scenarios

What do these scenarios have in common? The leaders are all different, but have valuable interpersonal skills. They also have some technical knowledge and experience, but fall short in specific areas that could be strengthened with training, education, mentoring, and coaching.

- If you were Elena's manager, you would need to maximize her strengths in customer relations while ensuring her technical shortcomings didn't negatively affect the company's reputation or sales figures.
- As Henry's supervisor, you would need to help him improve multiple skill sets, including prioritizing his tasks, becoming a clearer communicator, and improving his presentations to earn back his team's respect.
- As Blake's senior executive, you would try to harness their exceptional interpersonal skills while providing support and resources to bolster their project management and budgeting abilities.

Today, interpersonal skills, sometimes referred to as "soft skills," are at the forefront of employers' minds. These skills include the ability to communicate effectively, demonstrate humility and authenticity, express empathy, collaborate harmoniously, and build strong relationships with colleagues and customers. In terms of the Casciaro and Lobo (2005) study we previously mentioned, most employers value the "likable fools" (employees who demonstrate strong emotional and social competence but might be lacking in some specific skill areas) because they have the interpersonal skills to bridge gaps between diverse groups. However, when a person's soft skills are much better than their job performance, they may be underappreciated and vulnerable to downsizing, particularly if they are not adequately meeting their key performance goals and objectives.

We believe that the so-called likable fools' interpersonal skills are such valuable assets that investing time and money to develop their technical knowledge and skills can truly pay off. Leaders need to protect these employees and put them in positions where they can thrive.

Performance Enhancement Feedback Coaching

When you have a valuable employee with excellent people skills and some challenges that prevent them from reaching their optimum level of performance, that employee needs performance enhancement feedback coaching (Figure 8-1). The essence of this strategy is troubleshooting to figure out the source of the deficiency in knowledge or skills so that you can address it.

Figure 8-1. Performance Enhancement Feedback Coaching

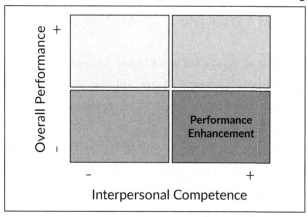

Does your employee lack some essential knowledge or a specific kind of training? Do they simply lack enough experience in the job, or do they lack fundamental motivation? Once you've identified the source of the performance deficiency, you will be able to put a development plan in place that fits the employee's needs and coach them to enhanced performance that meets your organization's needs.

Intellectual Ability vs. Emotional and Social Competence

Is it enough to have superior soft skills and emotional and social competence (ESC), or do employees also need a high intelligence quotient (IQ) to succeed in today's workplace? Obviously, intellectual ability is an asset on the job, but the relationship between IQ and job performance is not as clear-cut as we once thought (Treglown and Furnham 2023).

Complex factors are at play in how IQ is measured, and we can no longer rely only on standard tests. The value of IQ compared to structured employment interviews, job knowledge tests, biodata, and work-sample tests is a current topic of research, and the jury is still out (Richardson and Norgate 2015; Sackett et al. 2022).

What we can say at this point is that while a person's intelligence is important in developing skills for any job, people with high ESC often are *better* equipped to get their work done. High-ESC employees:

- Are high on empathy
- Ask good questions
- Demonstrate emotional regulation and control
- Are self-aware enough to reflect upon their successes and failures and develop their weaknesses
- Tend to be well liked and viewed positively by co-workers and supervisors

Launching a Performance Enhancement Analysis

Figure 8-2 is adapted from *Analyzing Performance Problems*, a classic book by Robert Mager and Peter Pipe (1997). It shows a series of troubleshooting questions you can answer to assess your employee's knowledge and skill deficiencies. You should begin by pinpointing the specific areas where their performance is lacking. Are their deficits related to productivity, quality, meeting deadlines, or specific job-related tasks? The flowchart will help you assess the employee's performance as precisely as possible.

Figure 8-2. Flowchart: Assessing Knowledge and Skill Deficiencies

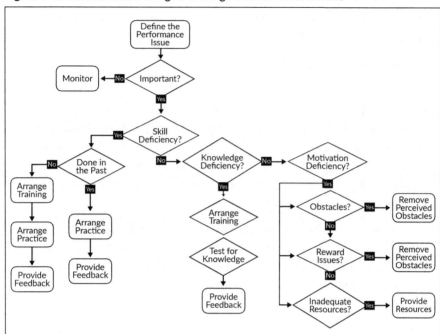

The more times you go through the troubleshooting process, the more you will develop your ability to correctly determine the cause of each employee's performance challenges. Always move through the process step-by-step:

1. Ask yourself if investing in developing a particular type of knowledge or addressing a specific skill deficit will have a worthwhile result.
2. If the answer is yes, then create a plan to develop the knowledge or skills needed.
3. If the answer is no, you may find it's more worthwhile to focus on leveraging your employees' strengths than addressing their deficits.

The Question of Motivation

Note, however, that employees may not be motivated to excel in the skills their leaders want them to. Early on, assess your employee's motivation level; if they aren't motivated, they likely won't excel even if you provide the best performance enhancement feedback coaching possible.

Sometimes, an employee simply needs to practice a skill they have not used often. Or perhaps they never learned to perform at the level the organization demands. As you can see in the diagnostic performance flowchart, asking the right questions will lead you to the best approach for each kind of challenge your employee faces. These questions include:

- What exactly is the performance problem?
- Is it important?
- Is it a knowledge deficiency?
- Is it a skill deficiency?
- Is it a motivational issue?
- Did the employee perform well in the past?
- Do the standards of the organization match the standards of the employee?
- Is there a favorable outcome for the employee for performing well?
- Does this favorable outcome match the wants or needs of the employee?
- Does performing well *matter* to the employee?
- Are there outside obstacles to performing well?
- Are there adequate resources to support improving the employee's performance?
- What are the best solutions to the challenge?
- What resources exist to help put the solution in place?

Which Skills Should You Try to Develop in Your Employee?

When an employee needs to develop multiple competencies, skills, or areas, it is important to identify and prioritize which ones the company should invest in. For instance, recall the scenario about Henry—he needs to work on prioritizing tasks, being more efficient, and improving his communication and presentation skills. As Henry's leader, you could define two things as you consider which skills he should focus on. Consider:

- Which of the competencies and skills are most important and relevant to Henry's job?
- How much is Henry motivated to work on those competencies?

The decision matrix in Figure 8-3 can help you determine which skills deficiencies need the most urgent attention. The model is based on:

- The relevance of each skill to the employee's job
- The employee's desire or motivation to work on a particular skill or competency

Figure 8-3. Decision Matrix: Where to Focus Employee Development Efforts

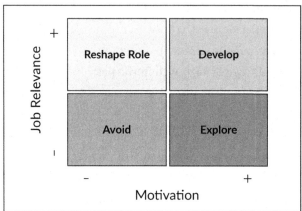

All employees can enhance their skills and competencies, but if the skills are not strongly related to their current roles and they don't want to develop them further, they will naturally ignore these potential development areas. If an employee isn't very motivated to enhance their knowledge or skills, it might be worth discussing whether specific tasks or roles could be reassigned to another team member or if parts of the job could be conducted differently.

Finally, an employee might also want to seek additional skills, experience, or training in areas that are not directly relevant, but are complementary to their current role or assignments. Although these new skills and experience would not add value to their current position, as a leader, you could explore how best to support the employee in their desire to continue learning new skills and evolving toward the future.

Define Key Performance Indicators

It is important to ensure that your employees have a clear understanding of their job responsibilities, key performance indicators (KPIs), and performance expectations. When KPIs are well defined, you can then help employees achieve their goals with a variety of specific strategies:

- **Define a specific skill set.** Start by defining the specific skills the employee needs to develop to contribute to your team or organization. Clearly articulate the goals and objectives associated with building these skills in a coaching conversation. For example, ask: "What are you trying to achieve in pursuing this skill set, and why is it important?"

- **Set quantifiable KPIs.** Ensure that KPIs can be measured easily and accurately. This may involve setting specific interim targets or benchmarks for improvement. Discuss the purpose of the KPIs. For example, ask: "How do the KPIs I have set affect your own goals and the organization's goals?"

- **Follow up on progress.** Regularly sit down to discuss your employee's progress toward the final goals. For example, ask: "Are these KPIs helping you achieve the skills and objectives you're pursuing?

Use Implementation Intentions

To help clarify goals and specific behaviors for employees, we suggested in an earlier chapter that research supports the use of *implementation intentions*—an "if/then" plan that helps people follow through on goals or build habits by making concrete statements about the *what, where,* and *when* of their intentions.

As we mentioned, research suggests that stated goal intentions alone may not result in successful maintenance of behavior over time (Lawton, Conner, and McEachan 2009). The road to unfulfilled goals is paved with good intentions! Remember all those people exercising with Ken on New Year's Day? The research tells us that half the people who make New Year's resolutions have failed to keep them by April Fool's Day. And only half translate their goal intentions into real action during the rest of the year as well (and this number is likely inflated).

For many years, SMART goals (specific, meaningful, attainable, relevant, and time-bound) have been the gold standard for changing behavior.

However, new research indicates that we can improve results by shifting away from goal intentions and toward *implementation intentions* (Nowack 2017). Simply adding *where* and *when* to your goal can boost the power of SMART goals and result in successful behavior change. Nearly 200 studies focusing on leadership, health, and interpersonal relations have shown that deciding in advance when and where you will complete a task can *significantly increase* your chances of doing it (Nowack 2017).

Practice Plan Activity Triggers

Practice plan activity triggers are a more formal version of implementation intentions you can deploy in performance enhancement feedback coaching. In these action plans, you link a situational cue (such as time of day) or an existing behavior (such as making your morning coffee) with a response that will bring you closer to fulfilling your goal. Reframe a goal as an "if/then" statement, with the "if" part as the situational cue and the "then" part as your planned response to that cue. Thus, a simple goal of "I want to work out more" becomes "If it is Monday, Wednesday, or Friday at 7 a.m., then I am going for a jog on the beach." If you are tying your goal to an existing behavior, you might say, "If I am brewing my coffee, then I am doing morning push-ups."

If used in connection with KPIs during performance enhancement feedback coaching, a practice plan activity trigger could look something like this:

- **Your employee's goal:** Remain calm in anxiety-producing situations.
- **Practice plan activity trigger:** "If my heart starts to race, then I will use a breathing technique and focus on how relaxed I begin to feel."

Create a Professional Development Plan

After a thorough analysis of the specific knowledge, skills, or abilities that will enhance your employee's overall performance on the job, you and your employee need to work together to translate these into a development plan. There are many development plan templates to choose from, probably even within your own company—just make sure it is specific about short- and long-term goals for enhancing knowledge, skills, competencies, and behaviors. We also recommend defining specific metrics to indicate what improvement looks like, as well as acceptable methods and approaches to obtain and practice important knowledge and skills (such as training programs and coaching).

Collaborate and Communicate

Collaborate with your employee to create a mutually acceptable development plan that outlines the steps and resources needed to improve their performance. This plan should communicate the short-term and longer-term goals and activities, as shown in Table 8-1.

Table 8-1. Template for an Example Employee Development Plan

	Training and Development Goal	Competencies or Skills to Be Acquired	Action Steps	Resources Needed
Short-term goals and activities (1 year)				
Long-term goals and activities (2-3 years)				

Provide Ongoing Feedback

Schedule regular ongoing feedback sessions with your employee to discuss their performance openly and constructively. Focus on their strengths in interpersonal skills and gently address areas that need improvement. Here are several key aspects of feedback to consider:

- **Encourage self-assessment.** One of the vital aspects of providing feedback is encouraging self-assessment. By assessing themselves, employees take ownership of their own progress. Help them to reflect on what they could do more, less, or differently to develop their skills. Encourage them to ask for feedback and ensure that you are approachable if they want outside feedback or validation. Emphasize the notion that "there is no wrong question."

- **Set regular check-in dates.** To monitor your employee's progress, schedule regular check-in meetings. During these meetings, you will be able to discuss challenges and adjust the development plan as needed. You will also ensure that the employee knows you are invested in their growth and are there to support them.

- **Initiate peer reviews.** Collect feedback from colleagues or team members about the employee's interpersonal skills and areas in which they excel. These reviews can provide valuable insights and help motivate the employee to improve.

Monitor and Reinforce Progress

When we conduct 360-degree feedback assessment reviews, many employees report that they feel they are not being recognized adequately for their efforts and accomplishments. Showing gratitude for a job well done does wonders for an employee's motivation to do great work. Research shows that there is a ratio for saying positive and negative things to employees to keep them motivated. Zenger and Folkman (2015) suggest that in low-performing teams, there are almost three negative comments for every positive one.

Providing constructive and critical feedback is an essential part of performance enhancement feedback coaching. Along with genuine praise and reinforcement of what employees are doing well, constructive feedback dramatically enhances both motivation and engagement.

Finally, when your employee's performance improves, it is important to provide timely recognition for the effort and results you have observed. Such positive feedback and praise will help you not only reinforce newly acquired skills and behaviors, but also celebrate goal attainment and success.

Encourage Mentorship and Coaching

There are distinct differences between the roles and responsibilities of coaches, mentors, managers, and sponsors within the organization (Table 8-2). People in each of these roles can work together to facilitate and enhance employee performance and discuss future career goals. In performance enhancement feedback coaching, leaders might suggest that employees consider internal or external coaching, working with an internal or external mentor, or seeking an internal sponsor to be part of their ongoing professional and career development efforts. Each of these individuals work collaboratively with the employee to help them address specific skill deficits, better understand and manage organizational politics, and become a useful sounding board to foster their ongoing growth and development.

Table 8-2. Development Roles of Managers, Coaches, Mentors, and Sponsors

Role	Perspective and Focus
Manager	• Has a vertical perspective • Provides direct authority • Gives advice on performance and career development • Promotes accountability • Shares concerns about performance
Coach	• Has an individual perspective • Provides an external mirror • Gives advice on development • Promotes self-reflection and behavior change • Shares concerns about personal growth
Mentor	• Has an internal or external perspective • Provides internal mirroring • Gives advice to broaden career options • Promotes self-responsibility • Shares concerns about learning
Sponsor	• Has a horizontal perspective • Provides influential power • Gives advice on obtaining high-visibility tasks and jobs • Promotes visibility • Shares concerns about opportunities

Facilitate Peer Coaching

Peer learning is an important part of the process for developing skills and building camaraderie. It is especially valuable for employees with high interpersonal skills who need to focus on developing other skill sets.

As a leader, you need to create a safe and supportive environment where team members feel comfortable sharing their experiences, insights, and challenges. You can do this by setting clear expectations, providing constructive feedback, encouraging openness and honesty, and celebrating successes and failures. As a leader, you should also model the behaviors you want to see in your team, such as asking for help, admitting mistakes, and acknowledging contributions.

We use the label "peer coaching" to broadly include specific educational and topical meetings designed to encourage team members to present and share knowledge, skills, and information (for example, using generative AI to enhance the effectiveness of work tasks or strategies and techniques in self-care and stress management). These sessions are typically voluntary and may be facilitated by HR or external coaches. For example, Sandra has designed peer and group coaching programs for a variety of companies and industries, including a leading entertainment company and other companies in healthcare, sales, finance, and media. These programs are specifically focused on enhancing emotional and social competence. The internal leaders typically meet for 12 bimonthly sessions, which are facilitated by Sandra, and take turns preparing and sharing case studies and current challenges they are having in a confidential setting. Sandra weaves in specific readings, assessments, and assignments to be done outside each session to enhance specific knowledge and skills.

Hold a Performance Enhancement Feedback Conversation

One feedback technique that we have found especially valuable in performance enhancement feedback coaching is called "Give-Get-Merge-Go." This technique provides a structured and participative way to deliver feedback in a supportive and developmental tone while allowing you and your employee to mutually define areas they need to work on. (The steps of Give-Get-Merge-Go are shown in Tool 8-1 at the end of this chapter.)

The technique starts by clearly stating the behavior areas you think the employee could consider working on (specific competencies) to enhance their overall performance. This is a participative technique because you're directly asking the employee for their input and point of view. By actively listening and summarizing areas you both agree on, you build their motivation for a specific development improvement plan. The feedback meeting should end with a clear agreement on specific coaching, training, and mentoring that will occur, as well as ways to follow up and measure improvement over time.

This coaching technique also works well for a variety of other performance situations, and it's embedded within the widely adopted GROW model (Whitmore 2009). Used in leadership coaching and for goal setting, the four-step GROW model can be introduced within the "Go" step in the Give-Get-Merge-Go feedback technique:

- **Goal.** Identify what you and the employee have agreed to focus on as a specific development goal to track and monitor.

- **Reality.** Discuss the current reality around the performance issues and specific barriers, challenges, and difficulties for the employee.
- **Options.** Brainstorm possible solutions, paths, and development plans to address the performance issues.
- **Way forward.** Define development actions, commitments, timeframes, metrics around improvement, and follow-up. What will the employee do? What will you do? How will it be measured? How can you best support the employee?

 **Key Points**

Let's review a few key points from this chapter:

- Performance enhancement feedback coaching is about building the skill sets of your employees with high interpersonal skills and inadequate knowledge and technical skill deficits contributing to poor performance. Examples of technical skills deficiencies can include project management, sales, budgeting, presentation, and communication skills.
- It is vital to identify the source of the employee's skill deficiency to address the issue appropriately. Some skills may not be important enough to address or the employee may not be motivated enough to address them.
- Once you've accurately identified a skill deficiency, there are a series of steps to take, including communicating expectations and setting implementation intentions, establishing KPIs, setting regular check-in times to track progress, effectively delegating tasks, and celebrating successes on the job.

Tool 8-1. Providing Feedback Using the Give-Get-Merge-Go Technique

Give: Express your perceptions, observations, suggestions, or point of view about the employee's current opportunities for development in a concise and open manner (e.g., "Here are my thoughts on this," rather than, "Here is what you need to do").

Get: Actively solicit the employee's point of view. Ask explicitly what reactions, thoughts, or ideas they have to what you just shared. Actively listen.

Merge: Confirm what you heard by paraphrasing what the other person said in a manner that clarifies and summarizes where you agree and disagree with each other.

Go: Finalize what you mutually agree are the next steps. Ask the employee to summarize what they have agreed to do more, less, or differently to enhance their current performance and sharpen their task, project, or administrative skills.

Tool 8-2. Questions for Analyzing Performance Deficiencies

Knowledge, Skills, and Abilities Analysis

Knowledge Deficiency	Questions
Did the employee know it in the past?	• How often is the knowledge used? • Has there been institutional forgetting? • Is it a one-time situation? • Can I provide a simple job aid or manual? • Can I store the needed information in an easy-to-access location (e.g., wiki, intranet, or phone app)?
Skills or Ability Deficiency	**Questions**
Could the employee do it in the past?	• Did they once know how to perform as desired? • Have they forgotten what to do? • How often is the skill used? • Is it a difficult skill to perform? • Is there regular feedback about how well the skill is performed? • How does the employee find out how well they are performing this skill? • Can I model, coach, or show them how to perform the skill? • What informal training can be used (e.g., peer instruction, mentoring, or coaching)? • What formal training programs might help improve skill performance?

Tool 8-2. (cont.)

Motivational Analysis

Motivational Deficiency	Questions
Does performing really matter to the employee?	• Were they motivated in the past? • Do the standards you have match the employee's standards? • Is there a favorable outcome for performing that matches the wants and needs of the employee? • Is there a source of satisfaction for performing? • Does the performance lead to positive recognition and outcomes that the employee values? • Can the employee take pride in their performance as an individual or member of a team? • Is there any competition or metrics of success that the employee can use to evaluate their performance?
Are there obstacles to the employee's ability to perform?	• Is the employee clear on what is expected? • Are there conflicting demands on the employee? • Is the employee overloaded and stressed? • Does the employee lack authority, control, time, equipment, or supplies? • Are there restrictive policies or norms that interfere with performance?
What solution is best?	• Does each solution address one or more of the problems identified during the analysis (e.g., knowledge, skill, or motivational deficiencies)? • What is the cost of each potential solution? • What are the consequences of not addressing the problem?
What resources exist to help the employee with this performance issue?	• Which solutions are most practical, feasible, and economical? • Which solution will add the highest value for the least effort? • Which solution is best for company culture? • Can your manager or human resources provide information and support? • Can the EAP provide information and support?

Tool 8-3. Five Critical Steps for Holding Performance Enhancement Feedback Coaching Conversations

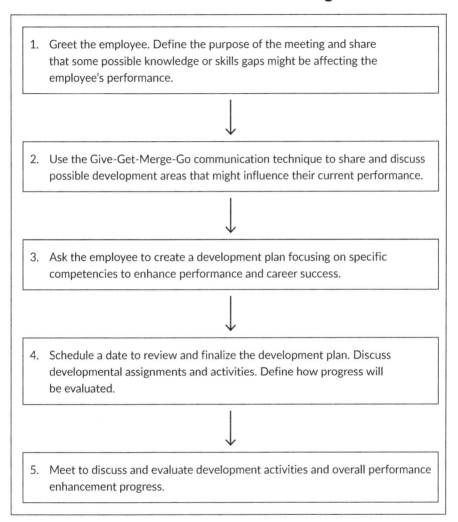

1. Greet the employee. Define the purpose of the meeting and share that some possible knowledge or skills gaps might be affecting the employee's performance.

2. Use the Give-Get-Merge-Go communication technique to share and discuss possible development areas that might influence their current performance.

3. Ask the employee to create a development plan focusing on specific competencies to enhance performance and career success.

4. Schedule a date to review and finalize the development plan. Discuss developmental assignments and activities. Define how progress will be evaluated.

5. Meet to discuss and evaluate development activities and overall performance enhancement progress.

Tool 8-4. Tips for Performance Enhancement Feedback Coaching

☑ Keep in mind that these individuals have some coachable areas of improvement to enhance their effectiveness and success. Focus on identifying and developing specific task and project management, communication, and job-related skills to enhance their overall performance.

☑ Expect this type of employee to be open and responsive to feedback. They will be motivated to create development plans that target specific knowledge, skills, abilities, and approaches to improve their current job performance and positively influence their professional and career growth within the company.

☑ There are several ways that employees learn, grow, and develop. Matching their preference and style for knowledge and skill acquisition is important to engender buy-in on the part of the employee and ensure they translate their new knowledge back to the job (e.g., from classes, conferences, workshops, coaching, mentoring, online seminars, and so forth).

☑ It is imperative to define what improvement looks like and how it can be measured to influence job performance. Put into place a supportive development plan with specific activities, benchmarks, and metrics to evaluate improvement over time.

☑ Consider using a 360-feedback assessment to provide concrete recommendations and suggestions to these individuals to help facilitate their development plans. Using a habit change or learning transfer platform like Envisia Learning's Talent Accelerator can help you measure actual behavior change success, along with repeating the 360 assessment as a follow-up measure.

☑ The more participative and interactive the feedback interaction and development planning (e.g., using the Give-Get-Merge-Go technique), the greater the likelihood these individuals will be intrinsically motivated to work to improve specific skills and abilities.

Chapter 9

Performance Improvement
How to Coach Low Performers
With Low Interpersonal Skills

A few years ago, Ken went into a favorite Los Angeles coffee shop with Vespa, a puppy he was in the process of training as a guide dog. For the past 20 years, he and his spouse have worked with a nonprofit organization to raise Labrador Retrievers to become service dogs for people who are blind or have vision impairment, children on the autistic spectrum, and veterans with post-traumatic stress disorder (PTSD). They raise the puppies from about six weeks to 20 months old, and then transition them back to the nonprofit to begin formal work with professional trainers.

That morning, the staff gave Vespa their usual warm greeting, and then the pup sat calmly while Ken placed his order. A stranger soon approached the counter, stood a little too close for comfort, and immediately started admonishing Ken for bringing a dog into the coffee shop. She rattled off a history of the misdeeds of irresponsible neighborhood pet owners in a tone that got louder and angrier as the lecture continued.

"Dogs like that are a menace," she said. "They carry diseases, just like rats! I run a cafe down the street, and I would never let a dog inside. If I see you and your dog near my place, I'll call the police!"

Ken was initially confused and then felt a rush of embarrassment, acutely aware that everyone in the coffee shop was watching and listening. *How can I cut this rant short and de-escalate the situation?* he thought. *Doesn't she know service dogs are allowed in public spaces? Why on earth is she yelling?*

Ken paid the barista, reached down to reassure Vespa with a quick pat, and took a breath. Before he could respond, the stranger walked out the door and disappeared.

Later, while talking about the incident with Sandra, Ken realized that the woman's fiercely combative way of communicating and ignorance about service animals and the law was a dangerous combination.

"Apparently," mused Ken, "she's a manager in the restaurant industry but doesn't know that the American's With Disabilities Act applies to service dogs."

"If only you could sign on as her coach," replied Sandra, only half joking. "She's a prime candidate for performance improvement coaching!"

In our work as leadership coaches, one of the most difficult questions we face is: How do you deal with people who lack the knowledge and skills required to do their jobs, as well as the basic interpersonal skills to get along with others? Remember that "no-clue gene" we talked about in chapter 1? When that is combined with poor job performance, it's always a challenging situation.

When confronted with what Casciaro and Lobo (2005) would call an "incompetent jerk," your first inclination as a leader might be to try to remove that person from your team altogether. Or you may be inclined to hang onto the employee and try everything you can to change their performance behavior, even if there's no improvement in sight. Either decision can mean high costs for your organization. You may prematurely terminate a high-potential employee who is experiencing hidden stresses that are influencing current performance. On the other hand, if you spend an enormous amount of time addressing someone's poor performance without making any progress, their behavior could have a lasting influence on their team's morale or a direct negative influence on customers and clients—or both.

When assessing employee performance problems, you must consider a variety of individual and organizational factors. As we mentioned in chapter 8, identifying the underlying causes of poor performance is critical. But unlike employees in the performance enhancement quadrant, those in the performance improvement quadrant not only lack emotional and social competence, but are also performing poorly overall; therefore, coaching and training tend to be less effective.

Managing poor performers who also exhibit interpersonal and social deficits is both time consuming and frustrating. Every company has protocols for managing poor performance, progressive discipline procedures, and the steps that trigger a performance improvement plan, probation, and termination. In this chapter, our aim is not to replace those protocols, but to explore some of the research that applies to those who need performance improvement and offer a variety of strategies and tools to make communicating with them easier.

"Quiet Quitting" and the Price of Poor Performance

Within our confidential executive coaching sessions, our clients sometimes reveal that they want to leave their organizations because they are bored, underutilized, placed in roles that don't deploy their skills and experience, pressured, disengaged, or all the above. These employees may try to perform at their best for a while, but if their feelings of disengagement continue, performance will eventually decline. When employees feel apathetic and disconnected from their work, they stop putting in the necessary effort. Additionally, they tend to disengage at a social level, which adds to the perception that they are interpersonally challenging and difficult to work with. These so-called "quiet quitters" constitute about 59 percent of all employees in most companies, according to a 2024 Gallup survey.

If you notice the following behaviors in employees who are performing poorly and have become even more interpersonally challenging, they are likely in a stage of quiet quitting; eventually, their performance will decline further, and they may resign:

- Increased absenteeism
- Lack of initiative and decreased productivity
- Missed deadlines and broken commitments
- Withdrawal from interactions with peers, team members, and customers
- Lack of enthusiasm when given tasks and assignments.
- Decreased communication about work-related issues

Sometimes, quiet quitting is more about bad bosses than bad employees (Zenger and Folkman 2022). As a leader, it's important to reflect on your practices and communication style when analyzing the poor performers on your team. (Tool 9-2 at the end of this chapter provides a helpful checklist.)

Sometimes, you will find opportunities to turn around a quiet quitter's performance and keep that employee at the company, particularly if you can mutually and adequately address their interpersonal deficits. These employees may be waiting for a candid conversation with a leader so they can identify the underlying factors impeding their performance. They may be hoping someone will inspire them to make changes in their behavior (Knight 2021). In other cases, poorly performing employees choose to seek employment elsewhere, which is a "win-win" for the employee and the organization.

One thing we know for certain is that your organization will pay a price for not addressing an employee's poor performance and lack of people skills—and not only financially. The price may include:

- **Other employees' compensating behavior and resentment.** When an employee's performance is poor and not addressed, other team members often pick up the slack to meet deadlines and customer expectations. This can cause resentment and job burnout for those who feel they need to pick up the work not completed on time or to a high standard.

- **Potential litigation.** It can seem that constructively confronting a single employee's poor job performance requires more work than ignoring it, but if you ignore problems, other employees may report a hostile work environment, take a medical leave of absence for stress, or even start legal proceedings. The resulting litigation and legal fees can come with a substantial cost.

- **Recruitment, onboarding, and training.** Sometimes, you will ask poor performers to leave, or they will do so voluntarily. Either way, their departure opens the door for a replacement—and all the costs of recruiting, selecting, onboarding, training, and coaching that go with hiring a new employee. Even if an employee is let go for well-documented underperformance, your organization may still be responsible for paying unemployment benefits. Specific state laws apply to each situation, so it is always important to get your internal legal department to collaborate with you when handling patterns of poor performance and all terminations.

- **Customer dissatisfaction and brand damage.** Poorly performing employees who lack interpersonal competence, especially those in customer service and technical specialists, can have a long-lasting and negative influence on external perceptions of your organization's products and services. Employees may use social media channels, such as Glassdoor, to broadcast their dissatisfaction with organizations and their leaders, which can harm their reputation.
- **Time devoted to addressing poor performance.** Managing poor performance is time-consuming work for conscientious leaders. When they inherit poor performers, busy leaders may feel like they have an additional full-time job.

Negative employee interactions have five times the impact of positive employee interactions on an organization (Glomb et al. 2011).

Performance Improvement Feedback Coaching

The goal of performance improvement feedback coaching is to seek immediate performance improvements or corrective action, often including the option of exploring new assignments or roles within the organization for the employee based on their current interpersonal and social skills (Figure 9-1 on the next page). For those in leadership roles, solutions might include removing their supervisory responsibilities or transferring them to another department. Some companies seek outside executive coaches for poor-performing individuals, but, in our experience, this tends to waste time and money and offers little return on investment. We usually see leaders and organizations offering employees executive coaching as "one last step" before considering termination to minimize the possibility of litigation.

With low performers who lack emotional intelligence, we believe it is important to address their performance, clearly communicate the behaviors and KPIs that should be improved, provide a timetable, and state clear consequences and next steps should they not improve. We agree with CEO Charles Bergh of Levi Strauss & Co, who says that too many leaders wait far too long to constructively confront and document employees' performance issues—or avoid the tasks altogether (Jacob 2023).

Figure 9-1. Performance Improvement Feedback Coaching

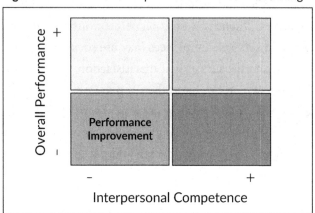

A Scenario for Performance Improvement

We will now walk through a hypothetical scenario for an employee who needs performance improvement coaching, outlining each step in detail.

Pat has been an employee of your company for more than four years. During the past few months, you have noticed that on several occasions, they didn't follow through on important commitments and deadlines related to key projects. Several times during the past month you noticed Pat arriving quite late to meetings, and they even missed two important project team meetings. Four times in the past two weeks, Pat has been unusually slow to respond to your emails and phone calls. Their assistant mentioned difficulty in locating Pat on several occasions when others called the office asking to speak to them, and that they seemed more moody, irritable, and preoccupied than usual. Two employees on your team said they don't think Pat has been working hard lately; one suggested that Pat was having some "personal problems," but wasn't specific about what they might be.

You recently overheard Pat complaining to colleagues about favoritism in the office and that "certain staff members" are always given preferential assignments and "visible projects." Someone outside your team reported that

Pat has been "bad-mouthing" senior management and posting negative comments on social media about recent changes in the organization. You have taken note of Pat's negative attitude, complaints, and criticisms, and believe they have influenced other employees, especially newer ones on the team. You are now concerned that Pat's behavior is harming the morale of your whole team.

In terms of personality, Pat is aloof, sometimes comes off as self-important, and impatient with others. They have been a solid but not outstanding performer for several years, and you believe their experience and skills could continue to be valuable to your team and organization, but first, you will need to do some diagnostic troubleshooting to assess the reasons for the absenteeism, performance decline, and poor interpersonal and attitudinal behaviors.

The first step is meeting with Pat to better understand their perspective on the current performance issues and to mutually agree on an improvement plan.

The Engagement Review Meeting

The best first step in approaching the situation with Pat or another such employee is to arrange what we call an "engagement review meeting" to determine the factors influencing their overall performance. At this time, you can explore the perceived barriers to improvement and how you can enable your employee to perform better on the job. Use Table 9-1 as a first step before the meeting to determine if the performance deficiencies are related to a lack of awareness or knowledge, a lack of motivation or engagement, or a lack of skills or abilities. With Pat, it appears that the poor performance is not directly related to a lack of skills or abilities.

Table 9-1. Template for an Employee Engagement Review Meeting

	Performance Coaching Challenge	Strategy to Address the Challenge
Enlighten (lack of awareness)		
Encourage (lack of motivation)		
Enable (lack of abilities)		

When you address Pat, start by exploring internal and external factors that might be influencing their level of engagement, motivation, or frustration. Why isn't Pat meeting deadlines? What is bothering them about senior management? Why isn't Pat motivated to attend project meetings?

Your task is to mutually define and implement realistic solutions to address declining performance. You should try to demonstrate an empathetic and solution-focused mindset and document the meeting.

Finally, some evidence suggests that the workplace environment also shapes employee performance (Zhenjing et al. 2022). An overall positive, trusting, and psychologically safe work culture improves employee commitment, engagement, and achievement. Ask Pat if they have found the culture at your company to be positive, trusting, and safe. If the answer is no, ask what specific changes could improve the environment.

Employee Engagement Review Meeting Checklist

Research suggests that key engagement drivers for employees are a demonstration of their leader's commitment to the direct report's success, an exploration of barriers to success, and a discussion of how the leader will enable the employee to perform better on the job. The purpose of the employee engagement review meeting is to assess their engagement level and all factors that might be influencing their motivation and behavior so you can follow up with practical solutions. Use this checklist to ensure you've accomplished each item during your meeting:

- ☐ Assess the employee's level of job satisfaction and personal success.
- ☐ Clarify and discuss what high performance looks like.
- ☐ Identify perceived barriers or issues hindering high performance.
- ☐ Demonstrate your support.
- ☐ Initiate an ongoing engagement dialogue.
- ☐ Define the purpose of the meeting, noting that it is not a performance review or disciplinary meeting.
- ☐ Share a line of sight about the employee's role and how it fits with the organization's goals and initiatives.
- ☐ Ask the employee about their top priorities and explore gaps.
- ☐ Ask about their signature strengths (or the skills they are interested in deploying and using more).
- ☐ Ask about job conditions: "What gets in the way of a great day at work?" "What support do you need from me?"

☐ Make a referral to your EAP or an outside allied health professional, if applicable.

☐ Discuss and clarify how you can work together moving ahead and schedule another meeting to follow up.

In our hypothetical scenario, if Pat's overall performance following the documented engagement meeting does not improve, then you'll need to schedule a second follow-up meeting and a formal performance improvement feedback coaching session, as described in the next section of this chapter. Seek input and advice from your own manager, human resources, and internal legal teams to ensure you are following proper policies and procedures related to progressive discipline.

The Performance Improvement Feedback Coaching Session

There are five essential steps in conducting this formal meeting; each is described in detail here and in Tool 9-1 at the end of this chapter. Before scheduling this session, check to see if your organization provides leadership training specifically around managing performance issues, corrective action, progressive discipline, and potential legal issues you should be aware of.

1. Define the Purpose of the Meeting and Describe the Performance Problem in a Specific and Supportive Manner

Introduce the meeting's purpose and spend some time creating a supportive and open environment to discuss performance issues and problems. Take an interest in your employee and demonstrate active listening by frequently summarizing, paraphrasing, and reflecting feelings they express. As you describe the performance problem, be as specific as possible. Avoid discussions about the employee's attitude and focus on overall performance based on mutually agreed-upon standards and expectations. You don't want to alienate the employee and put them on the defensive.

Remember, this is a discussion to uncover causes of the performance problems and work toward solutions, not to place blame. Always be as specific and as behavior focused as possible when describing your employee's recent changes in performance.

2. Solicit Input About the Causes of and Possible Solutions for the Performance Problem

Gather all the information you can about the cause of the performance problem by using open-ended questions. This is a good opportunity to actively listen and respond with empathy because your employee may express concern or frustration over factors that seem uncontrollable. Telling someone they must "do better" may be the most direct way to deal with a drop in quality of performance, but it doesn't stand much chance of success if the individual is not motivated or doesn't know what they need to do to improve.

The best way to build a commitment to change is to collaborate with your employee to identify the causes of the performance problems and viable solutions. List as many possible solutions as both of you can come up with. Build on the employee's ideas as you work toward acceptable solutions.

3. Reach Agreement With a Specific Action Plan to Improve Performance and Discuss Consequences if Performance Does Not Improve

It's time to choose the best solutions. At this point, you are ready to pinpoint exactly what must be done—by whom and by when—to correct the performance problem. Discuss specific actions you are both committed to. Remember to summarize the consequences of not improving. These consequences do not have to be extremely negative or punishing, but research suggests that individuals are most likely to change behavior when specific consequences (both positive and negative) are associated with the change effort.

4. Express Confidence in the Employee and Maintain Esteem

Remember to support the employee's previous accomplishments and current efforts to improve performance. Express your confidence that they can be a high performer. This will enhance the employee's self-esteem and build their commitment to carrying out the actions required to solve the performance problem.

5. Review What Was Agreed on and Schedule a Follow-Up Date to Track and Monitor Progress

Ask the employee to review and summarize the action plan you have agreed to verbally. It is easy to skip this step if the discussion was particularly difficult, but it's important. Agree on a specific follow-up date to track and monitor progress. By setting a date, you send a message to the employee that solving the performance problem is important to you. A follow-up meeting enables you and the employee to get together to discuss any progress or problems and plan further action.

End the discussion as you began it—on a friendly note—and give reassurance that you are available as a resource to support and help the employee along the way. Make sure you document the meeting and keep a copy in your employee records as a legal risk management procedure.

Our Practical Approach to Performance Improvement

Don't expect dramatic improvement from your performance improvement employees. In our example, Pat will likely fall short of meeting the goals you set together, but coaching can help. In this section, we outline the steps you can take in performance improvement feedback coaching to identify the underlying causes of interpersonal and skill deficits, strategies for communicating performance problems (clarifying standards and expectations that they need to reach), and guides for creating and tracking a performance improvement plan that leads to good choices in handling your low performers.

Preparation

Preparation is the most crucial step in the performance improvement feedback coaching process. It is essential to set your goals and objectives for success. We suggest you prepare as we do:

- **Identify performance gaps.** Ask yourself: What specific performance and interpersonal issues is the employee struggling with? What behavioral changes are critical for their personal and professional success? How are their behaviors affecting the team and organization's business results?
- **Provide specific feedback.** As you prepare your coaching and feedback sessions, take the time to identify specific examples so the person can better understand your message. Use current examples and focus on specific behaviors, actions, and words. Describe *when, where,* and *how often* you have seen these behaviors.

- **Identify specific areas for improvement.** What task and interpersonal behaviors need to be addressed immediately? What matters most to you? What matters most to the business? What matters most to the rest of your team?
- **Prepare for the reaction.** What reaction do you anticipate from the employee, given your relationship and their personality? How will you react if the employee is angry? Silent? Disagreeing with your perception? Defensive?

Set the Stage for Your Meeting

After you've completed your preparations, open the coaching session by setting the stage for success. During the first few minutes, do three things:

1. **Put the employee at ease.** After you state the purpose of the meeting, the employee might feel uncomfortable and even a bit defensive. This is an opportunity to build rapport and create an environment of trust and partnership. Help them relax and participate in the discussion by saying things like, "I'm not angry at you. This is not a serious problem. We're meeting now to keep it from getting serious."

2. **Clearly state the purpose of the meeting.** Get to the point. Be direct and candid. For example, in our scenario, you might say to Pat, "I'm concerned about your attendance over the past few weeks. We're meeting so I can find out what problems are keeping you away from the office and key team meetings and what we can do about them."

3. **Agree on the agenda for the meeting.** Review what is going to happen next in the process and explain why each step is important. For example, you could say, "Before we discuss what's wrong, we need to see if we agree on the standards we're working toward—in other words, the *shoulds* or *what's supposed to happen next.* We both need to agree on what the problem is before we discuss ways to solve it."

Make it clear that you do not have all the answers. You would like ideas from the employee, and you want to develop a two-way dialogue. The tone you set at the start of the meeting will carry through for the entire meeting. Think openness, optimism, and cooperation.

Determine the Cause

The most efficient and effective actions to eliminate a problem are those that fully address its cause. Comparing what the problem is and is not often prompts specific questions that lead to the cause. Another way to identify causes of performance problems is to work through a checklist. Ask yourself and the employee if the problem could be due to:

- Unclear goals, priorities, or expectations
- Lack of motivation
- Lack of skills or expertise
- Lack of resources
- External factors, such as family, health, or finances

Performance improvement feedback coaching works best when you and your employee *work together as partners.* By focusing on the problem and the performance, not on the person, you encourage open, two-way dialogue. This also helps avoid defensiveness or the temptation to agree to inappropriate quick fixes simply to end the discussion.

Review, Discuss, and Agree on KPIs

A frequent cause of performance problems is a difference in expectations. If standards are not clearly defined when you give assignments, performance problems often occur because you and your employees have different definitions of quality performance. If your direct report does not understand the standard you expected, simply restating and clarifying the standard may eliminate the problem.

Some performance standards, such as time, money, or units produced, are easy to quantify. Other kinds of standards, such as "provide good customer service" and "treat others with respect," are more difficult to measure. In these cases, agreeing on the standard is more likely if you discuss an *ideal.* If you and your employee can achieve a common understanding of the standard or results you expect when you give an assignment, you can avoid many performance problems and establish a framework for discussing actual performance. For example, "We expected a weekly production of 1,000 units. The actual performance was 750." In short, rather than jumping to conclusions about the cause of a problem and how to fix it, first *define it.* Useful questions to define any problem are:

- What is the problem?
- Where is the problem?
- When is the problem occurring?
- How big is the problem?

Plan Your Actions

The best way to identify effective solutions is to brainstorm possible corrective actions. We suggest you:

- **Generate as many possible actions as you can.** Don't evaluate them. Don't argue. Don't agree or disagree. Just generate ideas.
- **Test the ideas.** After generating several ideas, test each one against the cause. (For example: "Will this action achieve the results we want?" or "Could it cause undesirable side effects?") Work with the employee to agree on criteria for selecting the best actions before you jump to conclusions or begin to pass judgment on the ideas you've generated.
- **Create a performance improvement implementation plan.** Once you agree on the best actions, create a specific plan for implementing each one. Put it in writing, including who will do what and when. Without completion dates, good intentions will be forgotten and performance problems will persist. In our experience, people are more likely to leave coaching sessions feeling upbeat and confident if they have a specific plan.
- **Establish criteria for success.** This should answer the question, "How will I know when each action has been accomplished?" Figure 9-2 presents a sample template that you can use to create a plan of action. You may also check with your organization's HR and legal teams to find out if they have a standard performance improvement template.

Figure 9-2. Sample Performance Improvement Plan Worksheet

Performance Problem:			
Action Steps (What specific steps will be taken?)	**Person responsible?**	**Date to Be Completed**	**Success Criteria** (How will I know when each action has been accomplished?)
1.			
2.			
3.			

Monitor and Follow Up

Leaders often miss a critical step in performance improvement coaching feedback—observing, tracking, and documenting the employee's progress once a mutually agreed on improvement plan is in place. Leaders also need to be explicit about next steps and possible consequences if performance does not improve. Try these strategies for monitoring the employee's progress:

- **Schedule a time to meet again to discuss progress.** You will need to make sure your employee is implementing the action steps and find out if any adjustments need to be made. You follow up for three reasons:
    - » To modify the plan if it isn't working
    - » To show that you're serious and available as a resource
    - » To celebrate success
- **Say something about consequences.** You don't have to threaten or speak harshly, but effective coaching always involves specifying the consequences for continued poor performance. Be clear about what next steps, if any, might occur if the employee's subpar performance continues.
- **Sum up what you've done.** End your meeting by summarizing what you have agreed on, the actions you will both take, and why.

This helps ensure you both walk away with a clear picture of the situation.

Finally, it is imperative that you document your meeting and summarize performance improvement commitments, including mutually agreed on expectations, standards, and metrics to evaluate progress. This written documentation is important for legal risk management purposes and should comply with your company's policies and procedures around progressive discipline processes.

A Final Reminder

Employees who demonstrate performance deficits and interpersonal challenges are notoriously the most difficult to engage in the performance feedback process. But your role as a leader is to address lagging performance of all kinds and attempt to put a performance improvement plan in place. The plan should be specific, with clear timing expectations and consequences if performance does not improve.

The truth is, it's always easier to ignore or delay constructively confronting poor performance, but your team members will quickly lose respect for your leadership if you are unwilling to confront bad behavior and declining job performance in a fair, consistent manner.

 Key Points

Let's review a few key points from this chapter:

- Performance improvement feedback coaching is about directly addressing an employee's significant need for improvement in both technical and interpersonal skills. We recommend first seeking a consultation with your HR department to ensure proper communication, documentation, and corrective action steps are being taken to minimize potential negative legal or behavioral results.
- It is important to recognize that underlying personal, family, financial, and other factors may be interfering with an employee's performance and behavior. If your company has an external confidential EAP, you can share this information with the employee or suggest that they seek support from an allied health professional, if appropriate.

- Communicating clearly—both in writing and verbally—about specific incidents, observed behaviors, and inadequacies in meeting performance standards is critical. Mutually agreeing on a performance improvement plan with follow-up dates is also essential to facilitate improvement in overall performance.

Tool 9-1. Performance Improvement Feedback Coaching Steps

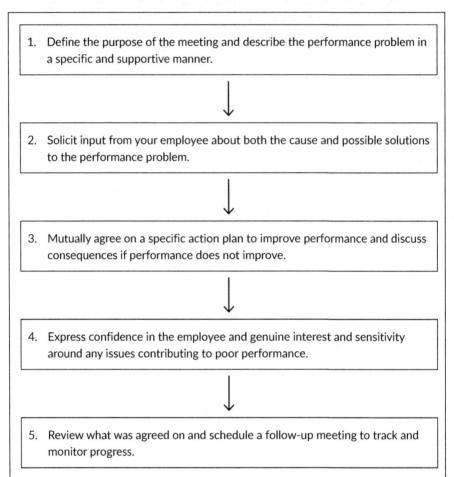

1. Define the purpose of the meeting and describe the performance problem in a specific and supportive manner.

2. Solicit input from your employee about both the cause and possible solutions to the performance problem.

3. Mutually agree on a specific action plan to improve performance and discuss consequences if performance does not improve.

4. Express confidence in the employee and genuine interest and sensitivity around any issues contributing to poor performance.

5. Review what was agreed on and schedule a follow-up meeting to track and monitor progress.

Tool 9-2. Performance Improvement Feedback Coaching Behavioral Checklist

As coaches, we need to monitor our own behavior to ensure we will make the most of our time with each employee. As you review and evaluate your meetings with employees to discuss performance issues, reflect on whether *you* demonstrated each of these valuable behaviors:

☐ I greeted the employee, defined the *purpose* of the meeting, and created a supportive climate to discuss recent changes in their performance.

☐ I shared specific events and changes in the employee's performance in a nonevaluative and factual manner (i.e., focusing on the problem, not the personality, of the employee).

☐ I solicited input from the employee about the cause of recent performance changes and possible solutions to improve their performance (i.e., involving the employee in the solution, rather than prescribing a solution).

☐ I maintained the esteem of the employee by recognizing their past accomplishments and providing encouragement for continued outstanding performance.

☐ I expressed genuine interest, concern, warmth, and sensitivity toward the employee's personal or family problems and expressed my open-door policy and desire to assist in any way I could.

☐ If applicable, I made a referral to the EAP.

☐ I discussed the consequences or next steps if the employee's performance does not improve.

☐ I defined a mutually agreed on action plan for performance improvement using practice plan goals (e.g., on-the-job training, outside education, scheduling changes, or coaching).

☐ I summarized the coaching meeting, asked the employee for their commitment to improve, and scheduled a follow-up date to review performance progress.

Tool 9-3. Tips for Performance Improvement Feedback Coaching

☑ Seek a consultation with your HR department and legal team to ensure you are following company best practices related to progressive discipline procedures, record keeping, and necessary risk management measures.

☑ Explore the employee's own explanation for changes in their recent performance. For non-work-related factors, listen for understanding and make a referral to an internal EAP or external support resources.

☑ Timeliness is critical in successfully addressing performance improvement issues with employees. Although most leaders dislike constructively confronting poor performance, the longer it is not addressed the harder it is to manage and the more it will affect the engagement level of the team working with the employee performing poorly.

☑ Redefining performance expectations, standards, and KPIs is critical for gaining understanding and acceptance by the employee about what aspects of performance need to be addressed.

☑ Asking employees for their ideas about how to solve their current performance challenges is important to engender buy-in for one or more solutions and to enhance intrinsic motivation to improve.

☑ Negotiating a reasonable follow-up date to monitor, track, and discuss performance improvement behaviors and efforts is imperative. Schedule the follow-up meeting after an initial conversation has occurred.

☑ Always share any resources, support, and assistance for the employee to address their current performance issues and challenges. You should be perceived as an ally and champion on behalf of the employee to increase trust and their commitment to seriously address performance shortcomings.

Chapter 10
Performance Feedback Meets Artificial Intelligence

Now that we've fully explained our Performance Feedback Coaching Model, we'd like to spend a little time discussing another way leaders can continue to grow, develop, and provide the most effective performance feedback for employees. Because our model emphasizes human communication and connection, it doesn't prescribe the use of artificial intelligence (AI) in the feedback process. However, we recognize that AI is already a valuable tool being used by leaders and will become more integral in our work in the years to come. By leveraging new and emerging AI-based tools, we expect leaders to be able to enhance their employees' learning opportunities and greatly improve the efficiency of feedback, coaching, and development in many ways. For example, AI could be used with the growing and changing landscape around digital coaching platforms, including AI-driven chatbots and interactive personal assistants (Passmore et al. 2024; Tavis and Woodward 2024).

Using AI for employee coaching and development, as well as performance management, could be especially useful for streamlining or simplifying frequent tasks, including:
- Setting employee development goals
- Providing employees with coaching tips and suggestions
- Identifying patterns in data related to employee performance, productivity, retention, and satisfaction

- Creating draft performance feedback emails and other communications that you could then customize for each employee
- Creating on-the-job simulations and exercises
- Writing draft performance evaluation reviews that you can then revise and edit
- Translating materials into a variety of languages
- Providing up-to-date research on employee mental and physical health
- Developing employee quizzes, tests, and assessments
- Creating employee development skill-building exercises
- Initiating reminders and nudges for implementing development plans
- Generating competency-based developmental resources, including books, videos, articles, and case studies

In addition, our model addresses several challenging aspects of performance feedback coaching that may be enhanced with the use of an AI-based assistant. For example, AI could help:

- **Reduce bias.** AI systems can be designed to minimize the cognitive biases that influence human decision making, including confirmation bias, the halo effect, and recency bias. By monitoring bias, AI could help leaders deliver fair, consistent, and less-biased feedback to their direct reports.
- **Gather data and improve feedback.** AI tools have the ability to track and monitor employee performance and provide real-time feedback. AI-generated performance data could then enable leaders to address issues promptly and offer timely feedback, coaching, and corrective action, if necessary.
- **Personalize feedback.** It's possible to use AI-based tools to analyze an employee's interpersonal communication style, personality, interests, values, and preferences to help facilitate more effective, tailored feedback delivery from leaders. In fact, some research suggests that using AI to provide performance feedback to employees is even more accurate, higher in quality, and more consistent than face-to-face feedback (Tong et al. 2021).
- **Analyze sentiment.** AI could be used to analyze the tone and emotions that come across in a written email conversation and

other communications, helping leaders identify potential areas of concern or misunderstanding so they could adjust their feedback approach accordingly.

Although AI will become an increasingly valuable and ubiquitous tool for supporting employee management and development, it can't and won't replace vital human interactions. Performance feedback coaching will continue to be interactive and personal—based on the dynamics and quality of communication you have with your employees.

Challenges and Risks

It is essential for leaders to be aware of current challenges, questions, concerns, and risks when using AI (Nowack 2023). As we know, humans are infinitely complex creatures, given the intersectionality of genetics, biology, experiences, upbringing, and other factors. AI models tend to aggregate current knowledge in ways that can oversimplify or ignore contextual factors related to feedback and might miss individual nuances, special situations, and needs, such as those of neuroatypical or neurodivergent employees.

In addition, many of the algorithms in current AI tools were trained using data full of human biases or by teams that were not alert to bias and were not especially diverse themselves. This results in what is called the "western, educated, industrialized, rich, and democratic (or WEIRD) bias," and leads to insensitivity to diversity in the growing global workplace. In short, leaders need to recognize not all employees will find the information supplied by an AI tool to be useful or appropriate.

Current research suggests that online coaching platforms and chatbots can be effective and perceived as caring by users (Terblanche, van Heerden, and Hunt 2024). However, AI currently lacks the human touch necessary to address performance and well-being issues for some employees. Relying on AI-based tools in such cases could lead to a sharp disconnect between leaders and their employees.

AI chatbots and other tools are also notorious for "hallucinating" and providing inaccurate (or completely made up) information. AI platforms can generate outdated, erroneous, and often misleading content in some circumstances. And even if the information is accurate, it is often quite generic and lacks specificity for an individual's situation. We need to continue relying on human expertise to ensure that any AI-suggested resources, references, and other learning and development content are up-to-date and accurate. In the near term at least, solutions to problems and performance feedback resources (including exercises, assessments, books, videos, and strategies for enhancing employee competencies) created by AI will also lack the spark of creativity we expect from human intelligence. Leaders must review all recommendations and resources to ensure they are getting the best match for their needs.

Privacy and security are among the biggest concerns for those using AI-based tools. AI engines and models already collect and track the user's personal information, and organizations must understand the limits of vendor confidentiality, privacy, and security. Leaders should never enter personal or confidential employee information into an AI platform or chatbot, even if it's generating useful suggestions and resources for employee development.

It's often difficult to discern what's behind current AI models, deep learning, and neural networks generating information and resources. This lack of openness and explanation by some AI vendors is an ongoing problem for leaders who rightly want to investigate and understand the AI tools they are using.

Legal questions related to copyright and data protection will probably continue to be complex and difficult for leaders to navigate. When using an AI tool to help create anything from a 10-minute assessment to an all-day skills-building exercise, it will be important to determine whether any of the source material is protected. Most AI platforms use content curated from the internet, and it is often unclear whether some or all of what is subsequently generated from that content violates copyright law within the United States or data protection regulations in other countries. Additionally, AI systems that generate original music, images, or text operate in an atmosphere of ambiguity around the true ownership of such output.

Finally, we suggest that leaders try not to become so enthralled by shiny new tools that depend on AI that they use them in all situations. You've spent years building your judgment and critical thinking skills through your work and life experiences. This knowledge is enormously valuable when it comes to providing performance feedback coaching and maintaining strong relationships with your employees. AI tools are useful in many situations but should not be used in every scenario with every employee.

With full knowledge that AI is changing rapidly—and many tools we find useful today will be displaced, improved, or gone within a few months or years—we've included a list of some of our favorite AI-focused tools in the appendix. We encourage you to continue exploring what AI has to offer and to keep abreast of how it grows and evolves in the years to come.

Conclusion

> I've learned that people will forget what you said, people
> will forget what you did, but people will never forget how
> you made them feel.
> —Maya Angelou, author, poet, and activist

We are pleased to share our strategies for driving successful behavior change through the four-quadrant Performance Feedback Coaching Model. We believe this model can help leaders in any organization better understand their employees' strengths and needs by applying a framework that tracks their current level of performance, emotional and social competency, level of engagement, and important individual differences.

The results of Wilson Learning's 2024 Annual Leadership Development Survey offered fresh support for the principles of our model and its emphasis on effective communication with diverse employee groups (Leimbach and Roth 2024). The survey found that some of the most effective core learning methods for leadership development were:

- Manager coaching
- Reinforcement
- Simulations and role play
- Structured on-the-job training

Our coaching model incorporates coaching, reinforcement, and on-the-job training and learning transfer by leaders for successful employee development.

Coaching for successful behavior change is multifaceted. It encompasses giving, receiving, asking for, and ultimately using feedback. We focus on all these facets, but place most of our emphasis on *how* leaders can frame and deliver feedback so employees will accept it and act on the messages delivered to achieve successful behavior change. We want to help all leaders deliver effective feedback that resonates with and motivates the people they care about and depend on.

We also recognize that leaders themselves must continue to grow and develop. They must ask those above them on the organization chart, their colleagues, and the people they supervise about how they are perceived and their impact on others. Increasing your self-awareness as a leader is crucial to enhancing your effectiveness. We have found that the most successful leaders are those who are most aware of their own strengths, blind spots, unconscious biases, and development opportunities.

According to Gallup surveys, employees who get frequent and continuous feedback from managers are 3.2 times more likely to strongly agree that they are motivated to do outstanding work and 2.7 times more likely to strongly agree that they are engaged at work (Sutton and Wigert 2019).

Throughout this book, we have emphasized that while there isn't a one-size-fits-all approach to leading and coaching employees, our model is designed to help leaders provide individualized development plans for each of their direct reports. We understand how complex people are and realize that employees won't always fit perfectly into one of our model's four typologies; in fact, most will move from one to another over time. We believe the exercises, checklists, and tools provided here can be adapted to your and your employees' evolving needs.

We now welcome *your* feedback for us! Please reach out and share your experiences using our model—what's working for you and what changes do you suggest? We'd love to be able to share your lessons learned with other readers. You can find Sandra at spectracoaching.com and Ken at envisia learning.com.

Acknowledgments

We wish to acknowledge and thank all our clients, both past and present, for their input, trust, and inspiration, which have been the foundation for this book.

A special thank you to Justin Brusino for initially approaching us to consider writing a new book devoted to a topic that is so special to both of us and is ongoing support to make it become a reality. We also very much appreciate the input and initial guidance by Jack Harlow, which helped shape the focus and initial outline that served as the architecture for the entire book.

We can't thank our development editor Shelley Sperry enough for her craft and skills at taking our initial drafts and not only making them tremendously more readable but also suggesting creative ways to organize and structure each chapter to improve them immensely. We truly enjoyed collaborating with her and without her sharp editorial eye, comments, and suggestions we would not have the professional finished product we do today. Just a really big thanks to making both of us look so good in print!

Maybe you can't tell a book by the cover, but we want to acknowledge and thank Melissa Jones and the entire ATD Press team for both the attractive cover and fabulous production editing and final copy edits that brought us all to the finish line!

A Selected List of AI Tools for Performance Feedback and Coaching

(As of December 2024)

AI Search Engines and Coaching Platforms for Leaders and Employees

- Aceup Coaching Platform (aceup.com)
- Andi (andisearch.com)
- Opera (opera.com)
- Bettercoach (bettercoach.io)
- Microsoft Bing Copilot (bing.com/chat)
- Bravely (workbravely.com)
- Butterfly Leadership Coaching (caterpillar.ai)
- ChatGPT (chat.openai.com/auth/login)
- Coachhub Digital Coaching Platform (coachhub.com)
- Cultivate Intelligent Coaching Platform (go.perceptyx.com/recording-cultivate-the-next-generation-of-leaders-with-intelligent-coaching)
- Google Gemini (gemini.google.com)
- EZRA Coaching (helloezra.com)
- Komo AI (Komo.ai)
- Ovida Skills Development Platform (ovida.io)
- Phind (Phind.com)

- Sharpist Coaching Platform (sharpist.com)
- Skillsoft Coaching Platform (skillsoft.com/coaching)
- Sounding Board Leadership (soundingboardinc.com)
- Torch Coaching Platform (torch.io)
- UExcelerate Coaching Platform (uexcelerate.com)
- Valence AI Leadership/Employee Coach Platform (valence.co)
- You AI Assistant (you.com)

AI Coaching Conversation Chatbots

- AIcoach Platform (aicoach.chat/about)
- AIMY Conversational AI Coaching Bot (coachhub.com/aimy)
- Coach M AI Chatbot (transferoflearning.com/services/chatbot)
- Coach Vici (coachvici.com)
- EVoach AI Coach Chatbot (evoach.com)
- Growth Mindset AI Coach (Rocky.ai)
- LEADx LiveCoach (leadx.org)
- PocketConfidant AI Coach Chatbot (pocketconfidant.com)
- SIX AI Well-Being App (your6.com)
- Tuesday AI Mental Health Platform (besttuesdayever.com)
- Yoodli communication skills coach (app.yoodli.ai)
- Youper Mental Health AI Chatbot (youper.ai)

References

Introduction

Abi-Esber, N., J.E. Abel, J. Schroeder, and F. Gino. 2022. "'Just Letting You Know . . .' Underestimating Others' Desire for Constructive Feedback." *Journal of Personality and Social Psychology* 123(6): 1362–1385. doi.org/10.1037/pspi0000393.

Cuddy, A.J.C., S.T. Fiske, and P. Glick. 2008. "Warmth and Competence as Universal Dimensions of Social Perception: The Stereotype Content Model and the BIAS Map." *Advances in Experimental Social Psychology* 40:61–149.

Eagle Hill. 2022. " Nearly Half of Workers Only Receive Feedback on an Annual or Semi-Annual Basis, New Eagle Hill Research Finds." Press Release. Eagle Hill Consulting, July 26. eaglehillconsulting.com/news/remote-and-hybrid-employees-say-getting-feedback-is-challenging.

Garr, S., and P. Mehrotra. 2023. "What's Holding Back Manager Effectiveness, and How to Fix It." MIT Sloan Management Review, January 11. sloanreview.mit.edu/article/whats-holding-back-manager-effectiveness-and-how-to-fix-it.

Guggenberger, P., D. Maor, M. Park, and P. Simon. 2023. *The State of Organizations 2023: 10 Shifts Transforming Organizations*. McKinsey, April 25. mckinsey.com/capabilities/people-and-organizational-performance/our-insights/the-state-of-organizations-2023.

Harter, J. 2024. "In New Workplace, U.S. Employee Engagement Stagnates." Gallup Workplace, January 23. gallup.com/workplace/608675/new -workplace-employee-engagement-stagnates.aspx.

Nowack, K. 2009. "Leveraging Multirater Feedback to Facilitate Successful Behavioral Change." *Consulting Psychology Journal: Practice and Research* 61:280–297.

Rock, D., B. Jones, and C. Weller. 2018. Using Neuroscience to Make Feedback Work and Feel Better." *Strategy + Business*, August 27. strategy -business.com/article/Using-Neuroscience-to-Make-Feedback-Work -and-Feel-Better.

Williams, J., and K.M. Nowack. 2022. "Neuroscience Hacks to Enhance Learning Agility in Leaders." *Consulting Psychology Journal: Practice and Research* 74(3): 291–310.

Chapter 1

Alvero, A.M., B.R. Bucklin, and J. Austin. 2001. "An Objective Review of the Effectiveness and Essential Characteristics of Performance Feedback in Organizational Settings (1985–1998)." *Journal of Organizational Behavior Management* 21(1): 3–29.

Alzina, R.B., and N.E. Escoda. 2007. "Las competencias emocionales." *Educación XXI* 61-82. 10.5944/educxx1.1.10.297.

Bottini, S., and J. Gillis. 2021. "A Comparison of the Feedback Sandwich, Constructive-Positive Feedback, and Within Session Feedback for Training Preference Assessment Implementation." *Journal of Organizational Behavior Management* 41(1): 83-93. 10.1080/01608061 .2020.1862019.

Cross, K.P. 1997. "Not Can, But Will College Teaching Be Improved?" *New Directions for Higher Education* 17:1–15. doi.org/10.1002/he.36919771703.

Gaze, E.C. 2023. "Debunking the Dunning-Kruger Effect—The Least Skilled People Know How Much They Don't Know, But Everyone Thinks They Are Better Than Average." The Conversation, May 8. theconversation.com/debunking-the-dunning-kruger-effect-the-least -skilled-people-know-how-much-they-dont-know-but-everyone-thinks -they-are-better-than-average-195527.

Gnepp, J., J. Klayman, I.O. Williamson, and S. Barlas. 2020. "The Future of Feedback: Motivating Performance Improvement Through Future-Focused Feedback." *PLoS One* 15(6): e0234444.

Green, P., F. Gino, and B. Staats. 2017. "Shopping for Confirmation: How Disconfirming Feedback Shapes Social Networks." Harvard Business School NOM Unit Working Paper No. 18-028.

Kluger, A. 2006. "Feedforward First, Feedback Later." A keynote lecture delivered at the 26th International Congress of Applied Psychology. Athens, Greece.

Kruger, J., and D. Dunning. 1999. "Unskilled and Unaware of It: How Difficulties in Recognizing One's Own Incompetence Led to Inflated Self-Assessments." *Journal of Personality and Social Psychology* 77(6): 1121–1134.

Luft, J. 1963. *Group Process: An Introduction to Group Dynamics.* Palo Alto, CA: National Press.

Nowack, K. 2013. "Development and Interpretation of the Emotional Intelligence View 360." Chapter in *Feedback to Managers: A Guide to Reviewing and Selecting Multirater Instruments for Leadership Development,* 4th ed., edited by J.B. Leslie. Center for Creative Leadership.

Nowack, K. 2014. "Taking the Sting Out of Feedback." *T+D* magazine, August.

Nowack, K. 2016. *From Insight to Improvement: Leveraging 360-Degree Feedback.* Envisia Learning.

Nowack, K. 2017. "Facilitating Successful Behavior Change: Beyond Goal Setting to Goal Flourishing." *Consulting Psychology Journal: Practice and Research* 70:1–19. dx.doi.org/10.1037/cpb0000088.

Sanchez, C., and S. Dunning. 2018. "Overconfidence Among Beginners: Is a Little Learning Dangerous Thing?" *Journal of Personality and Social Psychology* 114:10–28.

Schroeder, J., and A. Fishbach. 2015. "How to Motivate Yourself and Others? Intended and Unintended Consequences." *Research in Organizational Behavior* 35:123–141.

Tagliabue, M., S.S. Sigurjonsdottir, and I. Sandaker. 2020. "The Effects of Performance Feedback on Organizational Citizenship Behaviour: A Systematic Review and Meta-Analysis." *European Journal of Work and Organizational Psychology* 29(6): 841–861.

Taylor, S.E., M.E. Kemeny, G.M. Reed, J.E. Bower, T.L. Gruenewald. 2000. "Psychological Resources, Positive Illusions, and Health." *American Psychologist* 55:99–109. doi:10.1037/0003-066X.55.1.99.

Vergauwe, J., J. Hofmans, and B. Wille. 2022. "The Leadership Arena-Reputation-Identity (LARI) Model: Distinguishing Shared and Unique Perspectives in Multisource Leadership Ratings." *Journal of Applied Psychology* 107(12): 2243 -2268. doi.org/10.1037/apl0001012.

Zell, E., and Z. Krizan. 2014. "Do People Have Insight Into Their Abilities? A Metasynthesis." *Perspectives on Psychological Science* 9(2): 111–125. doi.org/10.1177/1745691613518075

Zenger, J., and J. Folkman. 2014. "Your Employees Want the Negative Feedback You Hate to Give." *Harvard Business Review*, January.

Chapter 2

Abi-Esber, N., J.E. Abel, J. Schroeder, and F. Gino. 2022. "'Just Letting You Know . . .' Underestimating Others' Desire for Constructive Feedback." *Journal of Personality and Social Psychology* 123(6): 1362–1385. doi.org/10.1037/pspi0000393.

Chen, Z., K. Williams, J. Fitness, and N. Newton. 2008. "When Hurt Will Not Heal." *Psychological Science* 19:789–795.

Danner, D.D., D.A. Snowdon, and W.V. Friesen. 2001. "Positive Emotions in Early Life and Longevity: Findings From the Nun Study." *Journal of Personality and Social Psychology* 80(5): 804–813. doi.org/10.1037/0022-3514.80.5.804.

DeWall, C., et al. 2010. "Acetaminophen Reduces Social Pain: Behavioral and Neural Evidence." *Psychological Science* 21:931–937.

Dickerson, S.S., and M.E. Kemeny. 2004. "Acute Stressors and Cortisol Responses: A Theoretical Integration and Synthesis of Laboratory Research." *Psychological Bulletin* 130(3): 355–391. 10.1037/0033-2909.130.3.355.

Eisenberger, N.I., M.D. Lieberman, and K.D. Williams. 2003. "Does Rejection Hurt? An FMRI Study of Social Exclusion." *Science* 302:290–292. doi: 10.1126/science.1089134.

Finkelstein, S.R., A. Fishbach, and Y. Tu. 2017. "When Friends Exchange Negative Feedback." *Motivation and Emotion* 41(1): 69–83. doi.org/10.1007/s11031-016-9589-z.

Fredrickson, B.L. 2004. "The Broaden–and–Build Theory of Positive Emotions." Philosophical Transactions of the Royal Society of London. *Series B: Biological Sciences* 359(1449): 1367–1377.

Gottman, J.M., and J.S. Gottman. 2015. "Gottman Couple Therapy." In *Clinical Handbook of Couple Therapy*, edited by A.S. Gurman, J.L. Lebow, and D.K. Snyder. The Guilford Press.

Gunnar, M.R., and B. Donzella. 2002. "Social Regulation of the Cortisol Levels in Early Human Development." *Psychoneuroendocrinology* 27(1-2): 199–220. doi: 10.1016/s0306-4530(01)00045-2.

Hambley, C. 2020. "CONNECT: A Brain-Friendly Model for Leaders and Organizations." *Consulting Psychology Journal: Practice and Research* 72(3): 168–197.

Keith, N., D. Horvath, A. Klamar, and M. Frese. 2022. "Failure to Learn From Failure Is Mitigated by Loss-Framing and Corrective Feedback: A Replication and Test of the Boundary Conditions of the Tune-Out Effect." *Journal of Experimental Psychology: General* 151(8): e19–e25.

Kiecolt-Glaser, J.K. 2018. "Marriage, Divorce, and the Immune System." *Am Psychol.* 73(9): 1098-1108. doi: 10.1037/amp0000388.

Kim, S.I., S. Hwang, M. Lee. 2018. "The Benefits of Negative Yet Informative Feedback." *PLoS One* 13(10): e0205183. doi: 10.1371/journal.pone.0205183.

Nash, R.A., et al. 2018. "A Memory Advantage for Past-Oriented Over Future-Oriented Performance Feedback." *Journal of Experimental Psychology: Learning, Memory, and Cognition* 44:1864–1879.

Neoh, M.J.Y., J.H. Teng, A. Lee, P. Setoh, C. Mulatti, and G. Esposito. 2022. "Negative Emotional Reactions to Criticism: Perceived Criticism and Source Affects Extent of Hurt and Relational Distancing." *PLoS One* 17(8): e0271869. doi.org/10.1371/journal.pone.0271869.

Nowack, K.M. 2013. "Coaching for Stress: StressScan." In *Psychometrics in Coaching*, edited by Jonathan Passmore. Kogan Page.

Nowack, K.M. 2016. "Toxic Bosses May Cause Health Risk." *Talent Management* magazine 12:26-29.

Nowack, K.M. 2017. "Sleep, Emotional Intelligence, and Interpersonal Effectiveness: Natural Bedfellows." *Consulting Psychology Journal: Practice and Research* 69:66–79.

Nowack, K.M., and P. Zak. 2020. "Empathy Enhancing Antidotes for Interpersonally Toxic Leaders." *Consulting Psychology Journal: Practice and Research* 72:119–130.

Parker, A., A. Gerbasi, and C.L. Porath. 2013. "The Effects of De-Energizing Ties in Organizations and How to Manage Them." *Organizational Dynamics* 42(2): 110–118. doi.org/10.1016/j.orgdyn.2013.03.004.

Pezirkianidis, C., E. Galanaki, G. Raftopoulou, D. Moraitou, and A. Stalikas. 2023. "Adult Friendship and Wellbeing: A Systematic Review With Practical Implications." *Frontiers in Psychology* 14:1059057. doi: 10.3389 /fpsyg.2023.1059057

Ruttan, R.L., and L.F. Nordgren. 2016. "The Strength to Face the Facts: Self-Regulation Defends Against Defensive Information Processing." *Organizational Behavior and Human Decision Processes* 137:86–98.

Shirom, A., S. Toker, Y. Alkaly, O. Jacobson, and R. Balicer. 2011. "Work-Based Predictors of Mortality: A 20-Year Follow-Up of Healthy Employees." *Health Psychology* 30:268–275.

Simon, L.S., C.C. Rosen, R.S. Gajendran, S. Ozgen, and E.S. Corwin. 2022. "Pain or Gain? Understanding How Trait Empathy Impacts Leader Effectiveness Following the Provision of Negative Feedback." *Journal of Applied Psychology* 107(2): 279–297. doi.org/10.1037/apl0000882.

Sleiman, A.A., S. Sigurjonsdottir, A. Elnes, N.A. Gage, and N.E. Gravina. 2020. "A Quantitative Review of Performance Feedback in Organizational Settings (1998–2018)." *Journal of Organizational Behavior Management* 40(3-4): 303–332.

Smither, J., and A.G. Walker. 2004. "Are the Characteristics of Narrative Comments Related to Improvement in 360-Degree Feedback Ratings Over Time?" *Journal of Applied Psychology* 89:575–581.

Stijovic, A., P.A.G. Forbes, L. Tomova, N. Skoluda, A.C. Feneberg, G. Piperno, E. Pronizius, U.M. Nater, C. Lamm, and G. Silani. 2023.

"Homeostatic Regulation of Energetic Arousal During Acute Social Isolation: Evidence From the Lab and the Field." *Psychological Science* 34(5): 537–551. doi.org/10.1177/09567976231156413.

Stroud, M.W., B.E. Thorn, M.P. Jensen, and J.L. Boothby. 2020. "The Relation Between Pain Beliefs, Negative Thoughts, and Psychosocial Functioning in Chronic Pain Patients." *Pain* 84(2): 347–352.

Taylor, S.E., L.C. Klein, B.P. Lewis, T.L. Gruenewald, R.A.R. Gurung, and J.A. Updegraff. 2000. "Biobehavioral Responses to Stress in Females: Tend-and-Befriend, Not Fight-or-Flight." *Psychological Review* 107:41–429.

Tian, Y.E., M.A. Di Biase, P.E. Mosley, M.K. Lupton, Y. Xia, J. Fripp, M. Breakspear, V. Cropley, and A. Zalesky. 2023. "Evaluation of Brain-Body Health in Individuals With Common Neuropsychiatric Disorders." *JAMA Psychiatry* 80(6): 567–576. doi: 10.1001/jamapsychiatry.2023.0791.

Thorson, K.R., and T.V. West. 2018. "Physiological Linkage to an Interaction Partner Is Negatively Associated With Stability in Sympathetic Nervous System Responding." *Biological Psychology* 138:91–95.

US Surgeon General. 2023. *Advisory on the Healing Effects of Social Connection and Community.* Department of Health and Human Services (HHS). hhs .gov/sites/default/files/surgeon-general-social-connection-advisory.pdf.

Xing, L., J. Sun, and D.M. Jepsen. 2020. "The Short-Term Effects of Supervisor Negative Feedback on Employee Well-Being and Performance." *Academy of Management.* doi.org/10.5465/AMBPP.2020 .14984abstract.

Xing, L., J.-m. Sun, and D. Jepsen. 2021. "Feeling Shame in the Workplace: Examining Negative Feedback as an Antecedent and Performance and Well-Being As Consequences." *Journal of Organizational Behavior* 42(9): 1244–1260. doi.org/10.1002/job.2553.

Yamanaka, Y., H. Motoshima, and K. Uchida. 2019. "Hypothalamic-Pituitary-Adrenal Axis Differentially Responses to Morning and Evening Psychological Stress in Healthy Subjects." *Neuropsychopharmacology Reports* 39:41–47.

Young, S.F., E.M. Richard, R.G. Moukarzel, L.A. Steelman, and W.A. Gentry. 2017. "How Empathic Concern Helps Leaders in Providing

Negative Feedback: A Two-Study Examination." *Journal of Occupational and Organizational Psychology* 90(4): 535–558. doi.org/10.1111/joop.12184.

Zak, P.J. 2018. "The Neuroscience of High-Trust Organizations." *Consulting Psychology Journal: Practice and Research* 70(1): 45–58. doi.org/10.1037 /cpb0000076.

Chapter 3

Abdulrehman, R. 2024. *Developing Anti-Racist Cultural Competence.* Newburyport, MA: Hogrefe Publishing.

Abi-Esber, N., J.E. Abel, J. Schroeder, and F. Gino. 2022. "'Just Letting You Know . . .' Underestimating Others' Desire for Constructive Feedback." *Journal of Personality and Social Psychology* 123(6): 1362–1385. doi.org/10 .1037/pspi0000393.

Amabile, T.M., and S.J. Kramer. 2011. "The Power of Small Wins." *Harvard Business Review,* May.

Austin, R.D., and G.P. Pisano. 2017. "Neurodiversity as a Competitive Advantage." *Harvard Business Review,* 96–103. hbr.org/2017/05/neuro diversity-as-a-competitive-advantage.

Bernstein, A.F. 2023. "Race Matters in Coaching: An Empirical Study of Coaches' Willingness to Have Difficult Conversations With Leaders of Color." *Consulting Psychology Journal* 75(1): 32–50.

Bhatti, K., and T. Roulet. 2023. "Helping an Employee in Distress." *Harvard Business Review,* September-October.

Cao, Y., L.S. Contreras-Huerta, J. McFadyen, and R. Cunnington. 2015. "Racial Bias in Neural Response to Others' Pain Is Reduced With Other-Race Contact." *Cortex* 70:68–78.

Carlin, B.A., B.D. Gelb, J.K. Belinne, and L. Ramchand. 2018. "Bridging the Gender Gap in Confidence." *Business Horizons* 61(5): 765–774.

Carlin, R., M. Carreras, and G. Love. 2020. "Presidents' Sex and Popularity: Baselines, Dynamics, and Policy Performance." *British Journal of Political Science* 50(4): 1359–1379. doi:10.1017/S0007123418000364.

Cho, I., B. Hu, and C.M. Berry. 2023. "A Matter of When, Not Whether: A Meta-Analysis of Modesty Bias in East Asian Self-Ratings of Job

Performance." *Journal of Applied Psychology* 108(2): 291–306. doi.org /10.1037/apl0001046.

Christov-Moore, L., N. Reggente, P.K. Douglas, J.D. Feusner, and M. Iacoboni. 2020. "Predicting Empathy From Resting State Brain Connectivity: A Multivariate Approach." *Frontiers in Integrative Neuroscience* 14(14): 3. doi: 10.3389/fnint.2020.00003.

Correll, S., and C. Simard. 2016. "Research: Vague Feedback Is Holding Women Back." *Harvard Business Review*, April.

Chopik, W.J., and K.J. Grimm. 2019. "Longitudinal Changes and Historic Differences in Narcissism From Adolescence to Older Adulthood." *Psychology and Aging* 34(8): 1109. DOI: 10.1037/pag0000379.

Croft, A., and T. Schmader. 2012. "The Feedback Withholding Bias: Minority Students Do Not Receive Critical Feedback From Evaluators Concerned About Appearing Racist." *Journal of Experimental Social Psychology* 48(5): 1139–1144.

Doldor, E., M. Wyatt, and J. Silvester. 2021. "Research: Men Get More Actionable Feedback Than Women." *Harvard Business Review*, February.

Doyle, N. 2020. "Neurodiversity At Work: A Biopsychosocial Model and the Impact on Working Adults." *British Medical Bulletin* 135(1): 108–125. doi.org/10.1093/bmb/ldaa021.

Dulebohn, J.H., et al. 2016. "Gender Differences in Justice Evaluations: Evidence From fMRI." *Journal of Applied Psychology* 101:151–170.

Dupree, C.H., and S.T. Fiske. 2019. "Self-Presentation in Interracial Settings: The Competence Downshift by White Liberals." *Journal of Personality and Social Psychology* 117(3): 579–604.

Eagly, A. 2023. "Once More: The Rise of Female Leaders. How Gender and Ethnicity Affect the Electability and Success of Women as Political Leaders." *American Psychological Association Research Brief.* apa.org/topics /women-girls/female-leaders.

Eagly, A.H., C. Nater, D.I. Miller, M. Kaufmann, and S. Sczesny. 2020. "Gender Stereotypes Have Changed: A Cross-Temporal Meta-Analysis of U.S. Public Opinion Polls From 1946 to 2018." *American Psychologist* 75(3): 301–315.

Finkelstein, L.M., E.C. Voyles, C.L. Thomas, and H. Zacher. 2020. "A Daily Diary Study of Responses to Age Meta-Stereotypes." *Work, Aging, & Retirement* 6:28–45.

Gerhardt, M., J. Nachemson-Ekwall, and B. Fogel. 2021. *Gentelligence: The Revolutionary Approach to Leading an Intergenerational Workforce*. New York: Rowman & Littlefield.

Gibson, S., and J. Fernandez. 2018. *Gender Diversity and Non-Binary Inclusion in the Workplace*. Philadelphia: Jessica Kingsley Publishers.

Goulet, J.D. 2022. "Stop Asking Neurodivergent People to Change the Way They Communicate." *Harvard Business Review*, October.

Hofstede, G. 2001. *Culture's Consequences: Comparing Values, Behaviors, Institutions, and Organizations Across Nations*, 2nd ed. Thousand Oaks, CA: SAGE.

Humiston, J. 2023. "Gender Inclusivity With Intention: There Are Several Ways to Enhance the Workplace Climate for Transgender and Nonbinary Employees." *TD* 77(6): 18.

Kelly, D., et al. 2008. "Three-Month-Olds, But Not Newborns, Prefer Own-Race Faces." *Developmental Science* 8:F31–F36.

Kirkland, R.A., E. Peterson, C.A. Baker, S. Miller, and S. Pulos. 2013. "Meta-Analysis Reveals Adult Female Superiority in 'Reading the Mind in the Eyes' Test." *North American Journal of Psychology* 15(1): 121–146.

Kunze, F., and J.I. Menges. 2017. "Younger Supervisors, Older Subordinates: An Organizational-Level Study of Age Differences, Emotions, and Performance." *Journal of Organizational Behavior* 38(4): 461–486. doi.org/10.1002/job.2129.

Livermore, D. 2015. *Leading with Cultural Intelligence: The Real Secret to Success*. AMACOM.

Longmire, N.H., and D.A. Harrison. 2018. "Seeing Their Side Versus Feeling Their Pain: Differential Consequences of Perspective-Taking and Empathy at Work." *Journal of Applied Psychology* 103(8): 894–915. doi.org/10.1037/apl0000307.

Martin, S.R. 2017. "Research: Men Get Credit for Voicing Ideas, But Not Problems. Women Don't Get Credit for Either." *Harvard Business Review*, November 2.

Mashihi, S., and K. Nowack. 2013. *Clueless: Coaching People Who Just Don't Get It*, 2nd ed. Santa Monica, CA: Envisia Learning.

McClean, E.E., S.R. Martin, K.J. Emich, and T. Woodruff. 2016. "The Social Consequences of Voice: An Examination of Voice Type and Gender on Status and Subsequent Leader Emergence." *Academy of Management Journal* 61(5).

Meyer, E. 2014. *The Culture Map: Breaking Through the Invisible Boundaries of Global Business*. Public Affairs.

Meyer, E. 2023. "When Diversity Meets Feedback: How to Promote Candor Across Gender and Generational Divides." *Harvard Business Review*, September-October.

Nowack, K.M., and S. Mashihi. 2012. "Evidence Based Answers to 15 Questions About Leveraging 360-Degree Feedback." *Consulting Psychology Journal* 64(3): 157–182.

Nowack, K.M., and A. Munro. 2019. "Emotional and Social Competency: The Female Advantage." *Training Journal Magazine* June, 29–31.

Nowack, K.M., and P. Zak. 2020. "Empathy Enhancing Antidotes for Interpersonally Toxic Leaders." *Consulting Psychology Journal: Research and Practice* 72:119–130.

Paolini, S., F.A. White, L.R. Tropp, et al. 2021. "Intergroup Contact Research in the 21st Century: Lessons Learned and Forward Progress if We Remain Open." *Journal of Social Issues* 77:11–37.

Paquette-Smith, M., H. Buckler, K.S. White, J. Choi, and E.K. Johnson. 2019. "The Effect of Accent Exposure on Children's Sociolinguistic Evaluation of Peers." *Developmental Psychology* 55(4): 809–822.

Praslova, L.N. 2024. *The Canary Code: A Guide to Neurodiversity, Dignity, and Intersectional Belonging at Work*. Oakland, CA: Berrett-Koehler Publishers.

Ravid, D.M., D.P. Costanza, and M.R. Romero. 2024. "Generational Differences At Work? A Meta-Analysis and Qualitative Investigation." *Journal of Organizational Behavior* doi.org/10.1002/job.2827.

Rudolph, C.W., R.S. Rauvola, and H. Zacher. 2018. "Leadership and Generations at Work: A Critical Review." *The Leadership Quarterly* 29(1): 44–57. doi.org/10.1016/j.leaqua.2017.09.004.

Salerno, J., et al. 2018. "Closing With Emotion: The Differential Impact of Male Versus Female Attorneys Expressing Anger in Court." *Law and Human Behavior* 42:385–401.

Schröder, M. 2023. "Work Motivation Is Not Generational but Depends on Age and Period." *Journal of Business and Psychology* 30:897–908.

Sheppard, L.D., T.M. Trzebiatowski, and J.J. Prasad. 2024. "Paternalism in the Performance Context: Evaluators Who Feel Social Pressure to Avoid Exhibiting Prejudice Deliver More Inflated Performance Feedback to Women." *Journal of Business and Psychology.* Advance online publication. doi.org/10.1007/s10869-024-09964-5.

Sherbin, L., J.T. Kennedy, P. Jain-Link, and K. Ihezie. 2017. "Disabilities and Inclusion: US Findings." Coqual, formerly Centre for Talent and Innovation Publishing. coqual.org/wp-content/uploads/2020/09/CoqualDisabilitiesInclusion_KeyFindings090720.pdf.

Simon, L.S., C.C. Rosen, R.S. Gajendran, S. Ozgen, and E.S. Corwin. 2022. "Pain or Gain? Understanding How Trait Empathy Impacts Leader Effectiveness Following the Provision of Negative Feedback." *Journal of Applied Psychology* 107(2): 279–297. doi.org/10.1037/apl0000882.

Stelling, D. 2023. "Do Applicants From Generation X, Y, Z Differ in Personality Traits? Data From Selection Procedures in Aviation (1987-2019)." *Frontiers in Psychology* (14):1173622. doi: 10.3389/fpsyg.2023.

Taylor, S.E. 2006. "Tend and Befriend: Biobehavioral Bases of Affiliation Under Stress." *Current Directions in Psychological Science* 15(6): 273–277. doi.org/10.1111/j.1467-8721.2006.00451.x.

Textio. 2023. "The Truth About Bias in Performance Feedback." Texico. textio.com/feedback-bias.

Textio. 2024. "Language Bias in Performance Feedback." Textio, textio.com/feedback-bias-2024.

UNDP (United Nations Development Programme). 2023. *2023 Gender Social Norms Index (GSNI): Breaking Down Gender Biases: Shifting Social Norms Towards Gender Equality.* New York.

Vaughn, D.A., R.R. Savjani, M.S. Cohen, and D.M. Eagleman. 2018. "Empathetic Neural Responses Predict Group Alliance." *Frontiers in Human Neuroscience* 12:1–10. doi: 10.3389/fnhum.2018.00302.

White Hughto, J.M., S.L. Reisner, and J.E. Pachankis. 2015. "Transgender Stigma and Health: A Critical Review of Stigma Determinants, Mechanisms, and Interventions." *Social Science and Medicine* 147:222–231. doi: 10.1016/j.socscimed.2015.11.010.

Wisdom, J.P., and M. Brancu. 2021. *Millennials' Guide to Workplace Politics: What No One Ever Told You About Power and Influence.* Winding Pathway Books.

Xiao, N.G., R. Wu, P.C. Quinn, S. Liu, K.S. Tummeltshammer, N.Z. Kirkham, L. Ge, O. Pascalis, and K. Lee. 2017. "Infants Rely More on Gaze Cues From Own-Race Than Other-Race Adults for Learning Under Uncertainty." *Child Development* DOI: 10.1111/cdev.12798.

Zenger, J., and J. Folkman. 2014. "Your Employees Want the Negative Feedback You Hate to Give." *Harvard Business Review,* January.

Zloteanu, M., P. Bull, E.G. Krumhuber, and D.C. Richardson. 2021. "Veracity Judgment, Not Accuracy: Reconsidering the Role of Facial Expressions, Empathy, and Emotion Recognition Training on Deception Detection." *Quarterly Journal of Experimental Psychology* 74(5): 910–927. doi.org/10.1177/1747021820978851.

Chapter 4

Berkman, E.T. 2018. "The Neuroscience of Goals and Behavior Change." *Consulting Psychology Journal: Practice and Research* 70:28–44. doi.org/10.1037/cpb0000094.

Bonezzi, A., C.M. Brendl, and M. De Angelis. 2011. "Stuck in the Middle: The Psychophysics of Goal Pursuit." *Psychological Science* 22(5): 607–612.

Boyatzis, R.E., and A.I. Jack. 2018. "The Neuroscience of Coaching." *Consulting Psychology Journal: Practice and Research* 70(1): 11–27.

Buyalskaya, A., H. Ho, K.L. Milkman, X. Li, A.L. Duckworth, and C. Camerer. 2023. "What Can Machine Learning Teach Us About Habit Formation? Evidence From Exercise and Hygiene." *PNAS Proceedings of the National Academy of Sciences of the United States of America* 120(17): 1–7. doi.org/10.1073/pnas.2216115120.

DePhillips, F.A., W.M. Berliner, and J.J. Cribbin. 1960. *Management of Training Programs.* Homewood, IL: R.D. Irwin.

Elfer, J., and Z. Belovai. 2024. "How to Lead Like a Coach." *Harvard Business Review*, September. hbr.org/2024/09/how-to-lead-like-a-coach.

Fogg, B.J. 2020. *Tiny Habits: The Small Changes That Change Everything.* Harvest Press.

Gollwitzer, P.M., and P. Sheeran. 2006. "Implementation Intentions and Goal Achievement: A Meta-Analysis of Effects and Processes." *Advances in Experimental Social Psychology* 38:69–119.

Grill-Spector, K., R. Henson, and A. Martie. 2006. "Repetition and the Brain: Neural Models of Stimulus-Specific Effects." *Trends in Cognitive Sciences* 10:14–23.

Lally, P., C. Van Jaarsveld, H. Potts, and J. Wardle. 2009. "How Are Habits Formed: Modeling Habit Formation in the Real World." *European Journal of Social Psychology* 1009:998–1009.

Macnamara, B.N., D.Z. Hambrick, and F.L. Oswald. 2014. "Deliberate Practice and Performance in Music, Games, Sports, Education, and Professions: A Meta-Analysis." *Psychological Science* 25(8): 1608–1618.

Miller, G.E., and C. Wrosch. 2007. "You've Gotta Know When to Fold 'Em: Goal Disengagement and Systemic Inflammation in Adolescence." *Psychological Science* 18(9): 773–777.

Neal, D.T., W. Wood, and J.M. Quinn. 2006. "Habits—A Repeat Performance." *Current Directions in Psychological Science* 15(4): 198–202. doi.org/10.1111/j.1467-8721.2006.00435.x.

Nowack, K.M. 2015. "Urban Talent Myths Exposed." *Talent Management* magazine 11: 35–37, 47.

Nowack, K.M. 2017a. "Facilitating Successful Behavior Change: Beyond Goal Setting to Goal Flourishing." *Consulting Psychology Journal: Practice and Research* 70:1–19.

Nowack, K.M. 2017b. "Sleep, Emotional Intelligence, and Interpersonal Effectiveness: Natural Bedfellows." *Consulting Psychology Journal: Research and Practice* 69:66–79.

Nowack, K.M. 2019. "From Insight to Successful Behavior Change: The Real Impact of Development-Focused 360 Feedback." In *The Handbook of Strategic 360 Feedback*, edited by A.H. Church, D.W. Bracken, J.W. Fleenor, and D.S. Rose. New York: Oxford University Press.

Nowack, K.M. 2024. "The Neuroscience of Successful Habit Change for Coaches: A One-Night Stand or a Lasting Relationship?" Association for Coaching, *Coaching Perspectives* 40:48–49.

Patel, M.S., et al. 2016. "Framing Financial Incentives to Increase Physical Activity Among Overweight and Obese Adults: A Randomized, Controlled Trial." *Annals of Internal Medicine* 164(6): 385–394.

Prochaska, J.O., and W.F. Velicer. 1997. "The Transtheoretical Model of Health Behavior Change." *American Journal of Health Promotion* 12:38–48.

Schoen, M., and K. Nowack. 2013. "Reconditioning the Stress Response Reduces the Inflammatory Cytokine IL-6 and Influences Resilience: A Pilot Study." *Complementary Therapies in Clinical Practice* 19:83–88.

Shen, L., A. Fishbach, and C.K. Hsee. 2015. The Motivating-Uncertainty Effect: Uncertainty Increases Resource Investment in the Process of Reward Pursuit." *Journal of Consumer Research* 41(5): 1301–1315.

van Donge, E.V., I.H.P. Kersten, I.C. Wagner, R.G.M. Morris, and G. Fernández. 2016. "Physical Exercise Performed Four Hours After Learning Improves Memory Retention and Increases Hippocampal Pattern Similarity During Retrieval." *Current Biology* 11;26(13):1722-1727. doi: 10.1016/j.cub.2016.04.071.

Williams, J., and K.M. Nowack. 2022. "Neuroscience Hacks to Enhance Learning Agility in Leaders." *Consulting Psychology Journal: Practice and Research* 74(3): 291–310. doi.org/10.1037/cpb0000231.

Woolley, K., and A. Fischbach. 2017. "What Separates Goals We Achieve from Goals We Don't." *Harvard Business Review*, April.

Chapter 5

Anseel, A., and E.N. Sherf. 2024. "A 25-Year Review of Research on Feedback in Organizations: From Simple Rules to Complex Realities." *The Annual Review of Organizational Psychology and Organizational Behavior* 12:51–5.25.

Casciaro, T., and M.S. Lobo. 2005. "Competent Jerks, Lovable Fools, and the Formation of Social Networks." *Harvard Business Review*, June.

Cuddy, A.J.C., S.T. Fiske, and P. Glick. 2008. "Warmth and Competence as Universal Dimensions of Social Perception: The Stereotype Content

Model and the BIAS Map." *Advances in Experimental Social Psychology* 40:61–149. doi.org/10.1016/S0065-2601(07)00002-0.

Eisenbruch, A.B., and M.M. Krasnow. 2022. "Why Warmth Matters More Than Competence: A New Evolutionary Approach." *Perspectives on Psychological Science* 17(6): 1604–1623. doi.org/10.1177 /17456916211071087.

Fiske, S., A. Cuddy, and P. Glick. 2007. "Universal Dimensions of Social Cognition: Warmth and Competence." *Trends in Cognitive Sciences* 11:77–83.

Fiske, S.T., A.J.C. Cuddy, P. Glick, and J. Xu. 2002. "A Model of (Often Mixed) Stereotype Content: Competence and Warmth Respectively Follow From Perceived Status and Competition." *Journal of Personality and Social Psychology* 82(6): 878–902. doi.org/10.1037/0022-3514.82.6.878.

Chapter 6

American Psychiatric Association (APA). 2013. *Diagnostic and Statistical Manual of Mental Disorders,* 5th ed. APA. doi.org/10.1176/appi.books .9780890425596.

Amabile, T.M., and S.J. Kramer. 2011. "The Power of Small Wins." *Harvard Business Review* 89(5): May.

American Psychological Association (APA). 2023. "Stress in America: Workplaces as Engines of Psychological Health and Well-Being." American Psychological Association, August. apa.org/pubs/reports /work-in-america/2023-workplace-health-well-being.

American Psychological Association (APA). 2024. "Work in American Survey: Psychological Safety in the Changing Workplace." American Psychological Association, June. apa.org/pubs/reports/work-in-america /2024/2024-work-in-america-report.pdf.

Braun, S. 2017. "Leader Narcissism and Outcomes in Organizations: A Review at Multiple Levels of Analysis and Implications for Future Research." *Frontiers of Psychology* 8. DOI: 10.3389/fpsyg.2017.00773.

Casciaro T., and M.S. Lobo. 2005. "Competent Jerks, Lovable Fools, and the Formation of Social Networks." *Harvard Business Review* 83(6): 92–999, 149.

Chong, A., et al. 2017. "ADP Ribosyl-Cyclases (CD38/CD157), Social Skills and Friendship." *Psychoneuroendocrinology* 78:185–192. doi.org/10.1016 /j.psyneuen.2017.01.011.

Eisenberger, N.I., M.D. Lieberman, and K.D. Williams. 2003. "Does Rejection Hurt? An FMRI Study of Social Exclusion." *Science* 302:290-2. doi: 10.1126/science.1089134.

Fisher, J., S. Cantrell, J. Bhatt, and P.H. Silverglate. 2024. "Workplace Well-Being Report 2024." Deloitte Insights, June 18. deloitte.com/us/en /insights/topics/talent/workplace-well-being-research-2024.html.

Galvin, B.M., D.A. Waldman, and P. Balthazard. 2010. "Visionary Communication Qualities as Mediators of the Relationship Between Narcissism and Attributions of Leader Charisma." *Personnel Psychology* 63(3): 509–537.

Grijalva, E., P.D. Harms, D.A. Newman, B.H. Gaddis, and C. Fraley. 2010. "Narcissism and Leadership: A Meta-Analytic Review of Linear and Nonlinear Relationships." *Personnel Psychology* 68:1–47. doi.org/10.1111 /peps.12072.

Ivcevic, Z., R. Stern, and A. Faas. 2021. "Research: What People Need to Work at a High Level?" *Harvard Business Review*, May 17.

Kaye, B., and S. Jordan-Evans. 2015. *Hello Stay Interviews, Goodbye Talent Loss: A Manager's Playbook*. Berrett-Koehler Publishers.

Korolevich, S. 2022. "Horrible Bosses: Are Americans Quitting Their Jobs or Quitting Their Managers?" GoodHire, January 11. goodhire.com /resources/articles/horrible-bosses-survey.

Kruger, J., and D. Dunning. 1999. "Unskilled and Unaware of It: How Difficulties in Recognizing One's Own Incompetence Lead to Inflated Self-Assessments." *Journal of Personality and Social Psychology* 77(6): 1121.

Nowack, K., and S. Mashihi. 2012. "Evidence Based Answers to 15 Questions about Leveraging 360-Degree Feedback." *Consulting Psychology Journal* 64(3): 157–182.

Nowack, K.M., and A. Munro. 2019. "Emotional and Social Competence: Old Wine in a New Bottle?" *Training Journal* magazine, May.

Society for Human Resources Management. 2020. "Survey: 84 Percent of U.S. Workers Blame Bad Managers for Creating Unnecessary Stress." shrm.org/about/press-room/survey-84-percent-u-s-workers-blame-bad -managers-creating-unnecessary-stress.

World Economic Forum (WEF). 2020. "Future of Jobs Report: 2020." weforum.org/reports/the-future-of-jobs-report-2020.

Chapter 7

American Psychological Association (APA). 2023. "Stress in America: Workplaces as Engines of Psychological Health and Well-Being." American Psychological Association, August. apa.org/pubs/reports /work-in-america/2023-workplace-health-well-being.

American Psychological Association (APA). 2024. "Work in American Survey: Psychological Safety in the Changing Workplace." American Psychological Association, June. apa.org/pubs/reports/work-in-america /2024/2024-work-in-america-report.pdf.

Avrane-Chopard, J., and J. Potter. 2019. "Are Hard and Soft Skills Rewarded Equally?" McKinsey & Company, November 4. mckinsey.com/capabilities /people-and-organizational-performance/our-insights/the-organization -blog/are-hard-and-soft-skills-rewarded-equally

Casciaro, T., and M.S. Lobo. 2005. "Competent Jerks, Lovable Fools, and the Formation of Social Networks." *Harvard Business Review,* June.

Deloitte. 2023. "Gen Z and Millennial Survey, 12th Edition." Deloitte. deloitte.com/global/en/issues/work/content/genzmillennialsurvey.html.

Digital Marketing Institute. 2022. "16 Brands Doing Corporate Social Responsibility Successfully." Digital Marketing Institute, January 2. digitalmarketinginstitute.com/blog/corporate-16-brands-doing -corporate-social-responsibility-successfully.

Fisher, J., S. Cantrell, J. Bhatt, and P.H. Silverglate. 2024. "The Important Role of Leaders in Advancing Human Sustainability." Deloitte Insights, June 18. deloitte.com/us/en/insights/topics/talent/workplace-well-being -research-2024.html.

Kaiser, R.B., and D.V. Overfield. 2011. "Strengths, Strengths Overused, and Lopsided Leadership." *Consulting Psychology Journal: Practice and Research* 63(2): 89–109. doi.org/10.1037/a0024470.

Kreacic, A., J. Romeo, L. Uribe. 2023. "How to Recruit Generation Z Workers—and Keep Them." World Economic Forum (WEF) Annual Meeting, January 16. weforum.org/agenda/2023/01/how -to-recruit-generation-z-workers-and-keep-them-davos23.

Lee, H. 2023. "Gen Z in the Workplace: How Should Companies Adapt?" John Hopkins University, April 18. imagine.jhu.edu/blog/2023/04/18 /gen-z-in-the-workplace-how-should-companies-adapt.

May, C. 2024. "Feedback for Better Performance." *TD at Work*. Alexandria, VA: ATD Press.

Pendell, R. 2023. *Engagement for Boomers: What They Want, How to Give It.* Gallup. gallup.com/workplace/509021/engagement-boomers-give.aspx.

Seligman, M.E.P., T. Rashid, and A.C. Parks. 2006. "Positive Psychotherapy." *American Psychologist* 61(8): 774–788. doi.org/10.1037/0003-066X.61.8.774.

West, T. 2022. *Jerks at Work: Toxic Coworkers and What to Do About Them.* Penguin.

Wisdom, J.P., and M. Brancu. 2022. *Millennials' Guide to Workplace Politics: What No One Ever Told You About Power and Influence.* Winding Pathway Books.

Chapter 8

Casciaro, T., and M.S. Lobo. 2005. "Competent Jerks, Lovable Fools, and the Formation of Social Networks." *Harvard Business Review* 83(6): 92-99, 149.

Lawton, R., M. Conner, and R. McEachan. 2009. "Desire or Reason: Predicting Health Behaviors From Affective and Cognitive Attitudes." *Health Psychology* 28(1): 56–65. doi.org/10.1037/a0013424.

Gailliot, M.T., R.F. Baumeister, C.N. DeWall, J.K. Maner, E.A. Plant, D.M. Tice, L.E. Brewer, and B.J. Schmeichel. 2007. "Self-Control Relies on Glucose As a Limited Energy Source: Willpower Is More Than a Metaphor." *Journal of Personality and Social Psychology* 92(2): 325–336. doi.org/10.1037/0022-3514.92.2.325.

Mager, R.F., and P. Pipe. 1997. *Analyzing Performance Problems: Or You Really Oughta Wanna—How to Figure out Why People Aren't Doing What They Should Be, and What to do About It*, 3rd ed. Center for Effective Performance.

Nowack, K.M. 2015. "Urban Talent Myths Exposed." *Talent Management*, 11: 35–37, 47

Nowack, K. 2017. "Facilitating Successful Behavior Change: Beyond Goal Setting to Goal Flourishing." *Consulting Psychology Journal: Practice and Research* 70:1–19. dx.doi.org/10.1037/cpb0000088.

Ogurlu, U. 2023. "A Meta-Analytic Review of Emotional Intelligence in Gifted Individuals: A Multilevel Analysis." *Personality and Individual Differences* 171. doi.org/10.1016/j.paid.2020.110503.

Richardson, K., and S.H. Norgate. 2015. "Does IQ Really Predict Job Performance?" *Applied Developmental Science* 19(3): 153–169. doi.org/10.10 80/10888691.2014.983635.

Sackett, P.R., C. Zhang, C.M. Berry, and F. Lievens. 2022. "Revisiting Meta-Analytic Estimates of Validity in Personnel Selection: Addressing Systematic Overcorrection for Restriction of Range." *Journal of Applied Psychology* 107(11): 2040–2068. doi.org/10.1037/apl0000994.

Treglown, L., and A. Furnham. 2023. "Are EQ and IQ Negatively Related? The Relationship Between Trait Emotional Intelligence and Fluid Cognitive Ability." *Psychology* 14:1136–1151. DOI: 10.4236/psych.2023 .147062.

Whitmore, J. 2009. *Coaching for Performance: Growing Human Potential and Purpose—The Principles and Practice of Coaching and Leadership*, 4th ed. London: Nicholas Brealey Publishing.

Zenger, J., and J. Folkman. 2013. "The Ideal Praise-to-Criticism Ratio." Harvard Business Review, March 15. hbr.org/2013/03/the-ideal-praise -to-criticism.

Zenger, J., and J. Folkman. 2015. "Feedback: The Powerful Paradox." Zenger Folkman Whitepaper.

Zetlitz, M., and A. Heivoll. 2023. "7 Key Corporate Learning Trends in 2023." eLearning Industry, January 31. elearningindustry.com/key -corporate-learning-trends-in-2023.

Chapter 9

Casciaro, T., and M.S. Lobo. 2005. "Competent Jerks, Lovable Fools, and the Formation of Social Networks." *Harvard Business Review*, June.

Deloitte. 2023. "Gen Z and Millennial Survey, 12th Edition." Deloitte. deloitte.com/global/en/issues/work/content/genzmillennialsurvey.html.

Glomb, T.M., D.P. Bhave, A.G. Miner, and M. Wall. 2011. "Doing Good, Feeling Good: Examining the Role of Organizational Citizenship Behaviors in Changing Mood." *Personnel Psychology* 64(1): 191–223.

Glomb, T.M., C. Hulin, and A.G. Miner. 2005. "Experience Sampling Mood and Its Correlates at Work." *Journal of Occupational and Organizational Psychology* 78:171–193.

Gallup. 2024. "State of the Global Workplace Report." Gallup. gallup.com /workplace/349484/state-of-the-global-workplace.aspx.

Jacob, C. 2023. "Levi's CEO Says His Biggest Mistake Was Not Firing the Wrong People Fast Enough." CNBC, September 27. cnbc.com/2023 /09/27/levis-ceo-my-biggest-mistake-was-not-firing-wrong-people-fast -enough.html.

Knight, R. 2021. "When You're Stuck Working With a Slacker." *Harvard Business Review*, May 14.

Pendell, R. 2022. "Employee Engagement Strategies: Fixing the World's $8.8 Trillion Problem." Gallup Workplace, June. gallup.com/workplace /393497/world-trillion-workplace-problem.aspx.

Zenger, J., and J. Folkman. 2022. "Quiet Quitting Is About Bad Bosses, Not Bad Employees." *Harvard Business Review*, August.

Zhenjing, G., S. Chupradit, K.Y. Ku, A.A. Nassani, and M. Haffar. 2022. "Impact of Employees' Workplace Environment on Employees' Performance: A Multi-Mediation Model." *Front Public Health* 13(10): 890400. doi: 10.3389/fpubh.2022.890400.

Chapter 10

Nowack, K.M. 2023. "Outgoing editorial for Consulting Psychology Journal [Editorial]." *Consulting Psychology Journal* 75(4): 315–321. doi.org/10.1037 /cpb0000268.

Terblanche, N.H.D., M. van Heerden, and R. Hunt. 2024. "The Influence of an Artificial Intelligence Chatbot Coach Assistant on the Human Coach-Client Working Alliance." *Coaching: An International Journal of Theory, Research and Practice.* doi.org/10.1080/17521882.2024.2304792.

Passmore, J., S.J. Diller, S. Isaacson, and M. Brantl. 2024. *The Digital and AI Coaches' Handbook the Complete Guide to the Use of Online, AI, and Technology in Coaching.* Routledge.

Tavis, A., and W. Woodward. 2024. *The Digital Coaching Revolution: How to Support Employee Development With Coaching Tech.* Kogan Page.

Tong, S., N. Jia, X. Luo, and Z. Fang. 2021. "The Janus Face of Artificial Intelligence Feedback: Deployment Versus Disclosure Effects on Employee Performance." *Strategic Management Journal* 42: 1600–1631. doi.org/10.1002/smj.3322.

Conclusion

Leimbach, M. 2024. "Seismic Shifts in Leadership Development." *Training*, May 9. trainingmag.com/seismic-shifts-in-leadership-development.

Leimach, M., and T. Roth. 2024. "The Leadership Development Mismatch." *TD* 78:34–37. td.org/magazines/td-magazine/the-leadership -development-mismatch.

Sutton, R., and B. Wigert. 2019. "More Harm Than Good: The Truth About Performance Reviews." Gallup Workplace, May 6. gallup.com /workplace/249332/harm-good-truth-performance-reviews.aspx.

Index

Page numbers followed by *f* and *t* refer to figures and tables, respectively.

A

Abdulrehman, Rehman, 69–70
acceptance, 18–20, 22*t*
acknowledge, respond, and change
  (ARC) model, 52
action
  commitment to, 20–21, 22*t*
  compassionate, 47
active listening, 128
*Advisory on the Healing Effects
  of Social Connection and
  Community,* 36
age, 72–76
age biases, 75
agendas, 192
AI (artificial intelligence), 201–205
Alphabet, 141
Americans With Disabilities Act
  (ADA), 50
Analyzing Performance Problems
  (Mager and Pipe), 165

Angelou, Maya, 207
anti-racist cultural competence,
  69–72
APA, 124
aphantasia, 49
ARC (acknowledge, respond, and
  change) model, 52
artificial intelligence (AI), 201–205
Asian employees, 59, 62
attribution bias, 57
autonomy, 142

B

baby boomers, 72, 73*t*, 76*t*
BDNF (brain-derived neurotrophic
  factor), 87
behavior change, 81–97
  coaching for, 208
  from feedback, 19
  goal setting, 82–84
  goal striving, 85–89

behavior change (*continued*)
neuroscience of, 89–90
3E Model of Successful
Individual, 89–96
Bergh, Charles, 186
Berkman, Elliot, 82
Bhatti, Kiran, 54
biases
age, 75
in AI, 203
AI reducing, 202
attribution, 57
confirmatory, 57, 202
conscious, 55–56
contrast, 57
cultural, 71–72
gender, 65
horns vs. halo, 56
in-group, 58–59
leniency, 56
minimizing gender, 65
negativity, 39
primacy, 56
racial, 60
recency, 56, 202
self-enhancement, 13–14
similar-to-me, 56
strictness, 56
unconscious, 54–58, 78–79
Black employees, 59, 62
blind spot, 16–17, 126–127
Boyatzis, Richard, 90
brain, 25
and goal setting, 82, 83*t*

and goal striving, 85*t*
and pain, 27
and unconscious biases, 57–58
brain-derived neurotrophic factor
(BDNF), 87
bright-side personality factors, 48*t*
broaden-and-build theory, 32
bullying, 24
burnout, 46–47
Buyalskaya, Anastasia, 87

C

The Canary Code (Praslova), 50
candid feedback, 20, 128–129
career paths, 148–153, 149*t*, 151*t*,
152*t*, 153*f*
Casciaro, T., 108, 112, 164
Case Western Reserve University,
87, 90
chatbots, 203–204
check-in dates, 171
Claremont University, 64
coach, role of, 173*t*
coaching, 172
coaching groups, 6
cognitive reappraisal, 52, 53
commitment to action, 20–21, 22*t*
compassionate action, 47
compassion-based approach, 90
competence, 6, 106
competent jerks, 106–107, 110
confidence, 15
confirmatory bias, 57, 202
confirmatory feedback, 40

conscientiousness, 49

conscious biases, 55–56

consequences, discussing, 190, 195

constructive feedback, 37–38

contempt, defined, 31

contrast bias, 57

corrective feedback, 18

COVID-19 pandemic, 36, 123, 141

cringe factor, 26

critical feedback, 26

criticism, defined, 31

Cuddy, Amy, 105

cultural biases, 71–72

The Culture Map (Meyer), 68

culture maps, 68

culture models, 68–69

cultures, 67–72
    and anti-racist cultural compe-
        tence, 69–72
    anti-racist cultural competence
        framework, 69–72
    and culture models, 68–69
    workplace, 138–142, 139*t*

Cyberball paradigm, 27–29

D

dACC (dorsal anterior cingulate
    cortex), 27, 85*t*

Danner, Deborah, 30

dark-triad personality factors, 48*t*

decision matrix, 168*f*

default mode network (DMN), 82,
    83*t*

defensiveness, 31, 127–128

DEIB, 141–142

Deloitte, 139, 142

derailment factors, 149

DESC technique, 130–131, 133

detachment, healthy, 47

*Developing Anti-Racist Cultural
    Competence* (Abdulrehman), 69

DeWall, C. Nathan, 28–29

disorders, interpersonal, 121–122,
    134

DMN (default mode network), 82,
    83*t*

dorsal anterior cingulate cortex
    (dACC), 27, 85*t*

Dunning-Kruger effect, 15,
    126–127

E

Eagle Hill Performance
    Management and Feedback
    Survey, 4

Eagleman, David, 55

EI. *See* emotional intelligence

Eisenberger, Naomi, 27–28

emotional contagion, 30

emotional intelligence (EI)
    and gender, 62
    importance of, 122–124
    and self-awareness, 13–14

emotional stability, 48

emotions, 25, 30, 31–32

empathy, 46–47, 46–49
    and gender, 64
    high trait, 46

empathy (*continued*)

    importance of, 12–13, 154

    and unconscious bias, 55

employee(s)

    disengagement of, 2–3

    engagement of, 51–54, 53*t*

    and gender, 64–65

    and race, 59

enable stage (in 3E Model of Successful Individual), 94–95

encourage stage (in 3E Model of Successful Individual), 93–94

engagement, 51–54, 52, 53*t*

engagement review meetings, 187–189, 187*t*

enlighten stage (in 3E Model of Successful Individual), 92–93

entrepreneurial career path, 148, 152, 152*t*

extraversion, 48

F

Faas, Andrew, 122–123

feedback, 11–22

    candid, 20, 128–129

    common mistakes when giving, 103–104

    confirmatory, 40

    constructive, 37–38

    corrective, 18

    critical, 26

    and Dunning-Kruger effect, 15

    factors affecting (*See* feedback factors)

    forward-in-time, 37

    hostile, 26

    ineffective, 104

    informative, 39–40

    limits of, 38–39

    negative, 18

    negative informative, 40

    outcomes of, 18–20

    and self-awareness, 13–17

    supportive climate for, 42*t*, 100

    tips for successful, 22*t*

feedback factors

    age, 72–76

    cultural differences, 67–72

    empathy, 46–47

    employee engagement, 51–54

    gender, 60–67

    and good relationships, 45

    neurodivergence, 49–51

    personality, 47–49

    race, 58–60

    unconscious bias, 54–58

feedback gap, 4–6

feedback loop, 17

feedback ratios, positive-to-negative, 29–32

feedback sandwich, 19–20

feedforward, 20, 37*f*

flow state, 95

fMRI, 58

Folkman, J., 73, 172

fools, likable, 106–107, 112

forward-in-time feedback, 37

Frederickson, Barbara, 31

The Future of Jobs Report 2020, 124

G

Gallup, 3, 183, 208

gender, 60–67

    and microaggressions, 65–67

    neurobiology of men and
        women, 62–64

    transgender and nonbinary
        employees, 64–65

gender bias, 65

generalist career path, 148, 151,
    152*t*

generational differences, 74, 140*t,*
    142–143

Generation X, 72–73, 73*t,* 76*t,* 140

Generation Y, 73*t,* 76*t. See also*
    millennials

Generation Z, 72, 76*t,* 140–141

Gentelligence (Gerhardt), 75

Gerhardt, Megan, 75

Give-Get-Merge-Go, 174, 176*t*

Gladwell, Malcolm, 87

goal (in GOAL model), 174

goal mentors, 95

goals

    hard-to-reach, 88

    if/then, 86

    SMART, 94, 169–170

goal setting, 82–84

goal striving, 85–89, 85*t*

good relationships, 45

Gottman, John, 30–31

GROW model, 174–175

H

habits, 95, 96*f,* 98–99

halo effect, 202

hard-to-reach goals, 88

Harvard Business Review, 54

healthy detachment, 47

HEC, 87

"Helping an Employee in Distress"
    (Bhatti and Roulet*),* 54

hidden window (in Johari Window
    model), 15–16

high trait empathy, 46

Hofstede, Geert, 68

Hofstede's 6 Cultural Dimensions,
    68, 69*t*

Hokkaido University, 34

horns vs. halo bias, 56

hostile feedback, 26

Hurt Feelings Scale, 29

I

IBM, 68

ICD-11 (International
    Classification of Diseases), 142

identity, defined, 15

if/then goals, 86

implementation intentions, 91, 94,
    169–170

implementation plans, 194

improvement plan, 195*f*

incompetent jerks, 112–113

independent contributor career
path, 148, 150–151, 151*t*

ineffective feedback, 104

informative feedback, 39–40

Ingham, Harrington, 15

in-group bias, 58–59

INSEAD Business School, 68

intelligence quotient (IQ), 165

intentions, implementation, 91, 94, 169–170

International Classification of Diseases (ICD-11), 142

interpersonal disorders, 121–122, 134

interpersonal skills, 121, 163–164

intersectionality, 61

interviews, stay, 145–147

intrinsic motivation, 83

IQ (intelligence quotient), 165

"I" statements, 129

Ivcevic, Zorana, 122–123

J

jerks, incompetent, 112–113

Johari Window model, 15–17, 17

Johns Hopkins University, 141

K

Kennedy, John F., 23

key performance indicators (KPIs), 169, 193–194

L

Lally, Phillippa, 86–87

leadership career path, 148–150, 149*t*

leniency bias, 56

Levi Strauss & Co, 186

lifespan lens, 74

lifespans, 30

likable fools, 106–107, 112

listening, active, 128

litigation, 184

Lobo, M. S., 108, 112, 164

loveable stars, 111–112

Luft, Joseph, 15

M

Mager, Robert, 165

managers, role of, 173*t*

Mayer-Salovey-Caruso Emotional Intelligence Test (MSCEIT), 14

McCovey, Willie, 23–24

McKinsey, 121

McNamara, Brooke, 87–88

men
feedback focus for, 64*t*
and gender biases, 60–62
neurobiology of leadership differences in, 62–64

mental health, 142

mentorships, 95, 172, 173*t*

Meyer, Erin, 68

Meyer's 8 Culture Map Dimensions, 68, 69*t*

Miami University, 75

microaggressions, 65–67

millennials, 72–73, 76*t*, 140

motivation
   levels of, 94
   performance acceleration and,
      153–154
   in performance enhancement,
      166–167
MSCEIT (Mayer-Salovey-Caruso
   Emotional Intelligence Test),
   14

N

narcissistic personality disorder,
   121–122
negative feedback, 18
negative informative feedback, 40
negative interactions, 30–31, 31
negativity bias, 39
Netflix, 141
neural links, 24–29
neurobiology, 62–63
neurodivergence, 49–51, 203
neurons, 86–87
neuroscience, 23–41
   of behavior change, 89–90
   feedback hacks based on,
      36–40
   neural links, 24–29
   positive-to-negative feedback
      ratios, 29–32
   of supportive relationships,
      34–36
   and when to give feedback,
      33–34
Nguyen, Lee, 131–132

nonbinary employees, 64–65
nucleum accumbens, 83t
nuns, 30

O

open window (in Johari Window
   model), 15–16
options (in GOAL model), 175
oxytocin, 37, 121

P

pain, 27–28
parietal cortex, 85t
peer coaching, 173–174
peer reviews, 172
Penn Positive Psychology Center,
   147
performance
   analyzing deficiencies in,
      177t–178t
   and employee disengagement, 3
   gaps in, 191
   indicators of, 168–169
performance acceleration feedback
   coaching, 137–160
   about, 111–112
   aligning strengths with,
      147–148
   and career path preferences,
      148–153
   case example, 143–145
   defined, 6
   generational comparisons
      with, 142–143

performance acceleration feedback coaching (*continued*)
and motivational drivers, 153–154
professional development plans, 154
role play exercise, 157
with stay interviews, 145–147
tasks and assignments for, 158–159
tips for, 160
and workplace culture, 138–142
performance enhancement feedback coaching, 161–180
about, 112, 164–165
analysis for, 165–166
case example, 161–164
critical steps for, 179
defined, 6
implementation intentions with, 169–170
motivators in, 166–167
performance indicators in, 168–169
professional development plans in, 170–175
selecting skills for, 167–168
tips for, 180
Performance Feedback Coaching Model
about, 108–109, 109*f*
exercises, 116–118
and feedback gap, 5–6
quadrants of, 110–113
using, 109–110
performance improvement feedback coaching, 112–113, 181–200
about, 185–186
behavioral checklist, 199
case example, 181–183, 186–187
defined, 6
engagement review meeting in, 187–189
formal meeting for, 189–190
guide for, 190–195
and quiet quitting, 183–185
steps for, 198
tips for, 200
performance management feedback coaching, 119–135
about, 110–111
blind spots, 126–127
candid and specific feedback, 128–130
case example, 122–128
defensiveness, 127–128
defined, 6
DESC feedback technique for, 130
emotional and social competence for, 122–128
and interpersonal disorders, 120–122
with motivational drivers, 125–126

and personal benefit, 126

    recognizing strengths, 132

    tips for, 135

personality, 47–49, 48*t*

personality disorder, narcissistic, 121–122

personality factors, 48*t*

physical pain, 27

Pipe, Peter, 165

positive emotions, 30, 31–32

positive feedback, 128

positive-to-negative feedback ratios, 29–32

posterior cingulate cortex, 83*t*

practice, 87–88

practice plan activity triggers, 170

Praslova, Ludmila, 50–51

primacy bias, 56

privacy, 204

professional development plans

    performance acceleration feedback coaching, 154

    in performance enhancement feedback coaching, 170–175

    template for, 171*t*

progress, monitoring, 172, 190–191, 195

project manager career path, 148, 151, 152*t*

psychological well-being, 31–32

Q

quiet quitting, 183–185

R

race, 58–60

racial bias, 60

rapport, building, 37–38

reality (in GOAL model), 175

reappraisal, cognitive, 52, 53

recency bias, 56, 202

relationships, 45

reputation, 16

retention, 3

rewards

    for entrepreneurial career path, 152*t*

    for generalist career path, 152*t*

    for leadership career path, 149*t*

    for specialist career path, 151*t*

    uncertain, 84

Rohn, Jim, 1

Roulet, Thomas, 54

S

San Francisco Giants, 23

security, 204

self-assessment, 171

self-awareness, 13–17

self-disclosure to others, 15

self-enhancement bias, 13–14

self-knowledge, 15

self-regulation, 33

Seligman, Martin, 147

signature strengths, 147–148, 156

Silani, Giorgia, 36

similar-to-me bias, 56

skills
  assessing deficiencies in, 166*f*
  interpersonal, 121, 163–164
sleep, 33–34
SMART goals, 94, 169–170
social feedback, 17
social pain, 27–28, 28–29
social support, 34–36
Society for Human Resource
  Management, 124
soft skills. *See* interpersonal skills
specialist career path, 148, 150–151,
  151*t*
sponsors, 173*t*
Spotify, 141
stability, emotional, 48
Stanford University, 55
stars, loveable, 111–112
stay interviews, 145–147
stereotypes, 55–57, 61–62, 76
Stern, Robin, 122–123
stonewalling, 31
strengths, signature, 147–148, 156
StressScan, 35
strictness bias, 56
subgoals, 84
support, social, 34–36
supportive feedback climate, 42*t*,
  100

T

task-positive network (TPN), 82
Taylor, Shelly, 64
teasing, 24

temporoparietal junction (TPJ),
  85*t*
Textio, 59
3M Model of Successful Individual
  Behavior Change, 21, 89–96,
  92*f*
TOMS, 141
TPJ (temporoparietal junction), 85*t*
TPN (task-positive network), 82
traits, defined, 15
transgender employees, 64–65
Treasure Corporation Worldwide,
  131–132
Trier Social Stress Test, 34
triggers, practice plan activity, 170
2024 Annual Leadership
  Development Survey (Wilson
  Learning), 207

U

uncertain rewards, 84
unconscious bias, 54–58, 78–79
understanding, 18, 22*t*
UNDP Gender Social Norms Index
  (2023), 61
University of Barcelona, 13
University of California, 4, 27
University of Kentucky, 30
University of Manitoba, 69–71
University of Michigan, 31
University of Oregon, 82
University of Toronto, 33
University of Vienna, 36
University of Washington, 30–31

unknown window (in Johari
Window model), 15–16
US Surgeon General, 36

V
ventrial striatum, 83*t*
ventrolateral prefrontal cortex
(vlPFC), 85*t*
ventromedial prefrontal cortex
(vmPFC), 83*t*

W
warmth, 6, 105
"the way," 85, 85*t*
way forward (in GOAL model),
175
WEIRD (western, educated, industrialized, rich, and democratic)
bias, 203
well-being, 31–32, 142
Well-Being at Work Survey
(Deloitte), 139
western, educated, industrialized,
rich, and democratic (WEIRD)
bias, 203
White employees, 59, 62
will, 82–83, 83*t,* 89–90
Williams, Alex, 131–132
Wilson Learning, 207
women
feedback focus for, 64*t*
gender biases against, 60–62
neurobiology of leadership
differences in, 62–64

and social support networks,
35
Work in America Survey (APA), 124
workplace culture, 138–142, 139*t*
World Economic Forum, 124
World Health Organization, 142

Z
Zak, Paul, 64
Zenger, J., 73, 172

About the Authors

Sandra Mashihi, PhD, is an organizational psychologist and leadership coach who has more than 20 years of experience coaching and training leaders to improve their behaviors in a way that leads to their team's high performance and effectiveness. Sandra has expertise in leadership development, executive presence, stress management, team building, talent management, managing corporate politics, and interpersonal relationships in the workplace. She has worked with leaders and teams throughout various companies including Fortune 500s. She works on a one-on-one basis, as well as facilitating group coaching programs along various topics, such as emotional intelligence, performance feedback coaching, and emerging leadership programs.

Sandra runs a boutique consulting firm called Spectra Coaching. She also serves as an adjunct professor at Pepperdine University's Graziadio School of Business and Management, The California School of Professional Psychology, and other professional institutions where she teaches leadership and organizational behavior for MBA and Doctoral students.

Sandra's expertise helping clients form new and lasting behaviors that become habits makes her coaching unique. She applies her expertise based on her experience working with various types of leaders and her research on best practices for effective behavioral change. Her approach with each client is tailored to what the client needs to thrive as a leader. She ensures that her clients become "the very best version of themselves."

Sandra lives in Los Angeles along with her husband and two very special young children who help her practice feedback skills each day! In her free time, Sandra loves hiking, painting, and being with her loving family and friends.

 **Kenneth M. Nowack**, PhD, is a licensed psychologist and the co-founder and senior research officer of Envisia Learning, a global leader in assessment and technology solutions. With more than 30 years of experience, Ken has made significant contributions to the fields of habit and behavior change, 360-degree feedback, leadership development, and health psychology. He holds a doctorate in counseling psychology from the University of California, Los Angeles.

Ken is the acclaimed author of *Clueless: Coaching People Who Just Don't Get It* and *From Insight to Improvement: Leveraging 360-Degree Feedback*. His extensive research and numerous publications have influenced best practices in human resource development and organizational effectiveness. His expertise spans executive development, career management, individual and team coaching, and corporate wellness programs, impacting public, private, and nonprofit sectors.

Recognized for his valuable insights in learning and development, Ken is a Fellow of the American Psychological Association's Division 13: Society of Consulting Psychology and served as the editor-in-chief of the *Consulting Psychology Journal*. He is also a member of Daniel Goleman's Consortium for Research on Emotional Intelligence in Organizations. Ken's speaking, writing, and consulting work continues to shape and advance the consulting psychology industry. For more information, visit envisialearning.com.

About ATD

atd The Association for Talent Development (ATD) is the world's largest association dedicated to those who develop talent in organizations. Serving a global community of members, customers, and international business partners in more than 100 countries, ATD champions the importance of learning and training by setting standards for the talent development profession.

Our customers and members work in public and private organizations in every industry sector. Since ATD was founded in 1943, the talent development field has expanded significantly to meet the needs of global businesses and emerging industries. Through the Talent Development Capability Model, education courses, certifications and credentials, memberships, industry-leading events, research, and publications, we help talent development professionals build their personal, professional, and organizational capabilities to meet new business demands with maximum impact and effectiveness.

One of the cornerstones of ATD's intellectual foundation, ATD Press offers insightful and practical information on talent development, training, and professional growth. ATD Press publications are written by industry thought leaders and offer anyone who works with adult learners the best practices, academic theory, and guidance necessary to move the profession forward.

We invite you to join our community. Learn more at **TD.org**.